Radicalisation, counter-radicalisation, and Prevent

Manchester University Press

Radicalisation, counter-radicalisation, and Prevent

A vernacular approach

Lee Jarvis, Stuart Macdonald,
and Andrew Whiting

MANCHESTER UNIVERSITY PRESS

Published by Manchester University Press
Oxford Road, Manchester M13 9PL

www.manchesteruniversitypress.co.uk

British Library Cataloguing-in-Publication Data
A catalogue record for this book is available from the British
Library

ISBN 978 1 5261 7273 0 hardback

First published 2024

Typeset by Newgen Publishing UK

Contents

List of Tables	*page* vi
Acknowledgements	vii
Introduction	1
1 Prevent and (counter-)radicalisation	8
2 Vernacular security and (counter-)radicalisation	31
3 Radicalisation and/in the vernacular	64
4 Knowing Prevent	88
5 Evaluating Prevent	110
6 Theorising (counter-)radicalisation in the vernacular	132
Conclusion	150
Bibliography	159
Index	178

Tables

2.1 Principles of vernacular security research   *page* 44
2.2 Topic guide and prompts   58
2.3 Excerpt from coding framework   61
3.1 Vernacular discourse on radicalisation   66
4.1 Vernacular discourse on Prevent   89
5.1 Vernacular discourse on evaluations of Prevent   111

Acknowledgements

Like all books, this one has been a long time in the making, and would not exist were it not for the work, generosity, and support of a large number of people. Most immediately, the material on which we draw was generated through a series of focus groups that were initially organised at the invitation of the team responsible for the Independent Review of the United Kingdom's Prevent Strategy. We are grateful to all of the individuals who participated in our focus groups, and for the time, experience, and knowledge they contributed to this project. These contributions – at a time of considerable uncertainty and difficulty in the UK due to the ongoing COVID-19 pandemic and the disruption it wrought – were vital for our efforts to explore 'vernacular' understandings of (counter-)radicalisation, and the book would not exist without them. Our thanks here, too, therefore to the researchers working for the independent review for reaching out to us with this initial proposal.

We are grateful, of course, to Manchester University Press for their support for this project – to Rob Byron, especially, for his enthusiasm, to the anonymous reviewers of earlier material whose comments certainly improved it, and to Lucy Brown and Andrae Fegalquin for their research assistance. All three of us have drawn on inspiration and advice from earlier writing projects, partnerships, and discussions with colleagues, collaborators, and students in writing this book which inevitably informs our argument and analysis. Although it is not possible to name all of those individuals here, important amongst them are: Huw Darling, Alan Finlayson, Gary Hazeldine, Tim Legrand, Michael Lister, Elizabeth Pearson, Sarah Pemberton, and Keith Spiller.

Finally, as always, we want to thank our families for the support and encouragement that has sustained us throughout this project. It wouldn't have been possible without them!

Introduction

Ultimately, I think [Prevent]'s a good idea. I know it's used in the wrong way and I know it's used to target the wrong people and I don't like that. And if I could change that, 100 percent I would. But knowing that the Government is trying to do something, and has finally realised how much of an issue terrorism is and how it does need to be addressed, is a good thing and does make me feel a bit happier.

Focus group participant

In March 2023, Lord Shawcross's Independent Review of the UK Prevent Strategy was published. Prevent is the UK's official strategy for countering radicalisation and Shawcross's review contained several important criticisms including concerns that that it had become overly focused on safeguarding 'vulnerable people' at the expense of robust counter-terrorism and that consequently the strategy was plugging gaps in other services, including mental health provision (Elgot and Dodd 2022). Particularly controversial, though, was the suggestion that Prevent had unduly focused on right-wing extremism to the neglect of its 'Islamist' counterparts. As one commentator argued when commenting on an early leaked version of the report:

Muslims were told to reserve our judgement of the Shawcross review into Prevent (a strategy launched in 2007 to stop people becoming terrorists) until its findings were released. But it is already turning out to be exactly what we feared – another direct attack on Muslims … Instead of a discussion about whether inherently racist Prevent policies should be scrapped altogether; the Shawcross review seems set to legitimise them.

Ezaydi 2022

Concerns such as these will be familiar to observers of Prevent, which has become one of the most discussed, debated and – for some – detested security instruments of the twenty-first century. Critics of Prevent, of whom there are many, argue it is racist and wasteful; that it poses major implications for longstanding freedoms of speech and association; that the conceptual framework of 'radicalisation' upon which it is based is both clumsy and

reliant upon vanishingly thin evidential foundations; that it introduces bur-
densome new responsibilities for ill-equipped, and already overworked
public servants such as teachers and doctors; that it stigmatises, and risks
criminalising, children and young people – especially from minority communities; and that it dramatically expands the state's security and surveillance apparatuses into what should be spaces of safety such as nurseries
and primary schools. As we shall see in Chapter 1, moreover, criticisms like
these gain considerable and continuing momentum from sustained media
reports on Prevent's failures and injustices: failures and injustices such as the
four-year-old Muslim boy recently referred to Prevent for talking at an after-
school club about *Fortnite*, a popular and widely played videogame (Stein
and Townsend 2021). Indeed, so widespread are such concerns now, that a
dedicated 'Prevent Watch' initiative was set up in 2015 to support 'people
impacted by Prevent' (Prevent Watch n.d.).

And yet, despite such criticism Prevent shows little sign of going any-
where anytime soon. The strategy remains a key component of the UK's
wider counter-terrorism framework, costing an estimated £40 million per
year (BBC 2017). For supporters, it plays a vital safeguarding role helping
to prevent vulnerable individuals from being drawn into violent extremism.
Such activity is seen to have wider import for national security, too, protecting potential victims of extremism as well as its perpetrators. The strategy's
recent emphasis on far-right extremism, moreover, is held up as evidence of
its reflexive engagement with its accusers; evidence, perhaps, that its focus
extends beyond those minority communities long deemed 'suspect' by the
state. Detractors, meanwhile, are accused of exaggerating their concerns,
as in Defence Secretary Ben Wallace's claim that the independent review of
Prevent would 'expect those critics of Prevent, who often use distortions
and spin, to produce solid evidence of their allegations' (UK Home Office
2019). Those who take issue with Prevent's lack of transparency, moreover,
can also be pointed toward the wealth of statistical information published
by the UK Home Office, including annual updates on the number of people
referred to and supported by the strategy (UK Home Office 2021a).

Political and normative debate such as this is, of course, vitally important for the implementation, review, reform, and contestation of security
instruments such as Prevent. It can tell us a lot about the workings and priorities of British politics, as well as shedding light on the impact of specific
policies upon, amongst other things, communities, citizenship, and security.
Our argument in this book, however, is that debate on Prevent – and on its
conceptual scaffolding of 'radicalisation' and 'extremism' – would benefit
from a far more detailed engagement with the perspectives, understandings, and experiences of citizens *themselves*. There is, to be clear, much to

be gained from theoretical critique of (counter-)radicalisation, from quantitative assessments of Prevent's impacts, from discursive analysis of policy documentation, and from interviews with those responsible for delivering counter-radicalisation initiatives – all of which are well-served in the existing academic literature, as we show in Chapter 1. There is *also*, however, much to be gained from providing space for more banal, everyday, understandings and experiences of (counter-)radicalisation and their implications for, or connection to, core political values and ideas. This book offers an attempt to provide such space.

Our overarching aim here is to offer a sustained investigation into how 'ordinary' citizens understand and make sense of 'radicalisation' as a security challenge, and how they interpret efforts to address this challenge via initiatives such as the UK Prevent Strategy. Drawing on original focus group research, the book sets out to answer three questions. First, how is (counter-)radicalisation understood or interpreted in vernacular discourse? How familiar, persuasive, and accepted is this vocabulary to 'ordinary' citizens? And do 'ordinary' or non-elite understandings of these issues reflect, reproduce, or challenge elite discourse? Second, what discursive resources are drawn upon when non-elites discuss (counter-)radicalisation in the vernacular? How important, for instance, are personal memories, anecdotes, cultural sources of knowledge, or vernacular experiences in 'lay' constructions of this framework? Third, what are the implications of vernacular constructions of (counter-)radicalisation for lived experiences and theoretical debate? How do everyday understandings of (counter-)radicalisation impact, for instance, upon security, or citizenship, or identity, or multiculturalism? By answering these questions, the book offers three primary contributions to existing knowledge in this area.

The initial contribution is the book's conceptual originality as the first sustained application of 'vernacular security studies' to counter-radicalisation initiatives such as the UK Prevent Strategy. As argued in Chapter 2, the concept of 'vernacular security' is a relatively recent one within critical security studies, coming to prominence via Nils Bubandt's (2005: 276) pathbreaking effort to highlight security's variability as 'a socially situated and discursively defined practice'. Vernacular approaches to security involve interrogating the 'richness and texture of localized security imaginaries', in order to ask 'what security means; how security feels; what conditions, objects, experiences, or relationships create security and insecurity; [and] with which values security is associated' (Jarvis 2019a: 116). Recent years have witnessed a burgeoning of interest in the potential of this framework to shed new light on a wide range of issues, including non-elite understandings of counter-terrorism in Nigeria (Oyawale 2022) and the UK (Jarvis and Lister 2015a; 2015b); public understandings of migration within the EU (Vaughan-Williams 2021); humiliation narratives within populist political mobilisations (Homolar and Löfflmann 2021); and the distinctiveness of 'security speak' on social media platforms such as YouTube and Twitter (Downing 2021). In this book, we offer the first dedicated reading of (counter-)radicalisation as a discourse and policy arena through this vernacular lens. In so doing, we seek both to build on and extend the insight of work such as the above, offering new reflection on the everyday politics of security as (re)produced in the lives and words of 'ordinary' citizens in this highly charged context.

Second is the book's analytical contribution, in which we explore vernacular discourse on (counter-)radicalisation as a way of shedding new light on several important and longstanding questions relating to (in)security. In the chapters that follow, for instance, we demonstrate the conceptual resilience of the language of 'radicalisation' by showing a vernacular willingness to use this terminology even amongst individuals who are most critical of this lexicon. This, we argue, offers new insight into the social resonance and sedimentation of security discourse. Also, by drawing attention to the importance of vicarious experiences of (counter-)radicalisation policy – such as the experience of Prevent training as recounted by family members – we offer new insight into the agency of particular individuals to speak authoritatively about (in)security to the persuasion of particular audiences. Engaging with everyday understandings such as these, we suggest, offers new resources for cutting into longstanding debates about the meaning, possibility, and desirability of 'security': the focus of the book's final chapter.

The book's third contribution lies in its development of a descriptively rich empirical examination of a significant body of original data documenting the vernacular politics of security in the context of (counter-)radicalisation. Although there is an increasing scholarship on practitioner understandings and experiences of Prevent – a literature that draws, for instance, on interviews with educators – there remains surprisingly little scholarship on understandings of the strategy and its implications for citizens and their encounters with (counter-)radicalisation in higher education settings, in workplaces, in their media consumption, in family conversations, in school assemblies, and beyond. By drawing on a large corpus of text totalling over sixteen hours and 96,000 words of original data generated through focus groups with one specific, but vitally important, community (see Chapter 2) – students in higher education institutions – the book offers a sustained attempt to centre such encounters and their social, political, and wider importance.

Book organisation

To make these contributions, the book begins by situating our own research in relevant policy and academic contexts. To this end, Chapter 1 offers an overview of the UK's Prevent Strategy which constitutes, we argue, one of the world's most prominent, and controversial, counter-radicalisation initiatives. Specifically, we outline the strategy's emergence and evolution since its introduction in 2006; its ambitions and the mechanics through which it operates in practice, and the many controversies that have surrounded its design and implementation, including its framing as a 'toxic brand'. The chapter's second section then turns to academic commentary on the strategy and its underpinning discourse of radicalisation and extremism, including critical accounts of Prevent's implications for minority communities and for the rights and entitlements of citizenship. Notwithstanding the importance of this work – much of which feeds into our own analysis – we argue that the continuing lack of sustained vernacular analysis of the sort offered by this book renders understanding of Prevent's socio-political consequences unnecessarily incomplete.

The book's second chapter then outlines our theoretical and methodological framework. We begin with an overview of changing understandings of security within the post-Cold War period. In doing this, we introduce important critical work from the field of security studies and beyond, that has focused attention on two vital issues: first, the construction of security in spoken, written, and visual texts; and second, the diverse ways in which security works in practice across heterogeneous social and political contexts. This enables us to then turn attention to a series of conceptual approaches that have, in different ways, foregrounded everyday, banal, or quotidian experiences, perceptions, and expressions of security, and, within this, to describe the vernacular approach employed in the book's three empirical chapters that follow. Here we set out the meaning and implications of a vernacular approach to (counter-)radicalisation, and how this influences the analysis and interpretation of our focus group research. The chapter concludes by detailing the focus group method employed here and the assumptions and value it brings to our understanding.

Chapter 3 begins our discussion of the empirical findings upon which our book focuses. Drawing on material generated in our focus groups, it explores different ways in which the concept of 'radicalisation' is understood in vernacular discourse. The chapter begins by contrasting two different models of radicalisation that dominated our focus groups. The first is a processual one, that speaks very closely to governmental understandings of this term. The second is a rather different attitudinal one, in which radicalisation is seen to involve a willingness to take action. A second section then explores heterogeneities in the understandings of radicalisation's drivers or causes that underpin these views. These differences – which include competing views on the importance of grievances and local communities – reflect, we argue, wider assumptions about the nature and interaction of structure and agency in the social world. The chapter then turns to vernacular reflections on the language of radicalisation, its ambiguities, and power, before exploring prominent vernacular concerns with this terminology as a framework for making sense of political violence.

In Chapter 4, we turn our attention to vernacular constructions of *counter*-radicalisation in general, and of the UK's Prevent Strategy more specifically. The chapter begins by exploring citizen understandings of Prevent, its aspirations, and its implementation in practice. A second section then reflects on sources of vernacular knowledge which include, we demonstrate, the views of family and friends, experiences in higher and secondary education, encounters with the strategy in employment and training contexts, and media representations. The chapter concludes by exploring the vernacular as a site of political imagination by exploring a range of suggestions encountered in our focus groups for improving the communication and 'selling' of the Prevent Strategy to publics.

Chapter 5 turns to vernacular evaluations of the Prevent Strategy as a framework for countering radicalisation. The chapter begins by highlighting the widespread support for (something akin to) Prevent that we encountered amongst participants in our focus groups, despite evidence of not-insignificant concerns with its current articulation and implementation. These concerns, discussed in a second section, focus on the strategy's empirical and theoretical underpinnings; on issues around training and the identification of vulnerability indicators; and on Prevent's impact upon citizenship including in relation to freedom of expression, and the day-to-day lives of 'suspect communities'. The chapter's third section explores proposals for reforming Prevent that emerged in the context of our discussion. These included suggestions for adjusting Prevent's public communication, recommendations for wide-reaching reforms to its underpinning assumptions, and views that Prevent is, effectively, unsalvageable and should therefore be replaced by something radically different.

Chapter 6 connects the empirical discussion of the previous three chapters to the vernacular security framework introduced at the book's outset. In this chapter, we argue that vernacular constructions of (counter-)radicalisation demonstrate important ambiguities and contradictions within commonly held assumptions about the meaning, possibility, and desirability of security. This includes, amongst other things, shedding new light on security's production in everyday contexts such as supermarket training rooms;

demonstrating the importance of relatively neglected securitising actors such as friends and family members, and highlighting heterogeneities within citizen responses to elite security discourses. These ambiguities, we argue, have significant implications for the study and practice of security far beyond counter-radicalisation and counter-terrorism policy.

In the book's Conclusion, we take time to summarise our argument and emphasise the significance of our findings. We argue that vernacular discourses such as those explored throughout the book are important because they first, broaden understanding of the policy implications of security initiatives such as Prevent; second, open new avenues for contestation and critique by enabling reflection on potentially subjugated knowledges; third, provide opportunity for new insight on wider social and political assumptions and imaginaries, and fourth, enable reflection on the resonance of dominant security discourses. These claims, we argue, demonstrate the relevance and resonance of our findings and argument for wider contexts and debates.

1

Prevent and (counter-)radicalisation

On 15 October 2021, MP Sir David Amess was meeting residents of his Southend West constituency. Amongst his appointments that day was a twenty-five-year-old man, Ali Harbi Ali, who had travelled from his home in London, having claimed to have recently moved to the area. A few minutes in, as Vikram Dodd (2022a), in *The Guardian*, reports: 'the meeting was interrupted when Ali's phone rang. He stood up from his chair, put his hand in his pocket and said "sorry".' As Dodd (2022a) continues, Ali then 'pulled a knife from his pocket, leant over the table and stabbed the 69-year-old repeatedly in the stomach. Amess screamed at times as the blows continued, raising his hands to defend himself.' Reports of the attack suggested that Ali made no effort to harm anyone else, and that he was subsequently taken into custody by local police to whom he confessed to the murder. Ali, as Dodd (2022a) writes, 'saw himself as a soldier of Islamic State and wanted to punish a British lawmaker for the UK's actions in Syria'. David Amess, who died less than an hour after the attack, was the unfortunate legislator upon whom Ali had settled.

Ali Harbi Ali's story bears unfortunate resemblance to a number of tragic incidents that will be well-known to readers. These include, of course, acts of violence against other politicians – including, most notoriously, the 2016 killing of Jo Cox MP by white supremacist Thomas Mair – and any number of so-called 'lone actor' attacks conducted in the name of terrorist groups by individuals with scant direct connection to the leaderships of Al Qaeda, Islamic State, or other organisations. Ali's attack on David Amess, however, was also *made* familiar to readers, viewers, and other media consumers in the UK and beyond because it was widely interpreted or narrated as yet another example of a hitherto successful, adjusted individual who had 'descended down a spiral of self-radicalisation' (Pennick 2022). This radicalisation frame – one of the most pervasive in contemporary discussion of political violence – was widespread in news coverage of this attack. The BBC, for instance, described Ali as 'a textbook study of radicalisation' generated through anger at the Syrian war and his vulnerability to Islamic State propaganda (Casciana 2022). For the right-leaning *Daily Mail*, similarly, 'The killer of Sir David Amess was a football-loving aspiring doctor who descended down the spiral of self-radicalisation after watching ISIS propaganda and Bashar al-Assad's brutality in Syria' (Chaudhary and Tingle 2022).

Although it is not uncommon for 'successful' terrorists to have previously attracted the attention of law enforcement or intelligence personnel, Ali's case generated additional interest because of his prior contact with the UK's counter-radicalisation framework: the Prevent Strategy. Although the specifics of that contact are, as we write this book, yet to be confirmed, it was widely reported that Ali had been directed to Prevent's voluntary Channel programme which aims at supporting those deemed at risk of radicalisation (Dodd 2022b). These revelations, as might be expected, served to reopen longstanding questions about the strategy's effectiveness, from *Sky News*'s 'Why key part of government's counter-terrorism strategy is under scrutiny after murder of MP Sir David Amess' (McGuiness 2021) to the *Daily Mail*'s 'Islamist "lone wolf" Ali Harbi Ali was able to secretly plot his murderous act for years despite being referred to "politically-correct" anti-terror programme' (Tingle 2022).

In this chapter, we address both the phenomenon of radicalisation itself, and the emergence and development of the UK's Prevent Strategy, by situating these in relevant political and academic contexts. We begin with an introduction to Prevent, exploring some of the ways it has evolved since its emergence in 2007. Here we preface themes explored in the book's analytical chapters, reflecting on the conceptual framing of radicalisation, extremism, and related terms in the strategy, before considering its delivery, outcomes, impacts, criticism, and international context. The chapter then provides a review of the voluminous existing scholarship on Prevent and the wider conceptual and political issues the strategy generates and reflects. In doing this, we highlight a number of important critiques of the politics of radicalisation and extremism, and of the wider consequences of counter-radicalisation frameworks and actions.

The UK Prevent Strategy

The UK Prevent Strategy was first introduced in 2003, made public in 2006, published as a standalone strategy in 2007 and since then has undergone several revisions. In 2011, the government published one of the revised versions and included within it a foreword from the then Home Secretary Theresa May. In this foreword, May took care to distinguish this incarnation from its predecessors, charging those earlier versions with incoherence, ineffectiveness, and even counter-productivity:

> The Prevent programme we inherited from the last Government was flawed. It confused the delivery of Government policy to promote integration with Government policy to prevent terrorism. It failed to confront the extremist ideology at the heart of the threat we face; and in trying to reach those at risk of radicalisation, funding sometimes even reached the very extremist organisations that Prevent should have been confronting.
>
> HM Government 2011: 1

At the time of writing, the most recent version of Prevent is the 2018 update that was published as part of the UK's overarching counter-terrorism strategy CONTEST. This document clarifies that Prevent is organised around three core objectives. First, tackling the 'causes of radicalisation' and responding to the 'ideological challenge of terrorism' (HM Government 2018: 31). Second, safeguarding and supporting vulnerable people 'most at risk of radicalisation through early intervention' (HM Government 2018: 31). And third, to 'enable those who have already engaged in terrorism to disengage and rehabilitate' (HM Government 2018: 31). Notwithstanding considerable, and important, conceptual ambiguities within the strategy discussed below, these objectives draw from a relatively coherent big-picture understanding of terrorism. Central here is the (contestable) assumption that the threat of terrorism is fundamentally ideational, such that 'the existence of a broadly consistent set of ideas and narratives is an important factor in motivating terrorist groups of all kinds' (HM Government 2018: 16). By using 'pernicious, divisive messaging and amplifying perceived grievances', terrorists encourage 'extremists within our own communities to subvert our way of life through simple, brutal violence' (HM Government 2018: 7). Prominent groups such as ISIS and Al Qaeda, 'hold in common an absolute rejection of democracy, personal liberty and human rights' (HM Government 2018: 16).

This emphasis on the ideological roots of terrorism underpins a processual understanding of terrorism's causal mechanics, in which vulnerable individuals are gradually radicalised. As set out in the UK Home Office's (HM Government 2020: 9), official guidance for members of Channel Panels which seek to support those at risk of being drawn into terrorism, vulnerability here could include cases where individuals:

- are accessing extremist materials;
- are espousing scripted extremist narratives;
- are demonstrating acute behaviour changes in relation to our working definition of extremism;

- have had potentially traumatic exposure to conflict zones; and
- are acutely intolerant towards people from different ethnic backgrounds, cultures or other protected traits as defined in the 2010 Equality Act.

As indicated elsewhere in this guidance, moreover, the incrementalism of radicalisation, as understood in Prevent, is seen to offer opportunity for intervention at different stages along the pathway to radicalisation. Responsibility for interventions of this sort, controversially, is distributed across a wide range of sectors including education, health, and local authorities, as well as within the community (HM Government 2018: 33–37). 'A successful integration strategy is therefore important' in order to address terrorism's ideological challenge and 'protect the values of our society – the rule of law, individual liberty, mutual respect, tolerance and understanding of different faiths and beliefs' (HM Government 2018: 23).

Conceptual moorings and delivery

The UK Prevent Strategy published in 2011 was relatively unusual amongst counter-radicalisation initiatives for providing a glossary of its core terms, many of which are, to its credit, explicitly recognised as contentious. Radicalisation, in the strategy, 'refers to the process by which a person comes to support terrorism and forms of extremism leading to terrorism' (HM Government 2011: 108). 'Extremism', in turn, is understood as 'vocal or active opposition to fundamental British values, including democracy, the rule of law, individual liberty and mutual respect and tolerance of different faiths and beliefs' (HM Government 2011: 108). To this broad understanding is added a more specific supplement, such that 'We also include in our definition of extremism calls for the death of members of our armed forces, whether in this country or overseas' (HM Government 2011: 108). More equivocal, though, is the strategy's definition of counter-radicalisation, which 'usually refers to activity aimed at a group of people intended to dissuade them from engaging in terrorism-related activity' (HM Government 2011: 108).

The Prevent delivery model operates across three levels: tackling the causes of radicalisation, early intervention, and rehabilitation (HM Government, 2018: 32). In order to do this, Prevent takes a whole-of-society approach to counter-radicalisation that engages with local communities, the public at large, and users of online spaces. These different levels combine, with the intention of amplifying credible voices in opposition to extremist narratives, or in order to provide multi-agency support for vulnerable people within different regions of the UK. For the government, Prevent represents the 'softer' strand of CONTEST and efforts were made in 2011 to more clearly separate direct counter-terrorism from pre-emptive work within communities. Subsequent updates to the UK's approach in the Counterterrorism and Security Act 2015 (CTSA 2015) and the 2018 CONTEST strategy further adapted Prevent's delivery mechanisms by introducing the Prevent Duty, explicitly framed as a safeguarding initiative.

The Prevent Duty refers to the introduction of a new statutory duty for 'specified authorities' to pay 'due regard' to 'the need to prevent people from being drawn into terrorism' (HM Government 2021a). This duty effectively deputises staff working across sectors such as public health care, education, local government, prisons, and policing into the UK's counter-radicalisation strategy. Guidance for employees within these sectors differs slightly, but common expectations upon them relate to the production of risk assessments, ensuring relevant institutional policies comply with the duty, developing, and delivering training for staff, and devising clear institutional responsibility for this framework (for specific details in the context of higher education, see Whiting *et al.* 2021b). The Prevent Duty guidance for schools and childcare providers, for instance makes clear that: 'schools and childcare providers are expected to assess the risk of children being drawn into terrorism, including support for extremist ideas that are part of terrorist ideology' (Department for Education 2015). The NHS Prevent Training and Competencies Framework, similarly, notes that 'Under the Prevent duty, the health sector is required to ensure that health care workers are able to identify early signs of an individual being drawn into radicalisation' (Department of Health and Social Care 2022). As these examples suggest, the duty's arrival has engendered a dramatic expansion of counter-radicalisation activities into the public sector, transforming the delivery of Prevent.

Outcomes and impacts of Prevent

Although the Prevent Strategy is often criticised for the opacity of its outcomes (as we shall see below), the UK Home Office now periodically publishes data on referrals to, and support offered through, Prevent. To give some sense of the strategy's reach, the November 2021 referral update, which contains data for the year ending 31 March 2021 (UK Home Office 2021a), saw the lowest total number of Prevent referrals since the availability of comparable data, with 4,915 referrals in total: a 22 per cent reduction on the previous year's 6,287 (UK Home Office 2021a). This decrease is explained, in the accompanying information, by the 'effects of public health restrictions that were in place throughout the year to control the spread of the COVID-19 virus' (UK Home Office 2021a), which included national and local lockdowns and a range of other restrictions on public movement and interaction. Indeed, the most recently published referral data for the year ending March 2022 saw a 30 per cent increase in referrals up to 6,406 – a number comparable to pre-lockdown levels (UK Home Office 2023).

Referrals to Prevent do not require the consent or approval of the individual concerned (Grierson 2020) and for the year ending March 2022, by far the largest two sectors for referrals made were education and the police, accounting for 36 per cent and 28 per cent respectively. For the same reporting period, 89 per cent of the referrals where gender was known were for male individuals, with the largest age demographic being the 30 per cent of individuals between 15 and 20 for referrals in which age was known (UK Home Office 2021a). Of the 6,406 referrals to Prevent, 1,486 were passed on to one of the UK's multi-agency Channel Panels which seek to 'determine the extent of an individual's vulnerability to radicalisation and whether a tailored package of support is necessary and proportionate to address the vulnerabilities' (UK Home Office 2023).

These reports categorise referrals by type, for example, 'Extreme Right Wing' (20 per cent) or 'Islamist' (16 per cent) (UK Home Office 2023). In a change from previous years' reporting, the most recent statistics for the year ending March 2022 have removed the aggregated category 'Mixed, Unstable and Unclear' (MUU) and where possible, instead sought to record these cases using a specific category. MUU was a broad and increasingly contentious category which included individuals with undetermined or conflicted ideologies as well as those holding a 'school massacre ideology' (UK Home Office 2021a). The statistics for the year ending March 2021 recorded 51 per cent of referrals as being MUU; however, with this category now removed, we can gain a clearer insight into emergent or less prevalent ideologies such as 'school massacre' (2 per cent) and 'incel' (1 per cent) (UK Home Office 2023). Despite these changes, 'individuals with vulnerability present but no ideology or CT risk' still make up the majority of referrals (25 per cent), a category that has increased year on year since 2019–20 reporting (UK Home Office 2023)

Prevent's evolution

It has now been over fifteen years that Prevent has been a public standalone strategy and in this time it has gone through several revised versions, two independent reviews, important amendments, and high-profile moments of reframing and refocusing. When first launched as a standalone strategy in 2007, Prevent was framed as a counter-radicalisation strategy that sought to adopt a 'hearts and minds' approach intended to sit comfortably alongside New Labour's Community Cohesion agenda (O'Toole *et al.*

2012). Criticisms of this iteration are addressed below, but it was in light of these – and a new Coalition government having taken office – that a revised version was published in 2011, following an independent review led by Lord Carlile of Berriew. This version saw several changes of emphasis including the decision to expand the strategy's focus to include non-violent extremism. In subsequent Prevent documentation, this broader remit was explained on account of non-violent extremism having the potential to 'create an atmosphere conducive to terrorism and [to] popularise views which terrorists can exploit' (HM Government, 2021b). This shift in focus towards non-violent extremism proved controversial both for its impact on free speech in general, and for its stigmatisation of conservative versions of Islam in particular.

This version of Prevent was also marked by a concerted effort to address concerns that the strategy had focused excessively on the threat of Islamic extremism despite the growth of alternative types of extremism and terrorism. Such efforts notwithstanding, the criticism has not disappeared, although the emergence of an increasingly prominent and credible far-right terrorist threat within the UK has seen impetus added to the strategy's refocusing. The reframing of Prevent as a *safeguarding initiative* with the CTSA 2015 and arrival into law of the Prevent Duty discussed above, finally, enabled the strategy to be positioned as a natural fit with the everyday work of doctors, nurses, teachers, and lecturers, all of whom have existing and well-established duties of care. For critics, though, a tension remains with the strategy's dual framing here as both a safeguarding initiative, and a prominent aspect of the UK's counter-terrorism strategy.

Criticisms and concerns

In March 2015, a retired senior Police Officer, Dal Babu, received widespread news coverage following an interview with BBC Radio 4's flagship news publication, *The Today Programme*. In the interview, the former Chief Superintendent pointed to the lack of non-white and Muslim police officers within UK counter-terrorism units, arguing, 'Prevent has become a toxic brand and most Muslims are suspicious of what Prevent is doing' (BBC 2015). Although serving officers and government ministers were quick to defend the strategy, this sense of toxicity has been difficult to shake, with victims of terrorism (Mughal 2019), think tank representatives (House of Commons Home Affairs Committee 2016: 31), and other politicians explicitly and publicly denouncing Prevent in this language. As Lord Sheikh (Hansard HL Debate, 12 November 2018) put it in a House of Lords debate on the Counterterrorism and Security Bill in November 2018: 'Some critics of the strategy have said that there is racial profiling, excessive spying and the removal of basic civil liberties from innocent individuals. It has also been mentioned to me that Prevent is perhaps a toxic brand'.

These claims of toxicity can be understood through reflecting on high-profile examples in which young people from Muslim backgrounds, in particular, have found themselves targeted by Prevent for innocuous, and at times farcical reasons. In August 2016, for instance, an eight-year-old boy was reported to Prevent by teachers at his primary school for wearing a T-shirt pronouncing 'I want to be like Abu Bakr al-Siddique' – a reference to an important historical figure within Sunni Islam. As the *Independent* newspaper subsequently reported, the boy's interview with police officers (from which the parents were absent) included questions about ISIS, and the boy's religious convictions, 'such as whether he believed Christians go to hell when they die' (Mortimer 2016). Three years later, in January 2019, a thirteen-year-old boy was questioned under the strategy for using the phrase 'eco-terrorist' in a discussion of environmental activism (Grierson 2019). More recently still, in June 2021, an eleven-year-old primary school pupil was referred to Prevent having been asked what he would do with a hypothetical sum of money. The boy's response – 'give alms to the oppressed' – was misinterpreted by the teacher as 'give arms to the oppressed' (Taylor 2021).

The negative publicity attracted by cases such as these has gained momentum through related incidents connected to, but not formally under the remit of, Prevent. The March 2016 questioning of two brothers – aged five and seven – by uniformed police because one had brought a toy gun to school, for example, required Bedfordshire local education authority to clarify that the visit 'was not in a Prevent capacity, but routine police attendance', in its subsequent admission of racial discrimination (Addley and Topping 2017). In other instances, the stigma of Prevent has generated unwanted, if erroneous, news coverage. The widespread reporting of a high-profile story – in which a ten-year old Muslim boy was allegedly visited by police having mis-described his terraced house as a 'terrorist house' – was denounced by Lancashire Police as a misrepresentation of a more complex situation (BBC 2016).

The striking sense of injustice generated by incidents such as these means they attract significant media, political, and public attention. Importantly, they also dovetail with and speak to more pervasive, if less dramatic, concerns articulated by think tanks, campaign groups, and beyond. A 2016 Muslim Council of Britain briefing on Muslim experiences of counter-extremism policies, for instance, argued that the 'fundamental approach is problematic and lacks an evidentiary base: Conservative religious and cultural practices (and more recently political beliefs) are classed as "non-violent extremism" and the first step in a "conveyor belt" towards violent terrorism, without any evidence underpinning this theory of radicalisation' (Muslim Council of Britain 2016: 4). This increasingly expansive conception of extremism, the report suggests, contributes to the construction of Muslims as a 'suspect community' within the UK today, fuelling Islamophobia and discouraging political participation amongst Muslims (Muslim Council of Britain 2016: 4).

An Open Society Justice Initiative report, also published in 2016, makes a related argument, suggesting that 'The UK's Prevent Strategy, which purports to prevent terrorism, creates a serious risk of human rights violations' (Open Society Foundations 2016: 15). The report continues: 'The programme is flawed in both its design and application, rendering it not only unjust but also counterproductive' (Open Society Foundations 2016: 15). Cage Advocacy (2015: 3) – an organisation established on behalf of those impacted by the post-9/11 war on terror – took the opportunity a year earlier, on the tenth anniversary of the 7/7 London bombings, to argue more stridently still with its claim: 'the Prevent Strategy is based on a flawed evidential basis, which criminalises innocent and democratic political activism and dissent, and perpetuates political grievances.' High-profile organisations like Rights Watch and Liberty UK oppose the policy, too, and have frequently published briefings and evidence against Prevent. Their joint briefing (Rights Watch and Liberty 2017) on the Higher Education and Research Bill, for instance, notes that the, 'policy, as well as being flawed in design, leads in practice to very real human rights violations.'

Concerns like these added momentum to calls for an independent review of Prevent to which the government committed in 2019 under the Counter-Terrorism and Border Security Act 2019. The former Independent Reviewer of Terrorism Legislation, Lord Carlile, was initially appointed to head the review, the terms of reference for which included evaluating whether the strategy was achieving its objectives; assessing the effectiveness and efficiency of its delivery, and asking how to respond to criticisms and complaints around Prevent (UK Home Office 2021b). Lord Carlile's appointment, though, proved controversial, in part for his previous support for the strategy (Bowcott 2019), leading to a legal challenge against the Home Office led by Rights Watch UK that saw him replaced by Lord Shawcross and a re-launch of the review in May 2021. This re-launch did not, for many, go far enough in addressing Prevent's controversies, and the review was boycotted by influential organisations, including Amnesty International and Liberty (Grierson 2021). Indeed, February 2022 saw publication of a competitor 'People's Review of Prevent' by academics, community organisers, and others, which argued that Prevent, among other things, is Islamophobic, discriminatory, undermines free expression and the safeguarding of vulnerable people, and relies on profiling mechanisms which target poor communities and Muslims (Holmwood and Aitlhadj 2022: 5–6).

International contexts

Before turning to the now-voluminous scholarship on radicalisation, extremism, and their policy responses, one final piece of useful background context worth noting here is that the UK's Prevent Strategy is not unique. A number of states around the world now have counter-radicalisation strategies of their own, as indeed do some multi-national institutions (Foret and Markoviti 2020). Within this broad trajectory, Prevent is important, in part, because it represents one of the most robust counter-radicalisation strategies and has served as a model of 'best practice' for several other European countries. The Netherlands, Denmark, and Norway, for instance, all offer examples of states who have followed the UK's approach in adopting a 'comprehensive' strategy with defined goals, methods, and budgets (Vidino and Brandon 2012: 164).

Outside of Europe, New Zealand recently revised their counter-terrorism and violent extremism strategy (New Zealand Government 2022), following the high-profile 2019 terrorist attack in Christchurch. In this document, the government outlines its vision for the strategy, which, much like Prevent, adopts a 'whole society'-based approach to this end, co-opting among others, local communities, public and private sectors, and the media in its delivery. In a similar vein, the Nigerian Government, in 2017, introduced a 'substantive policy framework and national action plan'. This document lays out a multi-stakeholder approach to countering violent extremism that again shares many of the features observable in the equivalent frameworks of states such as the UK or New Zealand. While the strategy adopts a broad national strategy, the Nigerian Government unsurprisingly positions it as, in no small part, a response to the threat posed by Boko Haram in the North of Nigeria (Federal Republic of Nigeria, 2017: 9).

Outside of these sorts of strategies, many other states have also employed forms of counter-radicalisation that are more targeted, for example, focusing on specific spaces or individuals. The substantive focus of this book – higher education – is one notable example of a sector regularly singled out for initiatives designed to (depending on the framing) counter violent extremism, build resilience, or safeguard young people. We address this in more detail below, but the perceived susceptibility of young people to extremist narratives has seen the emergence of educational initiatives designed to promote 'shared' or 'secular' (national) values such as the UK's Fundamental British Values (FBV) education framework, and the *Grande mobilisation de l'École pour les valeurs de la République* in France. At the individual level, Saudi Arabia's Religious Rehabilitation and Disengagement Programme (Boucek 2008) offers an example of a programme designed to promote disengagement from extremism for those perceived to have already been radicalised.

This initiative works exclusively with prisoners incarcerated for being sympathetic towards or supporting extremism, as well as those convicted of conducting acts of extremist violence.

While not exhaustive of Prevent equivalents, the above serves to illustrate the global proliferation of counter-radicalisation policies and initiatives. Not all states have adopted the same multi-stakeholder and 'whole society' approach that typifies Prevent today. Nevertheless, the influence of Prevent has clearly been felt internationally, and aspects of its design and delivery are undoubtedly evident across the globe. In the following, we turn now to some of the scholarship around radicalisation and counter-radicalisation, beginning with work on the former's utility as an explanatory framework for political violence and terrorism.

Academic scholarship and critique of (counter-)radicalisation

A first key focus of the relevant scholarship concerns the conceptual moorings of the term 'radicalisation' – a relatively recent addition to our vocabularies of political violence (Heath-Kelly *et al.* 2015: 4). This recentness is itself a source of reflection in the literature. For Cassam (2018: 188), the term has multiple attractions for policymaking communities in that – *contra* alternative or rival explanations – the 'radicalisation model' 'doesn't require one to conceive of terrorists as rational agents, it doesn't imply that terrorism might be justifiable, and it has policy implications that governments find congenial'. Kundnani (2012: 5), similarly, traces the term's popularity to political instrumentalism, arguing that 'the radicalisation discourse was, from the beginning, circumscribed by the demands of counter-terrorist policy-makers rather than an attempt to objectively study how terrorism comes into being.' This is why, for Kundnani (2012: 5), 'Answers to the question of what drives this radicalisation process are to exclude ascribing any causative role to the actions of western governments or their allies in other parts of the world.' Silva's (2018: 48) recent revisiting of Kundnani's genealogy argued likewise, that 'academic discourses of radicalisation can be approached as instrumental for government decision-making related to counter-terrorism.' Peter Neumann (2008: 4), of the International Centre for the Study of Radicalisation, casts the term's origins in similar light, seeing its emergence as a response to the political difficulties of explaining – without exonerating – terrorism (see also Butler 2002). Alex Schmid (2013: 6), meanwhile, argues that conceptual histories of 'radicalism' have value because they 'can offer some guidance as to what should be a defensible understanding of the term radicalisation'.

This appeal to a defensible understanding of radicalisation brings us to what is perhaps the most common focus within conceptual work on this term: its abiding ambiguities, such that 'Radicalisation is now part of our daily vocabulary, but … remains mired in controversy and confusion' (Coolsaet 2016: 4). Important work on this question has therefore set out to map the concept's heterogenous usage, and the academic and political importance of these ambiguities. Anthony Richards (2015: 371), for instance, situates the ongoing definitional confusion in terms of a blurring in the relations between concepts such as radicalisation, terrorism, and extremism. Mark Sedgwick's (2010) intervention remains influential in part because of his observation that the term 'radicalisation' functions both as an absolute concept with intrinsic meaning, *and* as a relative concept that is used to differentiate positions on policy continuums. This conceptual complexity is compounded, for Sedgwick (2010: 482), by the term's variable usage across security, foreign policy, and integration contexts, meaning that the lines between, say, 'radical' and 'moderate' are drawn in different places, and on different continua, depending upon the policy area. More sympathetic toward this concept, though, are authors such as Peter Neumann (2003: 873), for whom definitional confusion boils down to 'a principal conceptual fault-line … between notions of radicalization that emphasize extremist beliefs ("cognitive radicalization") and those that focus on extremist behaviour ("behavioural radicalization")'. Recognising this division, for Neumann, offers opportunity for resuscitating the concept which 'is likely to dominate public discourse, research and policy agendas for years to come' (Neumann 2003: 874).

This distinction between cognitive and behavioural conceptions of radicalisation is an important one that can be found within the UK Prevent Strategy itself, as well as within scholarly debate in this area (see Cherney *et al.* 2022: 99; Elshimi 2015: 112–113):

> This area of Prevent is based on the premise that people being drawn into radicalisation and recruitment can be identified and then provided with support. The purpose of that support is to dissuade them from engaging in and supporting terrorist-related activity. This support is sometimes described as 'de-radicalisation, a term which is sometimes used to refer to *cognitive or behavioural change*: in the context of our own programmes *we use it to refer to both*.
>
> HM Government 2011: 56, our emphasis

Cassam (2018: 195), drawing on Sageman (2016), argues that the term is understood to mean both 'the formation or acquisition of extremist beliefs', and 'a turn to violence', with understanding of the relationship between the two states both confused and contested. Hardy (2018: 79–80), similarly, notes that 'An important distinction is often drawn between "cognitive" radicalisation, which focuses on extremist beliefs, and "behavioural" radicalisation, which focuses on extremist behaviour.' This matters, he continues, because it 'gets at the question: has somebody radicalised once they adopt and internalise extremist views, or only if they engage in some criminal conduct (such as training for terrorism) as a result?' (Hardy 2018: 80). Monaghan and Molnar (2016: 395–397) add a third perspective here, distinguishing between cognitive, behavioural, and narrative approaches in their review of the relevant literature, with narrative approaches seen to move beyond the traditional focus on personality traits and social networks in order to emphasise the role of wider social contexts in radicalisation. This added complexity chimes with recent work by Clubb and McDaid (2019), for whom the very framing of debate around cognitive and behavioural approaches emphasises the agency (or lack thereof) of ideas as a driver of behaviour in a way that risks neglecting the wider structural contexts in which violence emerges.

Clubb and McDaid's (2019) critical realist take on 'radicalisation' helps us to interrogate the terrain upon which concepts such as 'radicalisation' are discussed. More critical still, though, is scholarship in which 'radicalisation' is simply seen as a discursive construct that *produces*, rather than reflects, reality. The work of Charlotte Heath-Kelly (2013) is particularly important here, with her approach to radicalisation as an 'invention' that supports and justifies UK counter-terrorism policy, including through enabling interventions toward communities deemed 'at risk of becoming risky' (see also Heath-Kelly *et al.* 2015: 1). In her more recent work, Heath-Kelly (2017a) identifies an epidemiological logic within radicalisation discourse that builds, in part, on historical public health policy efforts to protect the general population against contaminants (see also Heath-Kelly 2017b). Coppock and McGovern (2014: 246), in turn, situate radicalisation discourse within a wider 'psychologisation of social problems' that is particularly pronounced in social policies aimed at 'safeguarding' the vulnerable. This development, for them, should be located within broader neoliberal governmentalities that are geared toward pre-emptive intervention to avert future threats (Coppock and McGovern 2014: 252–253). Aistrope (2016: 183), finally, offers the different but related insight that the radicalisation discourse relies upon a 'Muslim paranoia' narrative in which 'resentment towards Western society is said to be motivated to some degree by a paranoid and conspiracy-driven worldview, which is thought to thrive in alienated and disempowered communities.'

Taken together, this literature points to the existence of considerable debate around ideas and understandings of '(counter-)radicalisation'. This includes, amongst other things, debate around the origins of radicalisation discourse and counter-radicalisation policy; around the (specific, or appropriate, or proper) meaning of 'radicalisation'; around the relationship between radicalisation and adjacent concepts such as extremism and terrorism, and around the relationship between radicalisation and the 'real world' of extreme ideas and violences. Questions and concerns such as these, as we shall see in later chapters, are prominent, too, in vernacular discussion of (counter-)radicalisation.

Mechanics and mechanisms of counter-radicalisation

Related to the primarily conceptual work considered above is a body of academic literature exploring the *effectiveness* of counter-radicalisation strategies such as Prevent. As Prevent has developed, the scope and focus of this literature has itself also shifted. When it was first introduced as an effort to win the 'hearts and minds' of British Muslims, critics such as Paul Thomas (2010) highlighted important reasons for scepticism toward Prevent, including its counter-productive targeting of Muslim communities (returned to below) and the inter-departmental conflicts generated by the new strategy's initial design and implementation. In his subsequent work, Thomas (2012, 2016) explores alternatives to Prevent, drawing on previous policy experiences (successful and otherwise) in areas such as education and multiculturalism.

A particularly prominent criticism of Prevent's effectiveness in its earliest incarnations was the way in which it problematically blurred counter-terrorism and community cohesion activities (Thomas 2014; Husband and Alam, 2011). O'Toole *et al.* (2012: 378), for instance, highlight how Prevent adopted a 'limited and securitised model of state-Muslim engagement' that led to dissatisfaction both locally and nationally. These early efforts were, for many, sorely lacking on account of Prevent's unwillingness to open into an honest dialogue about sources of dissatisfaction such as UK foreign policy (Brighton 2007), or the inequalities that continue to be experienced by Muslims in the UK (Kundnani 2009). Writing at a similar time, David Stevens (2009, 2011) argued that Prevent would be ineffective (if not counter-productive) for erroneously believing that the 'slide' towards violence could be addressed at the level of *ideas*, as well as on account of mistaken assumptions about why individuals join radical groups and how they operate. The idea that offering 'better thinking' would divert people from extremist groups operated, Stevens argued, on the 'outmoded assumption' that Preventing Violent Extremism (PVE) should be about 'rescuing the brainwashed' (2011: 173–174). Moreover, state support for and (crucially) *funding* of moderate religious groups, also risks reducing competition for potential moderate members that could allow extremism to flourish

(Stevens 2011: 177), while alienating those who hold different ideas to the state-backed 'centre ground' (2011: 183). Linked to this, Thomas (2009) argued that the community cohesion project that Prevent purported to be supporting suffered from not being 'whole community', but instead over-whelmingly focused on Muslims in the UK. This contradiction not only risked alienating young Muslims but also 'creating resentment among white working-class young people once again marginalised by a funding priority' (Thomas 2009: 290).

Turning our attention to the internal mechanisms of the Prevent Strategy, we return to Channel as one of the most significant here, with its aims to deliver, 'a multi-agency approach to identify and provide support to indi-viduals who are at risk of being drawn into terrorism' (HM Government 2020: 6). Evaluating Channel's effectiveness, however, has not been straight-forward, with the initiative scantly researched on account of its 'closely guarding its practitioners and working practices' (Pettinger 2020: 971). The recruitment of mentors, the training that they are offered, and the accreditation of intervention providers are all aspects around which very little remains known, and to date there has been no public evaluation of its outcomes (Thornton and Bouhana 2019). Nevertheless, the small body of research that has managed to secure privileged access to those involved in Channel, or with those who have worked or gone through the process, has raised concerns about how Channel approaches risk and vulnerability, on whom it focuses, and how it functions.

Much of the critique here stems from problems associated with observ-ing and quantifying risk. Tasked with identifying, assessing, and inter-vening upon risk in a context of worst-case scenarios (Bigo 2011: 113), Channel practitioners must quickly make visible and quantifiable that which is unknown and uncertain (Aradau and van Munster 2012: 102). The 'Extreme Risk Guidance' framework (ERG22+)[1] is the primary means with which to do this, which sets up a series of twenty-two broad 'hazardous' behaviours including 'engagement' factors such as 'Excitement, comrade-ship & adventure' and 'political, moral motivation' (National Offenders Management Service 2011). By interviewing Channel practitioners, Tom Pettinger (2020: 978–979) reveals how the combination of a very broad array of risk factors, a risk-averse environment, and an emphasis on 'intu-ition and gut feeling', create a system where effectiveness is not only very difficult to discern but where race becomes central in predictive efforts.

So, the effectiveness of Channel has been criticised, firstly, on account of so little being known about this subjective process and its outcomes that 'success' against its stated aims is impossible to ascertain. A second line of criticism, however, concerns the effectiveness of these interventions for the broader Prevent Strategy, on account of their role in alienating Muslims and stigmatising Islam. Arun Kundnani (2009: 34) refers to interviews he conducted with individuals working with young people going through the Channel programme, noting that – in their view – the process was merely about, 'identifying "naughty Muslims" rather than genuine cases'. Whether one views this as an unintentional consequence or an intended effect, Channel's preoccupation with young people who exhibit 'signs of extremism' in a pre-criminal space has repeatedly drawn the attention of critics for whom 'the pre-emptive framing of Channel effectively makes particular subjects problematic (Islam, politics, religion, etc.) through future potential, thus permitting mediation in the present' (Elshimi 2017: 154).

Finally, as argued above, one of the more contemporary and controversial developments within the Strategy has been the Prevent Duty. The Duty has enshrined in law the need for public sector workers to pay due regard to preventing people from being drawn into terrorism. The rationale for this expansion is a simple utilitarian one: the strategy's access to the public is significantly increased once millions of public sector workers are recruited to look out for those deemed, or suspected of being, vulnerable (Heath-Kelly 2017a). However, while there is much we do not know about the practice of counter-radicalisation, we *do know* it is a specialised field requiring careful work. Giving a counter-radicalisation responsibility to already overstretched public sector workers has therefore generated considerable concerns around how this work can be done effectively, given the resources and time allotted to this task (Spiller *et al.* 2018).

Consequences of counter-radicalisation

A third important critical literature emphasises the consequences of (counter-)radicalisation discourse and policy for individuals and communities. Of especial prominence here (and pointed to in our above discussion of discursive scholarship) is the contribution of (counter-)radicalisation initiatives to the production of Muslims as a 'suspect community'. Pantazis and Pemberton (2009) were amongst the first to apply this concept to Muslim communities' experiences of the 'war on terror', re-purposing it from Paddy Hillyard's earlier (1993) ground-breaking exploration of Irish communities' experiences under successive UK counter-terrorism regimes. Although the applicability of the concept to these new circumstances has generated conceptual debate (e.g., Greer 2010; Pantazis and Pemberton 2011; Breen-Smyth 2014), many have found it a productive framework through which to understand the impacts of the UK's Prevent Strategy.

Imran Awan (2012: 1158) argues that Prevent 'risks further marginalizing and stigmatizing Muslim communities', while O'Toole *et al.* (2016: 174) foresee a future in which Prevent will remain 'patchy, contested and/or resisted', yet retain its potential to facilitate a 'politics of unease' about Muslims in British society (Archer 2009: 332). Ragazzi's (2016: 725) theoretical reframing of the 'suspect community' concept to that of 'suspect category' sheds important light on the more insidious 'active participation and involvement of Muslims in their own policing', that is required of counter-radicalisation frameworks such as Prevent (see also Ragazzi 2015). Taylor (2020) has since applied Ragazzi's framing to explore the silencing of Muslim communities under the strategy, while Abbas (2019: 278) looks similarly at the endogenous, intra-communal, consequences of the far more complex network of power relations that runs through the production of Muslims as 'suspect':

> Co-opting Muslims to counter extremism means community members become accomplices of state terror tactics (Sofsky 1997: 130–144), reproducing conditions under which they are made suspect by policing Muslim identities and practices, stigmatizing members who have been subjected to counter-terrorism policing, informing on fellow Muslims to avoid becoming suspect themselves, or monitoring Muslims' activities under Prevent which, by engendering mistrust, is counter-productive for countering extremism or terrorism.

Work such as this intersects with a wider literature on the consequences of counter-terrorism more broadly for diverse publics. Where some of this work highlights significant incursions upon citizenship as this category is lived or experienced by those from minority communities in particular (e.g., Jarvis and Lister 2013a), other contributions are more optimistic in identifying creative and dissenting forms of political engagement with counter-terrorism initiatives, discourses, and professionals even under circumstances that may be extremely challenging (e.g., O'Loughlin and Gillespie 2012; Jarvis and Lister 2013b). Here, the structural relationship between security policy and its consequences is mitigated by the interests and agency of those individuals and communities through which the former works.

A significant body of theoretical work has explored the expansion of contemporary counter-radicalisation initiatives across civil society, especially in relation to notions of risk, surveillance, and governmentality (Mythen and Walklate 2006; De Goede and Simon 2013; Martin 2014; Elshimi 2015; Farrell and Lander 2019). Drawing heavily on Foucault's work on power, strategies such as Prevent are sometimes identified as fitting within a broader *dispositif* of precautionary risk management (Aradau and van Munster 2007: 103) that accelerated after the unanticipated events of September 11th, 2001 to include a raft of enhanced technologies and practices designed to counter terrorism and mitigate risk (Bigo 2014; Maguire and Westbrook 2020). At the same time, mitigation and preparation in the face of threats are not an entirely modern phenomenon, and the imagined carnage of what could occur within these *dispositifs* of risk serves as a constant reminder of the need to mitigate against the 'uncertain, unpredictable events that might never happen but are always possible' (Wichum 2013: 167). The subsequent production of a 'risk knowledge' has put emphasis on pre-emption and provides the conditions of possibility for a strategy like Prevent that renders subjects 'pre-emptively governable' (Heath-Kelly 2013: 395) 'risk repositories' (Mythen and Walklate 2006: 391).

With reference to the pre-emptive logic that underpins contemporary thinking about risk and security, a number of critics have also drawn attention to the ethical dilemma of having such a prominent aspect of UK counter-terrorism operating in a largely pre-criminal space (Innes *et al.* 2017). As with all pre-emptive or predictive initiatives, one must immediately answer the difficult question of 'how far upstream from the harm being countered is it viable or appropriate to go?' (Innes *et al.* 2017: 273). The legitimacy of political intervention upon those who have not committed any criminal offence is one important concern implicit in these comments. As, indeed, is the way state power has expanded (or overreached) where Prevent has become emblematic of the state's moving further beyond questions of emergency, 'to address more complex issues of community, integration and cohesion *through the lens* of security' (Rogers 2008: 52; original emphasis), such that security has increasingly become 'everyone's concern' (Jarvis and Lister 2010). As we have seen, the 2015 Prevent Duty formalised this shift in law, further entrenching disciplinary and governmental modalities of power and transforming 'how millions of public sector workers see and engage with their environments' (Martin 2018: 267). In this context, Rogers (2008: 53) therefore argues that the formal expansion of UK counter-terrorism powers represents a 'significant shift in … the focus of security-related strategic policy to underpin an emergent governmentality, that seeks to realign ideological thinking and thus citizens' conduct across the breadth of activities that are being generated'. Others have put it more simply: that the duty has required swathes of society to 'constantly look over our shoulder' (Carter, 2017: 24), and be vigilant to the 'enemy within' (Vaughan-Williams 2008).

Health has been a prominent area of empirical focus within work on the impact of Prevent, with research questioning the strategy's legitimacy and effectiveness here (Heath-Kelly and Strausz 2019), demonstrating the harmful effect it has had through encouraging self-censorship among staff (Younis and Jadhav 2019a), highlighting its negative impact upon clinical interactions (Younis and Jadhav 2019b) and arguing that it has, effectively, securitised mental health services and provision (Aked 2022). Even more scrutinised than the health sector, however, has been the field of UK education at all levels, from pre-school through to higher education. A recent but growing body of work here has sought to speak with practitioners within education, and on occasion, students, to gain a better understanding of attitudes towards the Prevent Duty in these spaces, and of the details within institutional implementation thereof. This literature has tended to focus on secondary and further education (Beighton and Revell 2020; Moffat and Gerard 2020; Busher *et al.* 2019; Elwick and Jerome 2019; James 2022), although a smaller body of work now exists with an explicit focus on UK higher education that we cover in greater detail below (Brown and Saeed 2015; Spiller *et al.* 2018; Whiting et al. 2021b).

It is interesting to observe the existence of significantly different expectations from the government toward different levels of the UK education system, such that primary, secondary, or further education tutors receive considerably more direction than do university lecturers, for example. The teaching of Fundamental British Values (FBV) is a requirement of all levels of education below higher education, for instance, and became a focal point of statutory guidance given to practitioners. This idea was pushed to the fore of the 2011 iteration of Prevent after the 'Trojan Horse' scandal (Revell and Bryan 2018), featured in the government's definition of extremism, and formed the basis of guidance produced for schools prior to the CTSA 2015 coming into law. Common concerns with the very idea of FBVs include the extent to which such values can be said to be distinctly British or comprehensively reflect the values of British citizens (Struthers 2017; Jarvis *et al.* 2020; Marsden *et al.* 2022). Revell and Bryan (2018: 7), for example, are amongst those who remind us of the contingency of these values when they say that 'there is no such thing as a set of values that is British; there are only the values that particular governments or policy documents at specific times insist are British.' Often unconvinced by their neutrality, academic criticism has therefore frequently turned its attention to the political functions they serve and how practitioners feel about delivering this content (Farrell 2016; Farrell and Lander 2019). Farrell and Lander (2019: 471) conclude that the requirement to reinforce FBVs in schools demonstrates how 'British education practice has become one of the racialised and securitised sites of the domestic war on terror.' Here, FBVs are seen as an attempt to reify a hegemonic version of Britishness that is conservative and racialised and in so doing, 'seeks to discipline, train, absorb and neutralise difference' and, indeed, define vocal opposition to these as "extremism" (Farrell 2016 294; see also Kaleem 2021).

The way vulnerability and safeguarding have been deployed at *all levels* of education in the name of counter-radicalisation has been another source of concern. Of course, the presence of a duty of care towards students – whether children or adults – is neither new nor in itself necessarily controversial. However, vulnerability and safeguarding have taken on new and concerning meanings in the context of Prevent that endangers the civil liberties of young people, especially young Muslims (Jarvis and Lister 2017), encouraging enhanced surveillance of, and data collection on, these populations in the name of intervening upon *suspected* vulnerability (Coppock and McGovern 2014: 244–245). Teachers are encouraged to utilise their professional judgement when considering potential vulnerability, but this will never be a consistent yardstick and, exercised in the absence of full and accurate information, may be highly speculative and involve a very open interpretation of behaviours that may constitute engagement with 'extremism' (Coppock 2014: 120). While there are serious reservations about including something as politicised as counter-radicalisation within existing safeguarding frameworks, it must be noted that other research has revealed how some practitioners have found this to be a useful means with which to navigate the new requirements of the duty (Jerome *et al.* 2019).

In the specific context of UK higher education (UKHE), where our own research is situated, we can observe overlaps with broader commentaries about counter-radicalisation in education as well as distinct lines of critique based on the specificity of this sector. Echoing the scepticism included above, research has explored how framing the duty as a form of safeguarding has been productive for 'depoliticised and psychosocial' explanations of radicalisation to dominate, justifying the 'medicalised language of intervention' (Qurashi 2017: 8) to conceal macro-level factors in favour of behavioural ones (Barrett 2018). The legality of the Prevent Duty within UKHE has also been the subject of discussion, especially with reference to possible infringements upon the Equality Duty and the European Convention on Human Rights (Barrett 2018; Cram and Fenwick 2018; Zedner 2018). However, this is not an opinion shared by all legal scholars (Greer and Bell 2018). Many of these legal arguments are predicated on the fear that the arrival of the duty within UKHE will have detrimental effects on freedom of speech, now that forms of expression are tied up with the potential for vulnerability. Linked to this, critics have lamented the 'chilling effect' the duty will have in classrooms and on campus (Spiller et al. 2018), something likely to be felt far more acutely by minority ethnic students given the 'racialised optics' of the radicalisation discourse (Puwar 2004: 51).

Despite the wealth of research on Prevent and its manifestations across British society, there is a surprising lack of work systematically engaging with the views and experiences of those likely to be subject to this framework. Work on the perceptions and understandings of students – the focus of this book – for example, has often concentrated on the lived experiences of Muslim students in particular (Brown and Saeed 2015; Abbas *et al.* 2021; Zempi and Tripli 2022). While understandable, and hugely significant, this focus also opens important questions about the wider implications of the UK's counter-radicalisation approach. Do the feelings of discrimination, depoliticisation, and so forth reported by Muslim students speak to wider concerns, or are these distinctive to the lived experiences of particular communities (Abbas *et al.* 2021; Zempi and Tripli 2022)? How generalisable, if at all, is Brown and Saeed's (2015: 1962) discovery that female Muslim students were being denied the opportunity to become 'students in the fullest sense' due to their exclusion from traditions of radical politics on campus? Our call for a wider focus here is not, to be clear, to trivialise the particularities of gendered, racialised, and other experiences of Prevent: at stake here is not simply a broadening move that involves adding the experiences of other individuals or communities to our understanding. Rather, our suggestion is that greater engagement with heterogeneous experiences and understandings of, here, (counter-)radicalisation adds context to the vital work already done in this area, shedding new light on the wider social and political contexts that surround particularised experiences and encounters.

Work by McGlynn and McDaid (2019) as well as Whiting *et al.* (2021a) takes us a little way towards this kind of understanding, with their adoption of similar research designs to the work above but wider recruitment of participants. Whiting *et al.* (2021a), for instance, found that students were broadly in favour of the placement of the Prevent Duty within UKHE structures, while remaining mindful of a series of important shortcomings and misgivings therein. For some students, the duty amounted to something of a pragmatic compromise where, on balance, the duty was justified given the risks associated with radicalisation. Reservations, however, included scepticism around efficacy, concerns about the way the duty would likely target suspect communities, the appropriateness of educators conducting this duty, and the coherence of vulnerability as an actionable concept (Whiting *et al.* 2021a: 19–22). McGlynn and McDaid's (2019) focus group research produced similar findings regarding the conceptualisation of vulnerability and revealed student's scepticism around a 'grooming' model of radicalisation. Interestingly, however, the study found no evidence of the duty producing a 'chilling effect' when discussing terrorism in class, or indeed upon any form of 'risky intellectual inquiry' (571).

Conclusion

In the preceding section, we set out to demonstrate that there now exists a significant body of research exploring the impacts and effects of the Prevent Strategy across social and political life, including in the health and education sectors. This work is valuable, in part, for emphasising the emphasis often placed on the susceptibility of young people to radicalisation (Ghosh *et al.* 2017), and for highlighting and tracing the ways in which the Prevent

Duty has formally extended counter-radicalisation into new settings. However, save for a few key pieces of work (e.g., McGlynn and McDaid 2019), there remains a striking lack of engagement with 'lay' individuals and their encounters with Prevent in the context of their everyday lives as citizens, as users of healthcare, or – as in our case – as students. As explored further in subsequent chapters, the absence of such voices in public dialogue about Prevent should be addressed for at least three reasons.

First, policies such as Prevent intervene in, and work through, everyday lives and encounters: encounters between doctors and patients, between teachers and pupils, between professors and students, and so on. To fully understand their operation and implications, it is, therefore, vital that we take seriously such encounters and how they are understood by their subjects. While abstract theoretical work or large-scale quantitative studies, for instance, have an important role to play in developing critique of government initiatives and actions, it is vital that interpretatively rich qualitative work aimed at *understanding* these dynamics is not neglected. Second, there may be normative reasons, too, for consulting with populations to whom security 'is done', and, in the process, attempting to provide space for those populations to speak for themselves, in their own words (Jarvis 2019a). Such work might be valuable, in part, for bringing forward neglected or marginalised stories and experiences. Finally, as detailed in Chapter 2, the perspectives and experiences of 'lay' people in relation to high-profile and contentious political initiatives such as Prevent also matter because they both draw upon, and tell us much, about wider political values and their understanding in everyday life. What people say about, and how people understand, say, radicalisation, tells us a great deal – we will argue – about the micro-level working of politics, citizenship, and especially security at everyday or vernacular levels. Taking this seriously, therefore, might open new ways of conceptualising or mapping such values, including by stepping away from the political elites on whose ideas and actions academic scholarship frequently focuses.

With these ambitions in mind, this chapter as a whole has sought to situate the book's central argument within relevant political and academic contexts. We began by introducing the Prevent Strategy, exploring its underpinning conceptual logics, its delivery methods, its evolution and, finally, its stated outcomes and variable impacts. Prevent is a controversial and widely debated political intervention, we argued, and having provided an overview of its rationale and functioning, we therefore addressed what has become a significant body of public criticism thereof. Accusations of Prevent as a 'toxic brand' responsible for compromising human rights and stigmatising Islam are criticisms regularly levelled at the strategy, and compounded by a growing body of critical academic research. Moreover, as the Strategy has expanded into the public sector via the imposition of a public duty, a small but growing body of research has also sought to explore the mandating of counter-radicalisation activity within public policy spheres such as health and education. A critical but currently under-researched aspect of this agenda has been talking to the ordinary people who inhabit these spaces and to/for which security is being done. In the next chapter, we outline the framework for vernacular security and argue for why everyday, non-elite, security utterances such as those from UKHE students warrant further attention both to develop existing research within this field as well as to diversify theoretical models of security.

Note

1 The risk factors within the ERG 22+ were later transferred to the Vulnerability Assessment Framework (VAF) for use in Channel guidance.

2

Vernacular security and (counter-)radicalisation

In Chapter 1, we argued that scholarship on the Prevent Strategy has shed important light on the emergence, working, and implications of the UK's approach to counter-radicalisation since 2007. Although this work has generated important theoretical and empirical insight into profound social, political, and ethical issues raised by the UK's approach, there remains significant scope for further analysis of the lived experiences of (counter-)radicalisation amongst specific populations. The neglect, to date, of the experiences and perspectives of university students is particularly important, we argue, because this population is at considerable likelihood of encountering the strategy in their everyday lives. First, for demographic reasons – due to the cohort's age profile, and Prevent's tendency to target younger populations. And, second, contextually – because of Prevent's prominence within contemporary Higher Education Institutions (HEIs) in the UK, not least since the imposition of the Prevent Duty upon HEIs under Section 26(1) of the CTSA 2015. This book's detailed and qualitatively rich engagement with the perspectives of students stands, in part, as an attempt to address this omission – an effort to centre their conceptions and constructions of Prevent and its targets.

To begin to do this, this chapter now sets out the theoretical and methodological foundations for the remainder of the book. We begin by arguing that security issues – such as radicalisation – and their solutions – such as the Prevent Strategy – are neither given nor inevitable. Rather, they are 'made' through the discursive work of particular actors and their experiences, perceptions and – crucially – constructions of the world. From this broad starting point, we then offer an overview of important work on the construction and functions of security discourse. In it, we argue that, notwithstanding important insight on the contingent (and therefore precarious) character of security paradigms, this scholarship has tended to focus on the security constructions – the security speak – of powerful or privileged actors such as governments and other political elites. This, in turn, has meant that alternative 'bottom up' discourses on security have tended to be neglected and taken seriously only by a small number of 'critical' theoretical approaches, such as within feminist and postcolonial traditions. Following a brief sketch of the importance of these critical alternatives, we then introduce the notion of 'vernacular security' as a productive framework for capturing 'bottom-up' understandings or constructions of the sort on which we focus in this book. A vernacular approach to (counter-)radicalisation, we argue, should: (i) centre 'everyday' experiences and understandings; (ii) pay attention to how those experiences and understandings are constructed, communicated, and contested, and (iii) be wary of generalising or abstracting from the distinctive specificities of concrete contexts and communities. An orientation of this sort has significant analytical, conceptual, political, and normative appeal for (re-)thinking security politics in this area and indeed beyond. The chapter concludes by introducing the methodological approach employed in our research. Here, we discuss the value and limitations of focus groups as a strategy for accessing (or, better, co-constructing) vernacular securities, reflecting on issues of recruitment and representation within our own focus groups, and the framework we employed for analysing the findings we generated.

Security challenges, security discourse

Security challenges like radicalisation, terrorism, or extremism can be understood (as we have seen in Chapter 1) through very different lenses. In the first instance, the characteristics, causes, and significance of such issues are fundamentally contested. As, in the second, are the appropriate mechanisms for their redress. Is radicalisation rooted, for example, in psychological or theological dynamics (Kundnani 2012)? Is the threat posed by terrorism truly existential (see Wolfendale 2016), or one comparable to the risk of DIY accidents or drowning in bathtubs (Mueller and Stewart 2021)? Should terrorism be addressed through military mechanisms, legal frameworks, or diplomatic initiatives (Jackson *et al.* 2011: 222–248)? What incursions on liberty, if any, are we willing to countenance to prevent the emergence or escalation of potential dangers (Waldron 2003; Macdonald 2008)?

Questions such as these are of profound importance in the design and delivery of measures aimed at improving human or national security. At the same time, however, it is possible to go a little further than this and ask not (only) how much of a threat to security something such as, say, extremism poses. But (also), under what conditions are issues such as extremism (or terrorism, or any others) even thinkable *as* security issues *at all* (see Krause and Williams 1996; Smith 1999). Every day, individuals and communities around the world suffer harm from a wide range of causes with varying degrees of avoidability – war, poverty, famine, pandemics, domestic vio-lence, and so on. Some of these are routinely understood as security issues, others far less frequently receive this treatment. Some issues – perhaps rec-reational drug use or communism – look emphatically like security threats to some observers in certain contexts, yet decidedly mundane or unremark-able to others. Other issues still are able to sustain very different, even oppo-sitional, interpretations of security. Is migration, for instance, a threat to national security? Or, are the practices of national security a threat to the security of would-be migrants (McDonald 2008: 567–68)?

These contestabilities have multiple diagnoses, and likely multiple roots. In some readings, they are a consequence of ambiguities that are integral to the notion of 'security' itself. For some, conceptual imprecision here might be deliberate: 'carefully calibrated' to invoke 'realities and necessities that everyone is supposed to acknowledge, but also vague generalities about eve-rything and nothing' (Walker 1997: 63). For others, security's contestability is a product of its derivative nature, such that its meaning emanates from and will be 'inexorably connected to a wider view of what constitutes poli-tics' (Smith 2005: 27). Perhaps the best-known intervention in this discus-sion is Arnold Wolfers's (1952) pioneering discussion of 'national security', in which he argues that although we know 'roughly what people have in mind if they complain that their government is neglecting national secu-rity or demanding excessive sacrifices for the sake of enhancing it' (Wolfers 1952: 483), it is still the case 'that the term "security" covers a range of goals so wide that highly divergent policies can be interpreted as policies of security' (Wolfers 1952: 484). Wolfers's (1952: 485) unpacking of these ambiguities led to his influential differentiation between the subjective and objective dimensions of security, whereby, for him: 'security, in an objective sense, measures the absence of threats to acquired values, in a subjective sense, the absence of fear that such values will be attacked.'

Wolfers's (1952) article, as Baldwin (1997: 6) points out, foreshadowed a veritable 'cottage industry' of efforts to redefine security toward the end of the twentieth century, and especially into the post-Cold War period. Such work helped to problematise taken-for-granted assumptions within the rapidly growing field of Security Studies, ushering in a period of meta-theoretical distraction or exciting new insight, depending on one's perspec-tive (compare, for instance, Walt 1991; Smith 1999). Baldwin (1997: 26) himself is sceptical of security's *essential* contestability, putting his faith in conceptual analysis and more rigorous specification to salvage this most (mis-)used of concepts. Barry Buzan's (2007: 28) highly influential *People, States and Fear*, offered something similar by responding to this 'weakly conceptualized but politically powerful concept' through delineating what he terms distinct 'sectors' of security and levels of analysis. This approach helped in the subsequent differentiation between military, economic, societal, environmental, and political security (Buzan *et al.* 1998): one that continues to influence the analysis and teaching of security issues today (see Collins 2013). In Buzan's more recent survey of the field with Lene Hansen, they offer a 'structured conceptual analysis' of security in which the term is seen to be supported or held in place by a series of adjacent concepts with complementary, parallel, and oppositional meanings (Buzan and Hansen 2009: 14–15). In so doing, they build on Jef Huysmans's (1998) earlier argument that security might be approached as a 'thick signifier', in which the term's meaning and consequences emerge contextually as a product of wider discourses.

The insight of authors such as those above was important, for our purposes, because it highlighted the contingent, precarious, and fundamentally discursive nature of security and insecurity. Along with a wide range of related literature – constructivist, feminist, postcolonial, and beyond – such work has enabled subsequent analysts to approach security as something that is constructed or produced rather than something essential, inevitable, natural, or given. Approached thus, questions such as what it means to be secure, what it is that threatens security, and whose security we should try to prioritise, can only be answered in the context of wider discourses that give meaning to the world, its inhabitants, and its objects (see Jarvis and Holland 2015). Terrorism, for instance, becomes a threat to national security in part because in our contemporary state-centric conceptions of world order, political violence is typically deemed legitimate only when conducted by nation states (Wight 2009: 101). Climate change was not typically discussed through the lens of security until relatively recently, in part, because of security's traditionally militaristic connotations (see Barnett 2003). Although alternative or dissenting conceptions of security will never be completely erased – such alternatives, of course, help explain how the meaning of security/threats changes over time – dominant or hegemonic discourses shape whether and how specific issues or threats can be comprehended *as* security at particular moments (Holland 2013).

If the meaning of security (threats) is socially produced rather than objectively given, the obvious next question becomes: *how* (see also Laclau 1990: 27). What are the dynamics or processes through which this takes place? Why is it that some issues become widely recognised as security threats, while others (that may be more dangerous in quantitative terms, say) do not? One of the most prominent answers to this question comes from 'securitization theory' which – in its initial incarnation at least – argues that 'normal' political issues become 'securitized' through the process of 'securitization' (Buzan *et al.* 1998). This process involves a 'securitizing actor' – typically someone who is able to speak with authority about a specific issue – successfully convincing relevant audiences that the issue – terrorism, migration, climate change, and so on – represents a genuine threat to the very existence of something that is valued, and therefore requires significant, even exceptional, counter-measures by way of response. Examples might include UK Prime Minister Boris Johnson making the case for national 'lockdowns' in light of the threat posed by COVID-19 to the lives of vulnerable people within the UK, or Russian President Vladimir Putin arguing for a 'special military operation' in Ukraine because of the threat posed to Russia by the continuing expansion of NATO. In both cases, we see a grammar of security that is structured around the 'urgency of emergency' (Salter 2011: 116), generated by 'a plot that includes existential threat, point of no return, and a possible way out' (Buzan *et al.* 1998: 33).

It is hard to overstate the impact of securitization theory for the study of security issues and threats. For Floyd (2011: 437), 'Securitization theory has established itself as one of the most influential non-traditional security theories in existence.' For Williams (2003: 528), likewise, 'The theory of "securitization" developed by the Copenhagen School provides an innovative, sophisticated, and productive research strategy within contemporary security studies.' This influence, unsurprisingly, has been accompanied by significant criticism (friendly and otherwise) around the approach's assumptions, implications, and relevance (e.g., Hansen 2000; Bertrand 2018; Howell and Richter-Montpetit 2020; Gomes and Marques 2021). Indeed, one recent survey article situated securitisation theory today 'at a crossroads' (Baele and Jalea 2022: 1), from which its ongoing relevance will be decided. One longstanding critical interlocutor (see Aradau 2004, 2006, 2008) went further still, arguing that 'While securitization theory has undoubtedly risen to dominance in critical security studies, it seems to have become more of an impediment to critical research than useful equipment' (Aradau 2018: 300).

For the purposes of the analysis developed in this book, it is the recurrent accusation of elitism within this influential approach to the discursive production of security issues that matters most (e.g., Stanley and Jackson 2016: 226–227). Despite the 'centrality of the audience' (Balzacq 2011: 8) to the framework, a suspicion remains amongst many critics and sceptics that securitisation theory 'implies an elitist vision of politics' (Huysmans 2011: 375). As Huysmans (2011: 375) continues: 'Securitizing analysis mostly focuses on leaders or politicians – "statesmen" – who speak security with sufficient clout while ordinary people continue their everyday lives.' For Innes (2014: 567), 'The study of securitization through speech acts has relied on political elites to perform the speech acts and produce security; security thus tends to be defined by elites.' Ken Booth (2007: 166), too, from a more overtly cosmopolitan starting point, makes a similar accusation: 'Securitization studies therefore suffer from being elitist. What matters above all for the school is 'top leaders', 'states', 'threatened elites' and 'audiences' with agenda-making power. Those without discourse-making power are disenfranchised, unable to join the securitization game.' Critiques such as these are important because they highlight the tendency of scholarship on security (discourse) to prioritise the language, ideas, and understandings of already privileged actors for analysis. And, although securitisation theory might be the most obvious example here, it is far from unique in so doing. Theo Farrell's (2002) review article on constructivism and International Relations, for instance, demonstrated the striking state-centrism within early contributions to this literature with its emphasis on international norms, security dilemmas, and balances of power (see also Edkins 2002: 66; Alkopher 2016: 50). Milliken's (1999: 245) earlier meth-odological review, relatedly, was explicit in identifying (and critiquing) the typically 'top-down' approach within critical work on discourses of global politics. In short, as Croft and Vaughan-Williams (2017: 21) summarise, there is, within security research an 'elitist bias [which] ... straddles so-called 'traditional' and 'critical' divides, both of which, for the most part, have privileged the rhetoric, speech acts and (in)securitising moves of politi-cians, policy-making communities, security professionals, private security companies, and so on'.

The reasons for this prioritisation of elites and their understandings of the world are likely diverse. They may be explicitly or implicitly concep-tual: a product, perhaps, of structural assumptions about where power lies in specific social contexts, or of specific conceptions of power which pull the attention of researchers toward particular actors and their capabilities. Alternatively, or also, they may reflect a normative desire to expose how elite political discourse engenders deleterious outcomes for individuals, commu-nities, citizenship, and so on. There may also be methodological reasons for this prioritisation, relating, for instance, to the better archiving of, say, leg-islators' speech than of speech from ostensibly more humble origins. There may, moreover, be sociological reasons within academia itself: a tendency, perhaps, of security scholarship to follow the path of earlier researchers and thereby (re-)produce a 'normal science' of security studies with established ideas and methods (Kuhn 2012).

The key issue for us, though, is that security, insecurity, risk, threat, and so forth are experienced, constructed, and imagined across a far wider socio-political topography than a traditional focus on authoritative figures would encourage us to believe. Non-elite individuals and communities encounter security discourses, technologies, policies, and professionals all of the time in their daily existence. Security is present in the media we con-sume on our tablets or telephones. It is there in the cameras we pass on our commutes, and in the checks through which we must go when travelling internationally. Security is present in our encounters with health professionals, educators, and others with duties of care and safeguarding mandates. And it is there in our videogames, novels, and films on ostensibly factual threats such as terrorism and war (e.g., Robinson 2015, 2016) as well as more creative cultural imaginations of future apocalypse engendered by nuclear war, climate breakdown, or zombie apocalypse (Drezner 2014; Hannah and Wilkinson 2016). To understand, then, how security issues are (re-)produced – to understand how they are understood, negotiated, contested, and recreated – we need to engage with security's working in a range of spaces less rarefied than parliaments, press conferences, and the situation rooms in which crises are managed. We need to look toward far more mundane or 'everyday' spaces and the experiences they generate.

Security from the 'bottom' up

Given the elitism within much work on security (and security discourse) described above, adjusting our focus toward everyday or non-elite understandings of issues such as terrorism and radicalisation might seem a significant task. Fortunately, there are a number of important literatures upon which we can draw for inspiration in redirecting our gaze in this way (for an overview, see Jarvis 2019b). In the first instance, and most obviously, we can take inspiration from a long history of feminist scholarship which emphasises the importance of everyday subjects, objects, practices, and experiences within international political life. Such entities are vital for reproducing security issues, policies, and outcomes, yet too often remain neglected within mainstream research precisely because they are seen as banal or mundane (e.g., Åhäll 2016; Wibben 2020). Cynthia Enloe's (2011: 447) reflections on this, in a forum on the international as everyday practice, are worth citing at length here, not least for her articulation of the potentially revolutionary implications of such an analytical (and political) shift, to which we return below:

> The most famous late twentieth-century feminist theoretical pronouncement is, "The personal is political." Its crafters were calling on women (and any men who had sufficient nerve) to look to the everyday dynamics in their lives to discover the causes of patriarchal social systems' remarkable sustainability. This call would have profound implications, we gradually learned, for understanding the flows of causality, the constructions of political cultures and the inter-locked structures of relationships between those actors we so simplistically call "states." The sites for research, these pioneering feminists argued, were not just states' corridors of power, not just political parties' or insurgencies' strategy sessions, not just corporations' board rooms. The sites where

we would have to dig for political causality were kitchens, bedrooms, and secretarial pools; they were pubs, brothels, squash courts, and factory lunch rooms – and village wells and refugee camp latrines. This was an astounding revelation: that power was deeply at work where it was least apparent. It was also disturbing for many social scientists, especially those who had found alluring the challenge of revealing the "Big Picture" of the international system, who certainly had not been initially attracted to their professions by images of themselves taking notes in a brothel, a kitchen, or a latrine.

Enloe's reflections draw out themes for which she is well-known, revisiting the thrust of her groundbreaking *Bananas, Beaches and Bases* with its claim that engaging with traditionally neglected landscapes, peoples, and voices leads to a fuller, and therefore more 'realistic' understanding 'of how international politics actually "works"' (Enloe 2000: 4). Work such as this gives us impetus, perhaps even permission, to populate our accounts of (in) security with a far wider cast of characters than is often typical. Wibben (2011: 19), citing Elshtain's (1987) *Women and War*, for instance, highlights how 'a much more nuanced and complicated story emerges when one tells "the story *from the ground up* as a narrative of men's experiences, rather than as an account of strategic doctrines or grand movements of armies and men seen from a bird's-eye point of view"' (original emphasis). As she argues in a subsequent piece, it is therefore imperative that we tell 'a multiplicity of stories about how, by whom, and for whom security is en*acted* in particular locations, realizing that they are likely to contradict each other' (Wibben 2016: 140).

This sense of interpretative richness that accompanies a move from elites and abstractions to 'ordinary' lives and stories is important, too, in Christine Sylvester's recent feminist scholarship. As she argues in the following piece, this move not only involves simply broadening our focus through the adding of new issues or people to our analyses of security contexts and problems (although it does, importantly, do this). It is a move that permits or even forces a fundamental rethinking of the purposes and point of research into issues of deadly seriousness from war to terrorism and other forms of violence:

> The idea behind studying people's experiences is to learn how the world looks and works according to those who actually, rather than theoretically, face forces of international relations. The point is not to test hypotheses that could help predict how others would react to similar or simulated conditions of international relations, or to gather true and accurate information on the ground. The point rather is to fill in the abstract contours of our knowledge by acknowledging that people are involved in daily and extraordinary activities of international relations.

> Sylvester 2013: 619

Feminist work, then, was amongst the earliest and most influential of attempts to 'fill in the abstract contours of our knowledge' (Sylvester 2013: 619) of how the politics of (in)security plays out in everyday lives. Such work has not, however, been alone in paying attention to the security experiences, perceptions, and speech of non-elites, and inspiration for the argument developed in this book can be taken from elsewhere too. Indeed, as Jarvis (2019b: 112–116) argues, we can discern similar efforts to rethink the subject of security 'from the bottom up' in scholarship as diverse as that on human security, Critical Security Studies, postcolonial security studies, and everyday security. In different ways, and from different starting points, such work contributes to what has become an increasingly 'rich and diverse scholarship engaging with security at the level of the banal, normal, or everyday' (Jarvis 2019a: 115).

Work on human security, for instance, although heterogeneous (Paris 2001: 87–88), has at its core a desire to orient 'all facets of security around, and in the interests of, individuals' (Newman 2001: 243), including through recognising the basic needs that humans have, and the diversity of ways in which those needs are threatened in everyday life (Newman 2010: 78–79). As the 1994 United Nations Development Programme (UNDP) Report famously argued: 'For most people today, a feeling of insecurity arises more from worries about daily life than from the dread of a cataclysmic world event. Job security, income security, health, environmental security, security from crime – these are emerging concerns of human security all over the world' (UNDP 1994: 3). Although critics of the approach – of which there are many – view this construction of 'new security challenges' as misleading or exaggerated (e.g., Chandler 2008), others (e.g., Wibben 2008) see within it opportunity for the longstanding critical project of broadening *and* deepening our understanding of international security. Deepening, here, is the revealing and unpacking of assumptions and politics underpinning claims that are made about security (Booth 2007: 149). Broadening involves recognising (or expanding) the range of relevant security challenges to far greater scope than the traditionally narrow focus on interstate war. In Ken Booth's (2007: 159) summary:

> It makes all the difference in the world to potential victims whether rape is defined as a security issue/war crime as opposed simply to a problem to be dealt with by 'women's studies' or 'sociology'. Equally, it matters whether global poverty is categorised as a security issue/global challenge rather than an item on the agenda of 'development studies'. Rape and poverty provoke more insecurity, day by day, for most people across the globe, than do the movements of a neighbour's army … on what justifiable basis can we deny space on the security studies agenda to the violence and insecurity done by world politics to many women, the poor, and those oppressed because of race?

Booth's comments here form part of a fleshing out of his 'Critical Security Studies' approach, sometimes referred to as the 'Welsh' or 'Aberystwyth' School. Although he is critical of the human security agenda's co-option by political elites (Booth 2007: 322–327), Booth's own approach mobilises a similar, if Marxian-influenced, 'wish to engage with the real world of lived lives and state practices' (Booth 2007: 57). As he argues, 'Like health and status, security is a condition that is not difficult to define; in each case, the starting-point should begin in the experiences, imaginings, analyses and fears of those living with insecurity, ill-health, or low status' (Booth 2007: 98). Similar arguments can be found in discussions of 'everyday security' with their focus on the 'lived experiences of individuals and groups who interact with security measures and practices', including 'the manner in which security projects and measures are interpreted, felt, understood, adapted to and resisted by different individuals and groups, as well as people's own perceptions and understandings of such measures' (Crawford and Hutchinson 2016: 1190). Postcolonial scholarship, too, while similarly diverse, often builds upon a related impulse to tell security's story from a different, bottom-up, vantage point aimed at 'pluralising the various subjects of social inquiry and analysing world politics from alternative, subaltern, perspectives' (Sabaratnam 2011: 789).

Work such as the above has been vitally important in foregrounding the security experiences of a range of populations that often go neglected in fields such as International Relations; these include women, subjugated citizens, security professionals, and others. Notwithstanding the significance of this work, and for reasons returned to below, our primary theoretical anchorage in this book is a distinct but again related literature on 'vernacular security'. An increasingly influential approach, 'vernacular security' first came to prominence through an influential article by anthropologist Nils Bubandt on 'the political imagination in Indonesia' (Bubandt 2005: 275). Security, Bubandt argued, should be thought of not as an unchanging, homogeneous, or singular entity, but rather as a 'socially situated and discursively defined practice' that emerges from complex interactions between different actors each with their own understandings of 'the problem of security' (Bubandt 2005: 276). Recognising this is important, precisely because it leads to a diversification of whose security speak we can (or should) take seriously in our efforts to understand how particular problems and threats are formed and addressed at different levels of social life.

Bubandt (2005: 277) is explicit in his article that his conception of vernacular security is not intended as 'a relativist assertion that there are multiple cultural constructions of security'. Indeed, as the above indicates, it is security's multi-scale nature that motivates his investigation as much as, perhaps more than, its social and idiomatic specificities (Jarvis 2019a: 116).

It is, however, fair to say that much subsequent work within this emerging 'tradition' has focused on the task of identifying and unpacking hitherto-neglected constructions of security as they are understood and articulated by non-elite individuals or communities in the context of their everyday lives (Croft and Vaughan-Williams 2017: 24) Vaughan-Williams and Stevens (2016), for instance, draw on focus group research across six British cities to explore the different ways in which citizens know, narrate, and construct threats to (their) security. Jarvis and Lister (2013b) also focus on the UK in their mapping of competing 'lay' conceptions of the term 'security' itself – a term, they argue, that is variously associated with survival, belonging, hospitality, equality, freedom, and insecurity. Where Jarvis and Lister (2015a, 2016) focused on citizen constructions of (counter-)terrorism as the empirical focus of their subsequent work, Vaughan-Williams (2021) more recently returned to the framework in order to 'understand border anxieties among EU citizens' in the context of the so-called 2015 'European migrant crisis' (also Löfflmann and Vaughan-Williams 2018).

Recent years have seen a proliferation of related work demonstrating the value of the vernacular security framework through its application to hitherto neglected, yet vitally important, spaces and contexts of (in)security (Jarvis 2023). This work includes Oyawale's (2022) exploration of non-elite understandings of counter-terrorism in Nigeria; Baker and Lekunze's (2019) mapping of vernacular securities in South-West Cameroon; Homolar and Löfflmann's (2021) exploration of the power of humiliation narratives within populist political mobilisations; and Downing's (2021) investigation into the distinctiveness of 'security speak' on social media platforms such as YouTube and Twitter (also Downing *et al.* 2022). Research such as this has been vital in expanding the thematic and spatial reach of vernacular security scholarship, while addressing risks of Euro-centrism through taking the framework to contexts and constructions beyond the Global North, upon which much relevant scholarship has concentrated (see also Mac Ginty and Firchow 2016: 313–315). In so doing, it brings us back toward the emphasis of Bubandt's (2005) initial framing with its focus, as noted above, on Indonesia.

Related scholarship here has also been productive in demonstrating the agility of a vernacular approach to (in)security by bringing this broad sensibility into contact with theoretical insights and assumption from other academic traditions. Fisher and Leonardi (2021), for instance, explore vernacular articulations of 'spiritual insecurity' via seventy interviews with individuals in Northern Uganda. George (2017: 58) combines it with a feminist perspective to investigate how vernacular discourses of (in)security in Fiji 'gender the everyday practice of state security agencies' and their policing of conjugal norms (see also George 2018). Croft and Vaughan-Williams (2017) connect work on vernacular (and everyday) security to developments within ontological security studies, highlighting the latter's emphasis on the importance of a consistent self-identity for an actor's security (see Mitzen 2006; Steele 2008). And Winch (2021), finally, links a vernacular approach to traditional 'human security' concerns such as personal security and food security (see UNDP 1994), in part to decolonise Eurocentric assumptions within the latter. Work such as this highlights the dexterity of vernacular security research with its capacity not only to comprehend the world of (in)security differently through highlighting 'the plurality of ways in which security is practiced' (Downing and Dron 2020: 4), but, in addition, to nuance, refine, extend, and adapt other approaches to, and understandings of, this most contested of terms.

A vernacular approach: Assumptions and priorities

Following Jarvis (2019b), a vernacular approach to security is one that begins with an ontological emptiness such that we abandon *a priori* expectations about the term's meaning. This involves recognising, in the first instance, that security only has meaning in relation to a subject (Walker 1997: 68); put otherwise, security only makes sense as the security *of* someone or something, whether an individual (e.g., a student), a collective (e.g., a religious community), or a non-human referent (e.g., biodiversity, or the ecosystem). Subjects such as these, of course, will likely have different conceptions and experiences of security – security for the ecosystem is likely to mean something very different to security for an individual person. To 'know' security, therefore, involves engaging *with* security's subjects in order to attempt to understand (or, better, to help co-construct) what security might mean in specific contexts (temporal, spatial, political). And, as for security, so too for security threats. Despite the plethora of efforts to catalogue threats by their significance and severity – in academic scholarship but also in national risk registers, security strategies, and the like – security threats again only make sense in relation *to* other things, not least of which being a subject of some sort that is deemed threatened. It is the subject's understanding or construction of security issues, then, that matters here: an understanding or construction which will be located within, and facilitated by, the wider contexts in which those subjects are embedded. Moreover, although this synopsis implies that the subject of security precedes the existence of security threats, the two should also be seen as mutually constituted: the idea of 'fundamental British values', for instance, is one that is created, in part, by the construction of threats to those values. The idea of national security, similarly, only makes sense in relation to real or imagined threats to that ideal.

Against these starting points, the fundamental ambition of a vernacular approach is to explore the 'richness and texture of localized security imaginaries', in order to ask 'what security means; how security feels; what conditions, objects, experiences, or relationships create security and insecurity; [and] with which values security is associated' (Jarvis 2019a: 116) for particular subjects in particular contexts. How do specific individuals or groups talk about security, for instance? What do specific individuals or groups see as the primary threats to their own security? How do they attempt to mitigate such threats? Such questions open space for vitally important second-order discussion around *how* security and security issues are known or constructed through different types of security claim, which may be 'factual and fabulous; qualitative and quantitative; normative and descriptive; logical, anecdotal, and hypothetical' (Jarvis 2019a: 117). The form through which (in)security is articulated, in other words, matters as much here as the content of security fears and imaginaries. As Fisher and Leonardi (2021: 386) summarise: 'Part of the appeal of a vernacular security studies framework is exploring notions and experiences of (in)security from a primarily inductive and bottom-up perspective; vernacular security studies seeks to put aside discursive and ontological assumptions and hierarchies.'

From these starting points, we can develop a small number of principles to guide the vernacular approach to (counter-)radicalisation offered in this book (see Table 2.1). First, knowledge of (counter-)radicalisation is not – or, perhaps, should not be taken to be – the preserve of privileged elites. 'Ordinary' people's perspectives and experiences of, say, the Prevent Strategy matter too, and merit the sort of sustained reflection typically reserved for elite political discourse. Although (some) citizens may lack access to particular types of knowledge through which (counter-)radicalisation is often constructed and communicated – from the analytical models of gated scientific papers to the classified briefings of intelligence services – those citizens should not be seen to be knowledge-less. Non-elite ways of knowing (counter-)radicalisation – which may draw upon other sites, from books to television series, to local anecdotes and stories – contribute to the construction of, here (counter-)radicalisation, its significance, and solutions in complex and multiple ways that cannot be known or assumed in advance. Citizens' perspectives and experiences matter, in short, even when we are dealing with ostensibly rarefied or classified issues such as those with which we are here concerned.

Second, how individuals articulate their knowledge or experiences is vitally important to a vernacular analysis of (counter-)radicalisation, because discourse is productive and not reflective of the world. Although our analysis of vernacular discourse on (counter-)radicalisation will, inevitably, be influenced by our own questions, concepts, and assumptions, we try to offer as

Table 2.1   Principles of vernacular security research

Principle	Explanation and rationale
Security is an ontologically empty concept.	Security only has meaning in relation to particular subjects and particular contexts.
Non-elite constructions of security have analytical, political, and normative significance.	Non-elite understandings of security are frequently – and wrongly – neglected. This may be because they are deemed unimportant, not 'really' security, or not equivalent to those of elites. A vernacular approach seeks to centre such understandings because they (i) are intrinsically worthy of reflection, and (ii) may offer resources for wider understanding and critique.
How security is constructed in the vernacular matters.	The language, logics, references, and examples within non-elite discussions are integral to vernacular understanding of security and related concepts and experiences. Security, in the vernacular, is produced *through* specific discursive choices, which may be conscious or otherwise.
Vernacular security research should be attentive to local particularities.	Security will likely mean different things in different times and places. Recognising this also involves guarding against deterministic assumptions about what security must mean in those times and places. This is, not least, because the meaning of security will never be fully and finally fixed.
Vernacular security research should be wary of generalisation.	The ability to speak security in the vernacular is shaped by specific contexts such as the presence of interlocutors, the spatial environment, and expectations about the appropriateness of particular constructions.

much space as possible in this book for participants to speak (or construct) the world via language that is meaningful to them. This ambition has a methodological component that involves enabling participants to guide the discussion as far as possible around their own interests and experiences. As discussed further below, we asked deliberately broad and open-ended questions within our focus groups to enable participants to speak about security issues and policies via their own categories (see Vaughan-Williams and Stevens 2016: 46). It also, however, has an analytical component in which we seek to offer space for these vernacular perspectives in the following chapters without over-editing or truncating the words of our participants. The challenge, and the appeal, of such an approach is in remaining open to surprising and unexpected findings which may include new criticisms of dominant security paradigms, or perhaps new understandings of seemingly settled conceptual terms such as 'radicalisation' or 'security' itself.

Third, developing the above, our vernacular approach also seeks to remain attentive to the particularities of local constructions of (in)security, even if this risks dissolving the historical privileging of 'security' as 'a conceptual and political referent' (Ciută 2009: 320). As Hultin (2010: 111) indicates, vernacular can be understood here in different ways. On the one hand, it points to the informality of citizens' 'security speak' which may proceed via different grammars or different examples, say, to those found within elite discourses. At the same time, the word 'vernacular' 'references specific cultural idioms without which issues of security, violence and politics can only be incompletely understood' (Hultin 2010: 111). Such cultural idioms and references – from traditional stories to local folklore, to shared or vicarious experiences of everyday life – will, of course, be fluid and contested within communities. And, because of this, we need to beware reductionist accounts of vernacular perspectives as somehow automatically determined by specific identities or 'ways of life', for instance, being a student, being from a city, being Welsh, or being male. The point is that a vernacular approach offers opportunity to *explore* specific grammars of (in)security and to unpack the differences, complementarities, and connections between them. An individual who discusses (and critiques) counter-terrorism practices through reference to an experience of personal humiliation at an airport check-in, to offer one example, is drawing upon a very different set of discursive resources than one who deduces the working of counter-terrorism from their reading of news coverage about government responses to terrorist attacks (Lister and Jarvis 2013; Jarvis and Lister 2015b).

A fourth principle is that vernacular security research should be wary of, and perhaps resistant to, generalisation. There are two reasons for this, both of which derive from the privileging of 'everyday' or non-elite expressions and constructions of (in)security within the approach. First is that these expressions are likely to be contextually specific, shaped not only by specific historical and cultural backdrops, but also by the circumstances of their utterance on or within specific sites (e.g., social media platforms), or encounters (e.g., in a response to a question in a focus group setting). As noted above, these contexts are generative rather than incidental to the expressions and experiences of (in)security they allow. Rather than assuming, say, that an individual comes to a focus group with a set of experiences or views to be shared, it is the process of sharing (and debating and arguing about) views and experiences within environments such as focus groups that helps to create an individual's experiences as meaningful. As Vaughan-Williams and Stevens (2016: 46) argue: 'The assumption in critical focus-group research work is not that the subject and his/her views pre-exist the situation in which the discussion takes place, but that it is via the interaction with others that this identity and knowledge are constituted.' The same, of course, would hold true for other research contexts, whether we are considering comments left on specific internet forums, or the sharing of jokes in a place of work.

A second reason to beware generalisation follows the privileging of qualitative richness that is typical of vernacular work on security. This emphasis on the detail or minutiae of everyday experiences of (in)security means that scholarship of this sort typically works with quantitatively small samples that are unlikely to be representative of larger populations (e.g., Vaughan-Williams and Stevens 2016; Oyawale 2022). The samples that are used, moreover, also tend to be generated purposively rather than probabilistically (e.g., Jarvis and Lister 2015a; Makki and Tahir 2021; Oyawale 2022), due to an interest in particular populations or experiences that will be built in to the research design. Vernacular constructions of security issues, then, may be seen as examples of – rather than synonymous with – wider experiences or understandings (Downing *et al.* 2022: 6).

The chapters that follow apply these principles to the case study of vernacular constructions of radicalisation and counter-radicalisation policy amongst students at higher education institutions in England and Wales. By approaching the experiences and understandings of these individuals as meaningful for the wider construction of security politics in this highly contested and controversial area, the importance of 'everydayness' in public encounters with (counter-)radicalisation is given especial treatment. This everydayness comes across, we hope, in a number of ways. First, in relation to the voices and experiences with which we attempt to engage in this book, given our attempt to centre analysis upon 'ordinary' citizens rather than privileged elites. Second, in the contexts through which these stories are told and shared, with participants joining our focus groups via digital technologies often from domestic, familiar spaces such as their living rooms and bedrooms. Although there are limitations to applying the focus group method within online contexts – discussed further below – our approach here draws on over twenty years of historical precedent for this sort of research, in which we have witnessed vast transformations in the potential, power, and ubiquity of computers and digital technologies (see Stewart and Williams 2005; Lobe 2017). Third, consistent with the above discussion, the following chapters also concentrate upon the vocabularies, concepts, and idioms of our focus group participants, eschewing anything more than superficial editing for presentational purposes. Although the selection and analysis of excerpts from our focus group discussions is an invention, perhaps even an intervention, on our part which must be recognised (see Jarvis 2009: 19–22), our ambition throughout is to stay as faithful to the words of our participants as possible, and to resist temptation to 'speak *for*, rather than *to* (or, perhaps better, *with*) "ordinary" people and the conditions of (in)security they experience, encounter or construct in everyday life' (Jarvis and Lister 2013b: 158, original emphasis). Fourth, as will become clear, participants in our research spent considerable time reflecting on their *own* everyday lives and experiences in their discussions of (counter-)radicalisation. This includes, amongst many other examples, detailed descriptions of lectures attended in the course of university degrees, or the remembering of school assemblies on terrorism and radicalisation, or the recounting of preparedness training at work. Such ostensibly quotidian experiences are vital, we will argue, for how people make sense of the Prevent Strategy, and 'much can [therefore] be gained by exploring how practices of security governance are experienced by different people and groups "on the ground" so to speak, and how they are implicated in, forged through and find expression via quotidian aspects of social life' (Crawford and Hutchinson 2016: 1185).

Why a vernacular approach to (counter-)radicalisation?

In the chapters that follow, we demonstrate the value of a vernacular approach to security issues – such as radicalisation – and security policies – such as Prevent – through the empirical research generated through our focus group methodology. Before moving to a more detailed discussion of that methodological approach, we bring this part of the chapter to a close by outlining the value of the vernacular approach developed in this book.

First, and most obvious, is the descriptive richness offered by research that is 'rooted in the experience and vernacular understandings of the people and groups who are "secured"' (Luckham 2017: 100). At a minimum, vernacular research enables the telling of different stories – and therefore the telling of more stories – about important and contested topics and issues. In a very immediate sense, as Luckham (2017: 111) argues, this has scope for shedding new light on the minutiae and intricacies of security dynamics, paving 'the way for more precise and detailed empirical scrutiny of how security … plays out in particular national and local contexts'. One implication of this is that specific research contexts are treated in their concrete complexity, without claim to comparison with other cases or to generalisation across cases. Abstraction, therefore, is treated with caution here, as a potential violence to the distinctiveness of specific contexts and experiences which, 'deserve to be respected for what they are and analysed in their own terms rather than those imposed upon them by … analysts writing, invariably, from altogether different vantage-points' (Hay 2002: 36).

This embrace of descriptive richness, though, extends beyond the unveiling of local nuance and variation, because it also opens scope for thinking through crucial epistemological and political questions around how security stories are told, by whom, and with what consequences. As Mac Ginty and Firchow (2016) note in their analysis of bottom-up perceptions of peace, safety and security within South Africa, South Sudan, Uganda, and Zimbabwe:

> The broad story of insecurity and precariousness is there in both the top-down and the bottom-up versions, but the 'stories' are often told differently. They contain different emphases, inflections and silences. These different stories are revealing not just about the different perspectives and ways of 'seeing' conflict and social change. They are also revealing about issues of epistemology and positionality. Crucially, they are also revealing about power: the power to write, to over-write and be heard.
>
> Mac Ginty and Firchow 2016: 309

Vernacular research is especially productive here, we suggest, because it avoids prioritising specific individuals, groups, or experiences as *a priori* starting points for analysis in the way that we sometimes find in related research traditions, such as some feminist or postcolonial scholarship (Jarvis 2019a). Vernacular research still involves methodological decisions, of course, about whose security speak is to be analysed. But the conceptual emptiness of the approach provides it with an analytical freedom to follow and foreground examples of security speak that are relevant to, or perhaps simply interesting within, specific research contexts.

Second, conceptually, vernacular scholarship poses potential for theorising security issues anew precisely by beginning with the 'bottom up' insight which researchers gain (or co-construct) through their analysis. In common with other interpretative approaches, this tends to involve an inductive approach to concept- and theory-building that might be organised through the vernacular of research participants, rather than through terminologies imported from elsewhere. Contextually specific security vernaculars, approached thus, may therefore help us to render visible hidden, forgotten, or excluded realities that – once recognised – become potential starting points for rethinking the construction and working of security in specific contexts.

A third advantage of a vernacular approach is its political potential for disturbing or critiquing dominant counter-radicalisation practices and knowledge. As Vaughan-Williams and Stevens (2016: 42) argue, 'vernacular constructions, experiences and stories of (in)security have the potential to disrupt "official" accounts and repoliticize the technocratic foundations of national security policies' (see also Nyman 2021: 321). Downing (2021), for instance, analyses the ways in which vernacular discussion on YouTube and

Twitter challenges elite constructions of threat, shedding light, in the process, on how 'more everyday practices of security have profound social consequences and may undermine, rather than reinforce the dominant conceptions of safety' (Shaykhutdinov 2018: 56). Atakav *et al.* (2020) employed digital storytelling to access vernacular expressions of 'British values' in order to disrupt, deconstruct, and otherwise challenge official discourse on this concept. In making this argument, we need to beware the temptation to valorise 'the vernacular' as an inherently authentic, progressive, or creative space (Gillespie and O'Loughlin 2009: 669–670; Shaykhutdinov 2018: 64). Everyday narratives may, of course, be sceptical of or hostile toward progressive political aspirations as much as supportive of them (Tonkiss 2016; Benzing 2020). Indeed, there is an important body of work on how localised security imaginaries can generate outcomes that are disempowering, even violent, such as in cases of vigilantism, domestic assault, homophobic violence, and mob killings (Risør 2010; Orock 2014; George 2017). This notwithstanding, there is, we argue, real value to 'listening to voices otherwise thought of as "noise" in the context of debates about national security policy' (Vaughan-Williams and Stevens 2016: 45), precisely because those voices might provide us with new opportunities, inroads, or resources for intervening in and reorienting those debates and associated policies (Jarvis 2019a).

Finally, and building on the above, such an approach also has normative potential, rooted in recognition that the neglect, exclusion, or forgetting of 'ordinary' experiences of government activities such as Prevent does a disservice, perhaps even an injustice, to those people themselves. In the chapters that follow, we discuss and engage with a range of perspectives on Prevent for which we have – as one would expect – varying degrees of sympathy. This discussion not only provides the richer mapping of vernacular discourses through which (counter-)radicalisation is produced in everyday life noted above. It also offers opportunity for those experiences to be heard and encountered, rather than forgotten, excluded, marginalised, or subjugated. As the feminist theorist Christine Sylvester (2013) argues, scholarship on security politics too often forgets that we are dealing, fundamentally, with people and their experiences. Formal models, abstract calculations, and the like serve to tidy up and obscure those experiences in ways that does a disservice to the people as well as to our understanding thereof:

> Individuals aggregated into data points cannot share their voices, their power, their agendas, and their experiences with international relations. And that is my point: in IR [International Relations], individuals are studied using someone else's script, not their own, which might be a reason why IR is on the back foot when it comes to anticipating people as stakeholders, actors, and participants in international relations.
>
> Sylvester 2013: 614

Whether or not we think 'ordinary' people matter as agents driving change in counter-radicalisation debate and policy (and, to be clear, they might do), they surely do matter *as* people whose ideas, understandings, criticisms, hopes, prejudices, and views may be heard and engaged with.

This normative claim that we might take vernacular, subjugated, or banal perspectives on (in)security seriously is sometimes taken to be an argument about the emancipatory potential or aspirations of work such as this. Importantly, we pull short of such a claim here, not least because of the paternalism associated with emancipatory political projects and their universalisms (Rengger and Thirkell-White 2007: 14–17). Instead, by highlighting the ethical implications of different understandings of (in)security (Ciută 2009: 323–324), and by reflecting on our own work in co-creating these understandings, we try to maintain what Nyman (2016: 834), drawing on Ciută (2009), refers to as a 'normative awareness' rather than a 'fixed set of normative commitments', involving the 'study [of] actors' different understandings and practices of security and what these do, considering their ethical implications in the context studied'. Muncey's (2005: 84) discussion of the normative and creative potentialities that accompany attentiveness to the minutiae of ostensibly banal stories within autoethnographic work resonates nicely with the ethos we seek to develop in the chapters that follow: 'Mainstream research [is] … tied up in rules and conventions that make the results appear dull and flat, and ignore completely the idiosyncrasies of the lived experience of the communities that it bypasses, so that in time, their stories become at best forgotten and at worst untold'. Our hope is that this book helps to counter the forgetting or un-telling of such everyday idiosyncrasies in the lived experiences of individuals around (counter-)radicalisation and the UK's Prevent Strategy.

Focus groups as research method

In the remainder of this chapter, we now seek to outline the methodological framework through which our research took place. In doing so, we describe and reflect on the planning, execution, and analysis of the focus groups we conducted and the implications of this process for the analysis that follows. This, we hope, adds context to our own findings while offering insight for future research in this vein.

Focus groups, their usage, and value

Focus groups offer a well-established method that is widely used by researchers throughout the academic, commercial, clinical, and entertainment sectors. The development and prevalence of focus group usage across the twentieth and twenty-first centuries (Stewart *et al.* 2007: 3) demonstrate their utility in helping to deliver the objectives of psychologists, advertisers, educators, marketers, and sociologists, to name but a few. While not the first to attempt to formalise this method (see, amongst others, Bogardus 1926; Edmiston 1944), American sociologist Robert Merton was a prominent proponent of focus groups in his time at the Bureau of Applied Social Research at Columbia University. Writing with Patricia Kendall in 1946, he reflected on the 'focussed interview' that he and his colleagues had conducted, differentiating the technique, in his words, 'from other types of research interviews which might appear superficially similar' (Merton and Kendall 1946: 541). The focused interview was one in which participants had experience of a 'particular concrete situation' which the researchers had previously studied. Thus, researchers could 'formalise an interview guide' around the case's 'hypothetically significant elements' and allow for a closer examination of the 'subjective experiences' of the participants thereof (Merton and Kendall, 1946: 541).

These principles remain useful today in part because they help us to distinguish what it is that makes focus groups distinct, as opposed to simply a 'catch-all' label, for group-based qualitative research or, indeed, for activities not really research-related at all, such as group-based decision-making, committees, or open forums (Kitzinger and Barbour 1999; Morgan 1998: 38–39; 2019: 4). Here, Kitzinger and Barbour (1999: 4) observe that the increased popularity in group methods has sometimes seen researchers adopt an uncertain tone when characterising their work as 'focus groups'. In their view, focus groups should be seen as 'group discussions exploring a specific set of issues. The group is "focused" in that it involves some kind of collective activity – such as viewing a video, examining a single health promotion message, or simply debating a set of questions' (Kitzinger and Barbour 1999: 4).

Alongside the principles outlined by Merton and Kendall, perhaps the most important defining feature of the focus group method is that it can achieve *interaction between participants*. Indeed, this is something actively sought by researchers who use this method to allow for the access of data that would otherwise be more difficult to obtain (Morgan 2019: 4). Rather than simply asking a series of questions to group members in sequence, 'focus group researchers encourage participants to talk to one another: asking questions, exchanging anecdotes, and commenting on each others' experiences and points of view' (Kitzinger and Barbour 1999: 4). This facilitating of semi-structured discussion around particular topics in a *group setting* is important, in part, because it allows participants and their interlocutors to independently *and* interdependently reflect on the meanings that lie behind groups' assessments, uncertainties, and ambiguities. And, in addition, it offers opportunity for the focus group analysts to reflect on these inter-subjective processes and the 'normative [and other] understandings that groups draw upon to reach their collective judgements' (Bloor *et al.* 2000: 4).

This emphasis upon interaction means that the focus group is also, 'particularly useful for allowing participants to generate their own questions, frames and concepts and to pursue their own priorities on their own terms, in their own vocabulary' (Kitzinger and Barbour 1999: 5). To achieve this, researchers typically attempt to provide a forum in which participants are able to express and discuss their views, while ensuring that sufficient flexibility exists for alternative and potentially unexpected avenues to emerge. A need for flexibility is not the same, however, as an improvised or 'loose' research design, and careful planning is required to allow enough structure for the most fruitful collection of views from group members (Langford and McDonagh 2003: 2). As detailed further below, our own use of focus groups involved a structured sequence of five overarching questions articulated in deliberately broad language.

The benefits of focus groups as a research method have been addressed extensively within academic literature across a range of disciplines (Bloor *et al.* 2000). Rather than retreading that ground here, we focus on the method's value for exploring how students across higher education in England and Wales experience, understand, and evaluate (counter-)radicalisation and Prevent. Given our desire to engage in a dialogue with those students, alternative qualitative methods of data collection were available to us, such as the individual interview. Interviews would have offered a similar means of data collection, while promising greater control on the part of the researcher and the likelihood of greater information from each participant (Morgan 1996: 10). However, beyond the confines of our topic guide and moderating role, tight *control* was not something we were keen to prioritise during this piece of research. Rather, returning to the above emphasis on interaction, our aim was to establish an informal and interactive forum in which group participants felt sufficiently confident to share their independent insights in relation to our questions, and to navigate uncertainty and ambiguity interdependently with their peers (Fern 2001: 132).

Another factor behind our employment of the focus group method related to its value in helping participants discuss sensitive and complicated subject matter (Liamputtong 2011). One might hypothesise that having an audience when discussing sensitive issues would make participants *less likely* to voice their own opinions and/or experiences. However, when compared to the individual interview, focus groups are able to provide a forum in which the researcher's power and influence is diffused (Wilkinson 1998: 114) allowing participants to discuss complex issues on their own terms (Seymour *et al.* 2004: 60). What makes a topic 'sensitive' is, of course, subjective (Farquhar and Das 1999: 49), and while our research does not explicitly address subject areas widely recognised as sensitive (sex, death, or mental health issues, for instance), we *were* aware that our discussions had the potential to be awkward for some participants. Race and racism, religion, multiculturalism, and the like were all likely topics to emerge in a conversation around the UK Prevent Strategy, and students may also have decided to disclose first-hand or second-hand trauma in the group setting. Thus, where interviews might provide 'straight answers to straight questions', focus groups were deemed a better fit for this project.

Alongside these methodological benefits, there were also important practical benefits to our use of this method. The purposive qualitative sampling we carried out prior to recruitment of participants, for instance, aimed to 'reflect the diversity within the group or population under study rather than aspiring to recruit a representative sample' (Barbour 2007: 58; see also, Kuzel 1992; Mays and Pope 1995). Representativeness was neither something we sought, nor something that was feasible for this project given time and resource constraints. However, through our sampling, *we did* seek to amass a population that reflected some of the diversity we see within the spaces of UKHE (covered in further detail below). Focus groups, therefore, provided an expedient means of organising and talking to multiple groups of students from different parts of the UK and from different types of HEIs, thereby providing a means of reflecting some of the diversity therein.

Additional constraints one could normally expect with this method were also removed on account of the focus groups taking place virtually via *Microsoft Teams*. With travel time and costs removed, participation in the study was rendered easier, albeit with some technological requirements for those seeking involvement in the research (again, covered below). It has been suggested that the convenience and comfort granted via virtual platforms such as this may help to explain the lower drop-out rates and higher demographic and geographic diversity when compared to in-person groups (Halliday *et al.* 2021: 2148). The value of hosting these particular groups virtually is further demonstrated when taken alongside other widely acknowledged benefits such as removing the need and cost of a physical set-up, allowing for immediate computer-generated transcription, and diminishing the 'interviewer effect' and its influence on the sort of responses we were likely to receive (Bloor *et al.* 2000: 83).

Considerations and limitations

Despite the benefits of virtual data collection considered above, the primary impetus for conducting our research online was the ongoing COVID-19 pandemic within the UK during the summer of 2021. With some restrictions still in place nationally, and many UK HEIs advising against face-to-face data collection, conducting the groups online offered the only feasible way to progress the research. Our experience with this approach, though, was a positive one and undoubtedly made easier coming at a time where both researchers and participants had considerable recent experience of HE in this form, given the widespread move to online teaching in this period. That is not to say that undertaking this research via an online platform was not without its challenges vis-à-vis more traditional offline formats, three of which in particular merit mention here.

First, the decision to conduct our research online meant there was no shared physical presence to the groups, and therefore aspects of the interactions we were interested in studying were either absent or very different in form to their offline equivalents. This was the first time any of our research team had conducted focus groups virtually, and as Morgan (2019: 122) warns, elements of nonverbal interaction were 'less available and more challenging to observe, which makes interaction more difficult to coordinate' for group moderators. In the traditional setting, body language provides many cues for moderators, allowing them to infer the desire or unwillingness of particular participants to contribute to a particular discussion, for instance. Something as overt as a raised hand is an obvious example, but other subtler cues might involve shifts forward or backwards in a chair, a raised eyebrow, or the shake or nod of a head. While we did not require that cameras were switched on during the focus groups, we were grateful that most participants opted to do this in order to allow some observation of these nonverbal aspects of communication.

Tied up with this were issues around the *informality* of interaction in focus group environments. Notwithstanding whatever efforts are made by moderators to soften the formality of focus groups, they remain *formal settings* that exist precisely because participants have been asked to provide 'certain types of contribution, and … require the interaction to be organized in certain ways' (Puchta and Potter 2004: 28). Formality, though, can stifle interaction and rapport, leading to stunted dialogue (Greenbaum 1998: 94), or a group taking on a 'call and answer' dialogue rather than one flowing more freely between members. However hackneyed it might sound, the moderator's refrain that 'the group is about you, not me' remains a useful one. Having participants feeling relaxed and safe in an informal setting can be crucial to achieving this.

Guidance on how to create a more informal environment that is more conducive to dialogue is a common feature of much focus group literature (see Stewart *et al.* 2007: 89–107; Bloor *et al.* 2000). Thankfully, much of this was transferable to the virtual format; however, notable aspects such as the physical arrangement of a room or the use of stimulus materials were, respectively, redundant or more difficult to replicate in our case. The fact that our participants were UKHE students who had experienced HE via virtual platforms such as *Zoom* or *Teams* over previous years undoubtedly made what we were doing less alien to the groups. Indeed, it is likely that some of our population felt *more* comfortable contributing via a virtual space as opposed to in-person, given this context. Nevertheless, as a research team, we felt that rapport was more difficult to establish when faced with a series of webcam feeds on a screen. To provide one brief example, the value of the time *before the focus group begins* to 'break the ice' with participants and to assess their characteristics (Liamputtong, 2011: 72) is incredibly valuable in in-person groups, but was completely absent within this study.

Mitigating some of these issues brings us to the second factor here: the role of the moderator when facilitating online groups. Stewart *et al.* (2007: 104) argue that the role of the moderator in a virtual focus group is rendered more difficult on account of the challenges of *controlling* the participants, quieting dominating individuals, and recognising those who are less active. While we remain less convinced by the requirement of control in focus group settings, Stewart *et al.* make the important observation that the dynamics of online groups can lead to time elapsing without the generation of valuable discussion. 'Value' is a loaded term, of course, but refers here not only to information that the researcher believes to be valuable, but in addition to those instances in which the *method is not working*, such as a hostile group member shouting down other participants, participants engaging in long asides that have no relevance to the objectives, or group members feeling sidelined from discussions. In instances such as these, it is the responsibility of the moderator to interject and get the group discussion and dynamics back on track.

On this point, Morgan (2019: 83) writes, 'along with the advice that the moderator should be more of a facilitator than a leader, there is a corresponding principle that the moderator should do as little as possible to accomplish a given goal.' So long as the discussion is 'on topic', having the participants lead and drive its direction via interaction is preferable to the moderator asking an ever more specific list of questions. Too much moderator influence and the focus group begins to resemble the group interview; with each question asked, the confines of the discussion become constricted. Moreover, given our status as educators in HE with research expertise on the topic, we were also acutely aware of a potential power dynamic here relating to our contributions in the group and those of our participants: that participants may think of us as 'the lecturer', here, and therefore treat our questions or contributions as more valuable than their own. Linked to this was the related concern that participants may begin to offer responses they thought we (as 'the experts') wanted or viewed as 'correct'.

The main challenge here – as with establishing rapport and informality considered above – was our ability to utilise or read nonverbal behaviour in an online context. The diminished opportunity for this made it more difficult, for instance, to interrupt particular speakers, or to bring quieter people into the discussion. An 'overtalker' as Morgan (2019: 85) describes them, may feel more able to speak at length when sat in a familiar and otherwise uninhabited physical space, whereas quieter participants may find it easier to slip into the virtual background where they will be much more difficult to reach with eye contact and a smile for reassurance or encouragement. In the absence of reliable nonverbal communication, we therefore offered verbal interjection and direction through the words we used and our delivery of these (Puchta and Potter 2004: 3538). While this meant that some of our groups involved more moderator speech than we had been accustomed to in other projects using this method, none of the groups suffered from a breakdown in dialogue or interaction.

Finally, something needs to be said about the inclusivity of this approach. In many parts of the Global North, internet connectivity rates are so high, and connectable devices so ubiquitous, that there could be a tendency to assume that virtual data collection offers unprecedented inclusivity with participation in research projects such as this. While barriers are undoubtedly removed without the need for travel and associated costs, involvement in this study required participants to have a stable internet connection, the necessary hardware, and a sufficient technological literacy to navigate the software. These barriers speak to what is commonly referred to as 'the digital divide' (Baker *et al.* 2020), and studies have emphasised the methodological concerns that can stem from digital inequalities (Robinson *et al.* 2015). However, not all barriers with virtual data collection are virtual, and recent studies have also demonstrated how participants may feel an increased social stigma that is associated with their home environment, for example, 'the lack of access to safe, quiet, and private spaces' (Lathen and Laestadius 2021: 6). Given the national circumstances we were operating in, conducting the research virtually delivered expediency, inclusivity, and safety. However, it is apparent that our approach also erected different technological and social barriers and should not be thought of as a silver bullet for participant inclusion.

Specificities of our method

In this section, we outline the different steps of the process we undertook to plan, organise, conduct, and analyse our focus groups. Here we pay particular attention to four key issues: the development of our topic guide, our sampling and recruitment strategy, the running of our focus groups, and our transcription, coding, and analysis practices.

Developing the topic guide

The topic guide for focus group research acts as a schedule of questions and associated prompts intended to facilitate and direct the discussion. This guide should flow directly from the research objectives (Stewart *et al.* 2007: 60), which in our case related to examination of the experiences, understandings, and evaluations of students in Higher Education in England and Wales. Our topic guide was drafted and reformulated over the course of a series of preliminary meetings between the three members of the research team prior to the recruitment stage. It is laid out in full in Table 2.2.

As Table 2.2 indicates, our questions were designed to be open-ended and avoid unnecessary qualification that could obscure our meaning, or limit the range of possible responses. For example, the opening question, 'What can you tell me about the Prevent Strategy?' had the benefit of allowing participants to 'pursue their own priorities' and begin interacting with one another (Kitzinger and Barbour 1999: 5), while at the same time offering an unsurprising starting point for the group. Of course, breadth can sometimes have a debilitating effect on group discussion, with participants unsure 'where to start' responding to a particular question. To defend against this possibility, the prompts set out in Table 2.2 served as an insurance policy to clarify the intention behind our questions with minimal steer. This was the primary rationale for the drafting of the prompts; however, even if discussion around a topic had been extensive, we still made use of these on occasions if we felt an important aspect remained unexplored.

Sampling and recruitment

Our study sought to recruit a specific population and consequently was non-probabilistic. The approach we adopted involved convenience, purposive, and snowball sampling techniques. The research team are all academics teaching in UKHE and the *convenience sampling* we conducted involved reaching out to students on modules and courses with which we were familiar, for instance, through our own teaching experiences. The *purposive sampling* involved reaching out to colleagues in other HEIs within England and

Table 2.2 Topic guide and prompts

Question	Possible prompts
What can you tell me about the Prevent Strategy?	• What are its objectives? • Who is it focused at? • Who is involved with its delivery?
Where does your knowledge of Prevent come from?	• News media? • Academia? • Personal experience? • Pop culture?
What does the term 'radicalisation' mean to you?	• Is it a useful term? • Is it a significant threat? • Are there any problems or criticisms of the term? • Where does your knowledge of the term come from? • Are there specific examples from popular culture or beyond?
How successful is Prevent in countering radicalisation?	• Does Prevent make us more secure? • Is Prevent proportionate to its objectives? • Are there any problems or criticisms with the strategy, its objectives and conduct? • Could Prevent do anything differently to address these problems?
If you oversaw the UK's counter-radicalisation programme, what would it look like?	• Would you keep Prevent as it is? • Would you change it? • Would you scrap it?

Wales and asking that they advertise the study to their students. Finally, we sought to *snowball* our sample by encouraging students who wanted to be involved in the research to let fellow students who might also be interested know about the project and the possibility of contributing.

Given this sampling strategy, our findings can only be illustrative rather than representative of wider student (or citizen) perspectives on issues around (counter-)radicalisation. As mentioned above, our aim was to reflect diversity across the population and to produce a depth of understanding in our findings, rather than prioritising replicability or generalisability. We cover the depth of our findings in subsequent chapters; however, the ability for our sampling strategy to deliver diversity was, we argue, a success. In total, we were able to recruit forty-three students from twelve different HEIs that reflected a diverse geographical distribution across England and Wales as well as consisting of variance in terms of institutional 'type' (e.g., Russell group, post-1992, or 'new' universities). Our overall sample of forty-three is comparable to other studies within International Relations and Security Studies that have sought to deliver similar research objectives in different topic areas (Johnson *et al.* 2018; Opiyo 2015) and, indeed, significantly larger than the only other studies of which we are aware, that attempt to explore Prevent with similar populations (McGlynn and McDaid 2019; Zempi and Tripli 2022). The research flyer we used to advertise our study directed participants to an online page where they could sign up to one of eight focus groups and provide some basic information confirming their status as a student in UKHE. The data collection phase ran throughout June and July of 2021.

Conducting the focus groups

Each focus group had two members of the research team in attendance. One member of the team acted as the group moderator, with the other tasked with introducing and observing the group. With each group taking place on *Microsoft Teams* – and the lack of an icebreaker beginning, discussed above – we used introductions to reassure participants of the group's purposes and form. Our introductions were therefore structured around seven pieces of information:

1. A brief introduction to the group's moderators, and to our role *as* moderators in the focus group format.
2. An explanation of the research project and the purpose of the group.
3. How the focus groups will operate, covering the structure and approximate timings.
4. The importance of consent forms and about obtaining consent.
5. Our intention to audio record the group and an explanation why we were doing this.
6. A read-through of each of the consent statements.
7. An opportunity for participants to ask any questions.

After these seven steps were completed, we asked for brief introductions from the group members. We invited each to tell us how they would like to be referred to during the focus group and their course of study before confirming verbally their willingness to participate. At this point, the first member of the research team handed over to the second, who would be moderating the focus group. Our groups lasted between sixty-five and eighty-one minutes, and at the end of each, we gave participants the opportunity to ask any question of us and to offer any additional comments or observations. Finally, we thanked participants for their involvement and pointed them toward an exit survey where they could reflect on the experience and opt-in to receive updates about our findings.

Transcription, coding, and analysis

One of the practical benefits of conducting the focus groups virtually via *Teams* was that we were subsequently able to upload the MP4 files to another part of the Microsoft 365 suite – *Microsoft Stream* – and make use of the auto-transcription feature. This was a significant time saver compared to transcribing by hand. At the same time, while the auto-transcription was surprisingly accurate, it was far from perfect and required subsequent editing for accuracy as well as to indicate the speaker of particular contributions. Two research assistants came on to the project at this stage to clean up the transcription documents ready for coding.

With the transcripts checked for accuracy, we were left with eight documents totalling 96,378 words in need of organisation. To achieve this, we embarked on a process of hybrid coding (Lester *et al.* 2021) in which the broad areas of interest from our topic guide served as overarching deductive codes. These deductive codes were:

1. Understandings / knowledge of Prevent.
2. Sources of knowledge.
3. Understandings of radicalisation.
4. Evaluations of Prevent.
5. Recommendations for Prevent/counter-extremism.

From this point, we began a three-step process that used these deductive codes to inform a first reading of the corpus, in which all three authors took responsibility for a section of each transcript and extracted 'analytically significant features' (O'Connor and Joffee 2020: 2) corresponding with the codes. This initial process served primarily to remove material from the corpus we deemed irrelevant to our research aims. With a more concise and workable corpus established, one author then went through the document, coding inductively to establish a more detailed coding framework (Hammond and Wellington 2020). To enhance accuracy and reliability, all authors met to review this inductive coding and make minor agreed-upon edits.

This process produced twenty-seven codes, each of which contained a range of more specific code values (Bauer 2000: 139). Table 2.3 is an excerpt of our coding framework demonstrating how the initial deductive code 'Understandings / knowledge of Prevent', consisted of nine additional inductively produced codes and a further thirty-four specific code values.

Table 2.3 Excerpt from coding framework

Initial deductive codes	Inductive codes	Code values
Understandings/knowledge of Prevent	What is Prevent?	Support
		Prevention
		Intervention
		Safeguarding
		Unsure
		A threat
	Links to other concepts	Radicalisation
		Extremism
	Context of Prevent	CONTEST
	Location of Prevent	School
		Welfare system
		Health
		University
		Third sector
		Education
	Aims of Prevent	'At risk' groups
		Root causes
	Targets of Prevent	'At risk' groups
		Communities
		Geographical
		Islamism
		Young people
		Are appropriate

(*continued*)

Table 2.3   (Cont.)

Initial deductive codes	Inductive codes	Code values
	Workings of Prevent	Channel
		Aims
		Targets
		Vulnerability risk factors
		Fundamental British values
		Referrals
	Developments in Prevent	Prevent duty
		Evolution of focus
	Controversies	Racial and religious bias
		Targeting communities
		Community backlash

Finally, we concluded this process by returning to the original eight raw transcripts and coding these anew with the inductive coding framework established and agreed upon by all members of the research team. This final part of the process was designed to test the reliability of our coding and to make certain there was nothing missed from the raw transcripts in the earlier stages of analysis.

Conclusion

In this chapter, we have set out the theoretical and methodological framework for our analysis of students' perspectives on the meaning and threat of radicalisation, and on the UK's Prevent Strategy as a mechanism for addressing this threat. We began by arguing that security should be approached not as an objective condition that exists outside of the understandings and lived experiences of citizens, but instead as something that becomes relevant and meaningful for individuals and collectives in specific discursive, historical, political, and cultural contexts. Because of this, we suggested, it is problematic to assume that the consequences (positive or negative) of specific measures aimed at enhancing security can be 'known', or deduced. These consequences can only be meaningfully known through empirical research. As for security, so too for threats thereto which are, again, 'made, not given' (Jarvis 2022a: 79). Something becomes an issue of security through its interpretation or production as such. There is nothing inherent to illicit migration, or climate change – or, in our case, to terrorism, extremism, or radicalisation – that renders them either security or non-security issues. They can be either, or neither, or, indeed, both, depending, amongst other things, on who we ask, where, and when.

In contrast to the emphasis of much existing traditional and critical scholarship, we then argued that security's construction takes place at 'everyday' levels as much as at the level of political elites. And, therefore, much is to be gained analytically and perhaps also politically by exploring, unpacking, and interrogating 'vernacular' constructions of (in)security. As noted above, a vernacular security studies approach involves taking 'the understandings, imaginaries, conceptions, fears, and insecurities of real people as experienced and lived within daily life' (Jarvis 2019a: 120), as a vitally important starting point for research. Analytically, our study offers a novel, indeed necessary, means of researching counter-radicalisation and its underpinning logics 'on the ground'. There are also, moreover, normative benefits stemming from our approach with its offering of opportunity to 'speak security' to those rarely empowered to do so.

In the second half of this chapter, we then introduced the methodological approach through which we have sought to access vernacular constructions of radicalisation and the Prevent Strategy. As outlined above, the chapters that follow detail and analyse findings from a series of focus groups conducted across twelve different HEIs within the UK. These empirical chapters explore how students have come to know about extremism and Prevent, as well as their evaluations thereof. To this end, we turn now in Chapter 3 to our participants' observations and thoughts around the strategy's underpinning logic: radicalisation.

3

Radicalisation and/in the vernacular

The underpinning logic of the UK's Prevent Strategy is one of radicalisation. As argued in Chapter 1, the strategy is justified on the grounds that terrorism poses a significant threat to the UK, and that people *become* terrorists through a process of radicalisation whereby the individual 'comes to support terrorism and extremist ideologies associated with terrorist groups' (HM Government 2021a). Prevent, then, offers an attempt to disrupt this process in its earlier stages, although, as we have seen, the strategy has also increasingly been framed as a politically neutral 'safeguarding' initiative designed to protect individuals from harming themselves and others (HM Government 2018: 31–42). This safeguarding logic does considerable work for Prevent and the interventions it justifies, providing it with a sense of pragmatism, even common sense (see Kaleem 2021), that has been vital for the strategy's expansion across the British state.

A great deal of academic – and activist – ink has been spilled exploring the discursive framing of radicalisation, its ubiquity, ambiguities, and problems, as we saw in Chapter 1. As yet, however, far less remains known about non-elite or vernacular conceptions of this concept, its coherence, and explanatory or political utility. How familiar is the term 'radicalisation' to 'ordinary' citizens in their efforts to make sense of political violence? Is the term deemed a useful or problematic one, and on what grounds? To what sorts of ideas or actions is the term applied in vernacular discourse? Under what circumstances is it problematised or challenged? This chapter offers an attempt to explore questions such as these, focusing on vernacular constructions of radicalisation encountered in our focus groups with students at Higher Education Institutions in England and Wales.

This chapter begins by exploring how students *conceptualise* radicalisation, how they explained it to us and their peers, and the different analogies and models they evoked in so doing. Here, we see a very familiar understanding of radicalisation as a process, on the one hand, competing with divergent framings in which radicalisation is seen as more akin to an attitude or willingness to act. A second section then turns to vernacular articulations of the enabling factors of radicalisation, in which overlapping agential and structural explanations are offered to make sense of this phenomenon. Here, we see a wide range of potentially significant variables discussed in our groups, from personal grievances to the role of communities in fomenting extremist ideology and action. The chapter then turns to the *terminology* of radicalisation and students' beliefs that an often ambiguous and imprecise language is frequently used to explain this phenomenon. Issues of power and subjectivity are important themes covered in this section, especially when determining who or what may receive the pejorative label 'radicalised' or the more positive one 'radical'. The chapter concludes by reflecting on the importance of these concerns. Table 3.1 summarises the chapter's findings.

What is radicalisation?

Contributors to our focus groups discussed the concept of radicalisation at considerable length, often demonstrating nuance and reflexivity in so doing. Notable in these discussions were two dominant conceptual framings relating to radicalisation as (i) a process, and (ii) an attitude. In the following, we discuss each in turn.

Radicalisation as a process

Most common amongst participants in our focus groups was a conception of radicalisation that echoes the UK government's processual understanding of this phenomenon. In the words of one of our participants, for instance:

> it's basically [a] process, [in] which an individual or maybe [a] group of individuals come to adopt an increasingly radical view … the more this process gets in depth, the harder [it is] to get out just basically because it makes so much sense for the person that is being radicalised.
>
> Focus Group 8, Participant 3

This processual conceptualisation of radicalisation is a prevalent one in contemporary academic and policy thinking. As Hardy (2018) notes, a range of models have been designed to flesh out how this process might work in practice that each differ in terms of the 'steps' and 'stages' involved along an individual's 'pathway'. What these models tend to share, though, is radicalisation as a dynamic that unfolds across a period of time. It is this temporal emphasis, indeed, that gives impetus to initiatives such as Prevent. This is because it offers a potential window through which to

Table 3.1 Vernacular discourse on radicalisation

	Cases	Discussion	Example
Understandings of radicalisation	(i) Radicalisation as a process	Vulnerable individuals are pushed toward the political fringes over a period of time by external influences.	'… the whole purpose of radicalisation is to target vulnerable people and it's like brainwashing … it's convincing this person that that's what they want to do'
	(ii) Radicalisation as (violent) attitude	Radicalisation as intolerance to the point of support for, and/or willingness to employ, violence.	'anyone who's willing to not only commit those acts, but even support those acts and support the people that do those acts become for me what would be considered a radical'
Causes of radicalisation	(i) Community dynamics	Online and offline in-groups act as echo chambers amplifying dangerous ideas	'… you're around like-minded individuals, you're really not getting much [sic] counter-arguments getting thrown your way … behaviours get normalised and not necessarily disagreed with'
	(ii) Grievance	Sense of individual disempowerment generated by alienation, ostracisation or dissatisfaction with social outcomes	'radicalisation, generally, is, I think, as sort of has been hinted at is sort of like ostracised, ostracisation, like feeling like you're not necessarily part of or not catered for by the community that you live in and then feeling like there is a voice being given to you from somewhere else'
Sources of concern and confusion	(i) Ambiguity	Vagueness of the term, and lack of differentiation from related concepts	'I would say that I don't think it is useful, mainly because I feel like theories of radicalisation are still way too broad and contested'

(ii) Pejorative connotations	Risk of demonising non-harmful forms of rebellion	'… the very word it makes it seem like being radical is a bad thing'
(iii) Subjectivity	Understandings of radicalisation are inherently contextual	'I think because it very much depends on your perspective … what a certain community finds radical, another community may find commonplace … '
(iv) Instrumental use	Governmental use of the discourse to justify security policies	'The term has been weaponised … to condone certain strategies in response to terrorism'
(v) Depoliticising effects	Used to discredit opposition, and restrict civil liberties	'Insofar as it's seen as a bad thing for people to be an oppositional force, for them to develop that opposition into some very active forms and potentially get to the point where they may not break the law'
(vi) Denial of agency of those 'radicalised'	Discourages engagement with the causes of extremism and terrorism.	Encourages ignorance of 'the content of what someone [has] started to believe and why'
(vii) Inconsistent application	Selective application, especially due to the racial or religious identity of potential targets.	'… you might find someone that commits a white supremacist attack wouldn't necessarily be considered radicalised, whereas if you were to get a Muslim terrorist, they would be considered radicalised'

observe radicalisation via cognitive and/or behavioural risk factors and, subsequently, to enable targeted intervention before any violence occurs.

The models within governmental explanations of radicalisation tend to work through physical metaphors such as conveyor belts, staircases, and pyramids (see Eroukhmanoff 2015; Muro 2016). The participants in our focus groups also drew upon metaphorical resources to convey this term's meaning, although the most frequent of these was a less specific, geometric one, that framed radicalisation as a process through which individuals 'move away from the centre'. This framing often worked, in our focus groups, through the conjoining of binary pairings – normal/radicalised and inside/outside:

> It's this idea that someone goes from being a normal person eventually they're, uh, they kind of get indoctrinated with the ideology and that becomes gradually more extreme, so you kind of *go from* a radical to an extremist to a terrorist.
>
> Focus Group 1, Participant 1, our emphasis

Here, the student draws upon an understanding of radicalisation as moving from a 'normal' middle to the 'radical', 'extremist', and 'terrorist' outsides defined by their structural relation to the centre. Although there is no indication here of the inevitability of negative outcomes following deviation from the centre, the assumption here, clearly, is that the process of radicalisation ends in bad news: the 'normal' person becomes a 'terrorist'.

This geometric conception of radicalisation was evident when contributors to our groups began to reflect on the drivers and dynamics underpinning this process. In the following example, for instance, we encounter a sense that radicalisation may stem from feelings of disenfranchisement and alienation, and the accompanying belief that the 'establishment … [has] pushed them outward' (Focus Group 1, Participant 4). Radicalisation, here, feels to the individual like 'an outside … which is being internalised' (Focus Group 7, Participant 3). In contrast to some of the earliest official models of radicalisation, however, we encountered little sense that this radicalising move away from 'the centre' was a straightforward, or irreversible one, with frequent recognition in our groups that the process was, 'not necessarily linear' (Focus Group 1, Participant 1), and 'complicated' because 'you can go back and forward, you can jump steps' (Focus Group 2, Participant 1).

Reflections on social and political agency were an important aspect, too, within these discussions on the radicalisation process. Students in our groups tended to view radicalisation as something that occurred because of a lack of agency on the part of the individual being radicalised. In some instances, this lack of agency was couched in the language of vulnerability; a language prevalent, of course, within official radicalisation discourse and strategies (Heath-Kelly 2013; Coppock and McGovern 2014). In the words of one participant, for instance, the process typically started 'from a space of vulnerability' (Focus Group 1, Participant 1). This sense of vulnerability was important to a participant in another group, too, although here the process of radicalisation was understood in instrumental terms: as one that is purposively *occasioned upon* vulnerable people for nefarious ends:

> the whole purpose of radicalisation is to target vulnerable people. Like brainwashing? [As] opposed to just someone going up to them asking them to join their terrorist organization, it's convincing this person that that's what they want to do, rather than it being just like recruitment. It is more kind of like targeting someone's ideological views.
>
> Focus Group 4, Participant 3

For this student, the process of radicalisation was as much, if not more, about the person *doing the radicalising* than the individual being radicalised, who was reduced to a soft target who could be manipulated or 'brainwashed' into a particular way of thinking or acting. This explicitly cognitive framing of radicalisation (see Chapter 1) was described elsewhere as the process of internalising the views of 'whoever is putting the views on you', until that 'becomes your thought process' (Focus Group 7, Participant 1). One student in our focus groups, for example, voiced their surprise that there had not been greater linkage between radicalisation and 'mental illness', 'addiction', or 'the tactics which might be used to groom young people' as these all seemed 'quite a fair analogy' to radicalisation with its emphasis upon 'someone's capability being reduced because of being abused or targeted and drawn into something' (Focus Group 6, Participant 1). Other references to radicalisation drew instead upon literary resources, as in discussion of this process as a 'falling down the rabbit hole' (Focus Group 1, Participant 4). Importantly, as the following illustrates, discussions such as these all militate against recognition of any meaningful agency on the part of the 'radicalised': the movement toward terrorism is understood here as far removed from any rational, let alone political, process of decision-making (Cassam 2018):

> there are some kids who get brainwashed by these communities and then they are ready to lose their lives for … they have been brainwashed to think that is right … that person has lost the ability to think for themselves and are following this … very violent ideology, they've been brainwashed to believe.
>
> Focus Group 6, Participant 4

A final point to note within this first conceptualisation of radicalisation was a sense amongst students within our groups that the process was a very difficult one from which to extricate oneself. As we noted earlier, many participants viewed this process as a non-linear one, with the capacity for movement back and forth along a 'pathway' or 'staircase'. At the same time, a number also argued that the further entrenched one became within this process, 'the harder [it was] to get out', not least, 'because it makes so much sense for the person that is being radicalised' (Focus Group 8, Participant 3). Getting 'tunnel vision' was seen as symptomatic of this process, meaning that the (hypothetical) radicalised individual, 'can't really be swayed' from their 'us versus them' thinking (Focus Group 1, Participant 4).

This conceptualisation of radicalisation as a process was prominent across our focus groups, and hearing how students understood it provides useful insight into its specific internal workings. As we have seen, students often worked with a geometric model of political sensibilities comprising a 'normal' centre and a radicalised fringe. The process of radicalisation was therefore seen to occur when vulnerable people lacking agency were led astray by external influences that took them from the centre toward the fringes. There was an acceptance that this was a very difficult process to undo, and was rarely, if ever, a rational and autonomous decision on the part of the person becoming radicalised.

Radicalisation as (violent) attitude

Thinking of radicalisation as a process is, as we have seen, a popular vernacular one, and the frequency with which it was mentioned in our focus groups may reflect its accuracy, intuitiveness or, indeed, the currency it enjoys within wider political and media discourse. However, this conception was not entirely uncontested within our groups, and we also encountered a divergent understanding of radicalisation as an intolerant attitude that supports, or is willing to use, violence. This framing differs from that discussed above in at least two ways. First, the passage of *time* is of far more limited significance within this attitudinal understanding. And, second, this alternative conceptualisation offers space for greater agency, as we shall see, on the part of the radicalised individual.

Sketching out their thinking in broader terms before linking the term 'radicalisation' to terrorism, one student likened the verb 'radicalise' to 'taking matters into your own hands':

> even if you consider in music like a radical, it's like they're going against the norms, the fixed rules and to create something that's a bit more bold and so it does sort of suit terrorism in a way because it's ignoring figures of authority and what the consensus in that population is about what's right and wrong. And it also suggests that people have already fixed on that path and that they can't be dissuaded by other figures.
>
> Focus Group 3, Participant 4

Other participants in our groups offered specific, and explicitly political, examples of what this attitude entailed including, for instance, being 'anti-democratic ... anti the rule of law' (Focus Group 7, Participant 4), and being 'hostile to particular groups' (Focus Group 7, Participant 4). The most common characteristic attributed to radicalisation as an attitude, though, concerned an individual's willingness to engage in violence:

> I think for me, it's anyone willing to do any acts that the UK or even Western society deem unlawful and so, I think a lot of times when we think of a terrorist attack, it's often to do with murder. So, anyone who's willing to not only commit those acts, but even support those acts and support the people that do those acts become for me what would be considered a radical.
>
> Focus Group 2, Participant 2

This excerpt reflected what several other participants conveyed to us: that radicalisation involves the harbouring not only of an intolerant attitude, but, also, a sense that violence represents a justified and instrumental form of action in the minds of the radicalised. Radicalisation, here, involves, 'being ok with turning to violence' (Focus Group 2, Participant 4) and having beliefs that 'make you so intolerant of other people's behaviour that you want to commit violence against strangers' (Focus Group 2, Participant 5). In the words of another student, radicalisation combines 'the internalisation of ... views', with a thoroughly modern sense of agency (see Gray 2003), in the 'perception that there's something that can be done to enact those views' (Focus Group 7, Participant 3).

It is noteworthy, we argue, that when asked to reflect on the meaning of radicalisation, participants in our focus groups offered two conceptualisations that differed in quite significant ways. The most popular of these – radicalisation as process – understood the concept as a dynamic of manipulation whereby a party with greater agency warped the thinking of their vulnerable victim, grooming them over time to think and act according to the former's interest. Conversely, when understood as a violent attitude, significantly greater agency is attributed to the radicalised individual. Radicalisation here is still largely depicted as a negative, unwanted dynamic. At the same time, in this instance. the radicalised subject is seen as actively taking control of their situation through the use of violence in order to express an extreme political agenda.

The contrast between these two conceptualisations is instructive. The former, as noted above, seems closely to reflect dominant discourse on this term – especially, although not exclusively – within the UK. The latter, in contrast, provides an alternative that may help reveal important contingencies or ambiguities in the concept of radicalisation itself. The former's promise of effective intervention to protect the vulnerable, moreover, draws upon a far more explicitly gendered logic in which vulnerable, passive, and affective (feminised) victims are to be protected from powerful, active, and rational (masculinised) agents. This gendering of the different parties is compounded by a masculinised reading of time, where Prevent is situated as the saving grace that acts to contain destabilisation and deliver a reassuring linear transition (Brown 2021) from the radicalised outside back to the normalised centre.

What causes radicalisation?

In designing the framework for our focus group discussions, we left space for – but did not explicitly ask about – the causes of radicalisation. As we expected, this topic emerged frequently within our conversations, perhaps reflecting the question's importance in the minds of our participants. As one student put it:

> But it's also this idea of actually putting time into understanding why people do become radicalised because I think it's a huge step, for example, to leave your family and go to Syria or to actually put your life at stake and do this causing harm to others … ending your life in suicide bombings, it's not easy and there must be something going into it. I think it's really important to understand why people take those steps and then sort of working out what can be done?
>
> Focus Group 3, Participant 5

In the following, we explore some of the explanatory factors offered by students in these discussions, grouping these into two broad, interlinked categories: community and grievance.

Community

Across our focus groups, we frequently encountered a sense that radicalisation is something that is enabled by a community. In the words of one participant, for instance: 'it involves a community for sure … it is a welcoming community to those who are in that community' (Focus Group 1, Participant 3). This student references the idea of an in-group characterised by an element of exclusivity, offering support and succour to its members. The role of the community may go further than this, though, to incorporate a transactional element that encourages further involvement in extremism in exchange for something of value to the 'recruit'. Such an understanding highlights parallels with the analogy of "grooming" mentioned above; as one student put it: "'they're" trying to get other people on the same level as their ideas by sort of offering them things, maybe like benefits to this, and trying and persuade them to join so they think it's this amazing thing' (Focus Group 5, Participant 1).

Communities are also seen, in vernacular discourse, to act as *echo chambers*, reflecting and amplifying potentially dangerous, minority ideas. Understood thus, communities are not plural spaces encouraging hetero-geneous views, disagreement, and debate. Rather, they exist to reproduce and reaffirm the (extreme) views of a membership, such as ideas of white supremacy and 'radical nationalism' amongst those attracted to the far right (Focus Group 6, Participant, 2):

> you're around like-minded individuals, you're really not getting much [*sic*] counter-arguments getting thrown your way … behaviours get normalised and not necessarily disagreed with. I think that possibly plays a bit of a role in rad-icalisation, but in human behaviour more broadly also.
>
> Focus Group 1, Participant 4

Participants in our groups were also often quick to point out that communi-ties facilitating radicalisation need not exist in physical space, such that 'you can now become radicalised over the Internet' (Focus Group 8, Participant 1). For one student, for instance, community involved a collection of like-minded people rather than any reference to physical proximity:

> I think community is more nowadays it's more about just people who have a similar mindset or similar set of beliefs. I think less and less it's becoming rel-evant where you are located geographically. In terms of this sort of radicalisa-tion process. I don't know necessarily that there's any real or any meaningful distinction between online and offline. I feel like one feeds into the other, and the other feeds into the other. But uhm, I think, yeah, that's sort of what I mean by community like. I think it's less important, like geographically. You know who you necessarily live next to or with.
>
> Focus Group 2, Participant 3

The significance that students placed on the role of a community in cases of radicalisation made clear that for many with whom we spoke, radi-calisation was a collaborative phenomenon involving other parties and external stimuli. As with vernacular constructions of radicalisation as a process, this understanding of radicalisation as an *inter-personal* dynamic chimes with dominant understandings of this term. A belief that such dynamics occur within like-minded communities does not, in itself, deny any role for individual agency within these processes. At the same time, however, we encountered much discussion in our groups about the une-qual power dynamics and possibility for manipulation within particular communities.

Grievance

Alongside the role of community, students in our groups also discussed individual grievances, such as dissatisfaction, ostracism, and a sense of external threat, as important factors in radicalisation dynamics. There was no suggestion, though, that these more agential dynamics should be considered in isolation from the community-based explanations considered above. Indeed, grievance and community were frequently connected to one another, with the former leading into the latter, as in the following example:

> a lot of people will turn to, or become radical, when they perceive a threat against their community as a threat against themselves. So, they take that threat very seriously ... really, very personally and so then their knee-jerk reaction is to go to the extreme.
>
> Focus Group 2, Participant 2

Alienation and ostracisation, when read alongside the community-oriented explanations above, seem to reveal a linear sequence within these vernacular accounts that helps provide evidence of how participants in our focus groups saw *the process of radicalisation* taking place. Here, alienation was typically approached as the originary point of this process, leading to a desire to have grievances heard in a like-minded and understanding community. As participants in two separate groups argued:

> Yeah, I think the key part of radicalisation, generally, is, I think, as sort of has been hinted at is sort of like ostracised, ostracisation, like feeling like you're not necessarily part of or not catered for by the community that you live in and then feeling like there is a voice being given to you from, from somewhere else.
>
> Focus Group 2, Participant 3

> alienation, dissatisfaction, etc., and then I think it just grows from there ... their end focus could be anything, whether it be going somewhere else or killing someone, you know, [it] tends to be violent.
>
> Focus Group 1, Participant 4

The presence of community-based *and* grievance-based factors here suggest that in the minds of many of our participants, at least, radicalisation has an agency/structure dynamic. The existence of these different factors and their interlinkage seems also to lend itself to greater support for *process*-based conceptualisations of radicalisation, whereby dissatisfaction at the individual level progresses to a desire for recognition within a wider community in which these sentiments become more entrenched. The nuances identified by students make clear, though, that participants in our groups view this as a complex phenomenon that should not be glossed over with simplistic and reductive explanations:

There's so many different cases, most of those terrorism fighters, they are educated people. They are not mentally ill people with big problems in their life, most of them are university undergraduates, so we can't just say 'mental illness', there are plenty of other factors that can influence radicalism.

Focus Group 6, Participant 2

No seriously, what *is* radicalisation?

Our conversations with students about how they understood radicalisation operated on two levels. The first was typified by the sort of content in the previous sections and proceeded within a context of good faith around the existence of radicalisation as a stable concept. In the discussions outlined above, students tended to accept the premises of our questions and discussed radicalisation with the ambition of providing a workable or even accurate version of radicalisation (albeit while recognising the term's many complexities). For example, one student might view radicalisation as a process while another might instead view it as an attitude. Such students, clearly, have different conceptions of how radicalisation works while sharing, at the same time, an effort to capture the truth of this phenomenon. However, as discussion within our focus groups progressed, a second level of conversation also tended to emerge in which participants began to critique the concept on more fundamental grounds, including through interrogation of the meaning and premises *of our questions*. The emphasis of these discussions saw students become less focused on radicalisation itself, and more concentrated on questions of ambiguity, subjectivity, logic, and power within the term's usage, by us and by others.

Ambiguity and conflation

The most frequent criticism of the language of radicalisation that we encountered in our groups is a familiar one from the literature reviewed in Chapter 1, and relates to the term's vagueness and conceptual ambiguities. In the preceding sections, we identified different accounts and explanations of radicalisation with which students were working. For some of our participants, however, the very plausibility of these diverse understandings spoke to the problematic breadth of the concept itself. Radicalisation, here, was seen as a 'blanket term' (Group 1, Participant 4), 'quite ambiguous' (Focus Group 5, Participant 3) and 'too vague' (Focus Group 7, Participant 4) to be helpful. Thus, when asked whether, with this ambiguity in mind, the students found the term useful, one replied: 'I would say that I don't think it is useful, mainly because I feel like theories of radicalisation are still way too broad and contested even between academics' (Focus Group 8, Participant 5)

Students in our groups seemed divided as to whether this issue was predominantly a definitional one that could be addressed with further efforts to pin down the concept (see Chapter 5), or an inescapable problem tied up in insurmountable dynamics of subjectivity and power (see below):

> I think within anything to do with humans in any terms you're going to have to be relatively nebulous because everything with humans is difficult to pin down, so I don't know that there's any term that you could use that would be more useful.
>
> Focus Group 2, Participant 3

Given this conceptual instability, confusion was apparent within our groups when determining exactly what it was that was being discussed. In the third group, for instance, as our discussion on radicalisation was approaching a close, one student made a point of saying that they 'still didn't have a clear idea of what is intended by radicalisation' (Focus Group 3, Participant 1). This sort of confusion was particularly apparent when students sought to navigate the differences between closely associated terms such as 'radicalisation', 'extremism', and 'terrorism':

> That's a difficult question to answer. So, maybe radical is someone on the fringes of society's acceptable norms. So, maybe something unusual, but not necessarily wrong, or something that's tolerable? Then an extremist is just outside of those acceptable norms and then you start to incorporate things like harms and things like that. Maybe that's the border.
>
> Focus Group 1, Participant 1

And, yet, as this student went on to argue:

> I think radicalisation gets lumped in with extremism almost synonymously these days. I think to be a radical isn't necessarily a bad thing but if you see 'radicalisation' or 'radical' and a news headline, you're immediately, or at least for me, you're immediately thinking towards extremism and terrorism.
>
> Focus Group 1, Participant 1

The conflation of terminology clearly made demarcating radicalisation difficult for some, and participants in many other groups pointed out how 'radicalisation has now been associated to terrorism' (Focus Group 8, Participant 1), or even more specifically, is 'used interchangeably with the idea of Islamic terrorism' (Focus Group 8, Participant 6).

Pejorative connotations

Terminological ambiguities and instabilities were significant points of concern for students trying to make sense of radicalisation in our groups, many of whom seemed to work with a sense that clarity of concepts is inherently virtuous (see Horder 2019). The criticisms considered above therefore tended to operate within a logic that saw potential for further demarcation of the meaning of terms: a view, put otherwise, that although the meaning of radicalisation may be contested, it is not, necessarily, essentially so. However, these sorts of conflation were further complicated given that radicalisation's stem, 'radical', was often viewed positively in a way that did not translate to its denominalisation: 'Well, it's interesting, so I've got quite a lot of friends who I would describe as radicals, but I certainly wouldn't consider them to be radicalised' (Focus Group 2, Participant 5).

As many commentators have remarked on the pejorative connotations of the term 'terrorism', radicalisation was also felt by some students to be a label associated with the 'bad guys' (Richardson, 2006: 19), one that brought with it powerful delegitimising effects. This association served to diminish the term's utility in the eyes of many of our participants, with the media deemed to play an important role in the amplification of this link:

> I personally don't know how much of a useful term it is, looking more from an academic perspective, because it's incredibly subjective and you find a lot in the media [that] they will use it very subjectively and as a kind of pejorative term to sort of diminish what someone's done.
>
> Focus Group 4, Participant 4

A student in our eighth group was vocal about the language's use to stigmatise those desirous of radical change:

> The very word it makes it seem like being radical is a bad thing, which I would argue radical is not always a bad thing. I think we need a lot of radical stuff to be honest, radical change. So yeah, the whole connotation of it being, you know, 'God forbid you being radicalised', it's just interesting.
>
> Focus Group 8, Participant 7

Another student, similarly, spoke about how two very different understandings of 'radical' or 'radicalise' had been collapsed into one another:

> It's definitely possible to say that radicalised has had a very particular meaning, in this context [of extremism], radicalisation before that or outside of that context doesn't appear to me to mean the same thing. There is for example, radical in the context of music [which] is really a positive objective and radical in terms of politics before this period was definitely seen with nothing other than a positive spin.
>
> Focus Group 3, Participant 1

The student went on to observe how this conflation could be used to reinforce certain political positions and delegitimise others: 'You could argue, and it has been argued, that saying something is radically bad is convenient for a particular political perspective to say that certain other perspectives aren't necessarily bad' (Focus Group 3, Participant 1)

Clearly there are linkages to the above discussion here. Criticism such as this serves as a specific form of conflation between something potentially positive (being rebellious) and something typically viewed as negative (being radicalised). In the above, Participant 4 in Focus Group 4 appears to lament that the concept has lost its potential for objective application on account of its contemporary negative associations. The latter two students, in contrast, are more concerned with the potential for the pejorative connotations of radical/radicalisation to serve as a blanket means of delegitimising anything oppositional to the status quo. The inconsistent application of this term, and its potential to be used for strategic political purposes, chimes with fundamental questions students asked about the subjectivity of radicalisation and its use in particular relations of power.

Subjectivity and power

Subjectivity and power were two themes that ran throughout all our discussions. Already in the section above we can see them operating in the foreground and background. The student who mentioned their radical friends but baulked at the idea they had *been radicalised* was presumably viewing these friends as 'the good kind of radical'. The student might have been using the word 'radical' in explicitly political terms (perhaps their friends have engaged in direct action) but, equally plausibly, may have been making reference to their friends' association with counter-cultures, say. Where these friends might have developed a 'critical resistance' to the status quo through their experiences or education and presumably expressed this in a non-violent way, the terrorist has had radicalisation *done to them*, becoming the 'bad kind of radical', with unequivocally extreme ideas about the world and a propensity to use violence. The radical friend and the radicalised terrorist share something semantically, but for many students in our focus groups, they remain very different because it is permissible to be rebellious on certain issues and in certain ways but not on all issues and in all ways.

Delving into the insights a little further here reveals that students recognise the subjectivity of radicalisation and explain this with reference to the overarching term 'context', which was understood along ideological, temporal, and power lines. For example, the students below reference how variations in identity or ideology between groups and communities structure how these groups can view issues as permissibly radical or problematically extreme:

> It's really quite tricky, isn't it? Because every group is quite context-dependent and then I suppose each group would have some very real existential threats and grievances that they would then hold and use them to justify whatever

actions they want to take. Because there's such a wide variance between the different ideologies, it tends to be along boundaries of identity and because there are so many of those on this planet there's quite a lot of variances.

Focus Group 2, Participant 5

For a student in another group, similarly:

I think because it very much depends on your perspective … what a certain community finds radical, another community may find commonplace … Therefore it very much is based on the community that you are in and so, I think pinning down what is radical and what isn't is very much about politics and about opinion.

Focus Group 1, Participant 3

A further complicating factor here is recognition that political judgement does not differ only across spaces or ideological sympathies, but also across *time*. Our first group, for instance, highlighted the example of Martin Luther King, Jr. as a man who at one time was viewed by the establishment as a dangerous radical, but who subsequently has come to be viewed very differently. This exchange began with a student offering the following observation:

If you look at like a Martin Luther King [he could] easily be described as a radical, right? But now he's you know, kind of in the 'Hall of Fame' of influential people associated with like human rights and things.

Focus Group 1, Participant 1

Prompted by this, another student linked the example to the role of state power in fixing 'the normal centre' and demarcating its outside as extreme:

I mean, it's a slippery slope because the governments decide what is what, right? Martin Luther King was for a time period, a terrorist and civil rights leaders were also terrorists, and they weren't allowed to fly, own guns, a lot of the things that. So, I'm not sure that is a useful distinction, the difference between radical and extremist.

Focus Group 1, Participant 3

A student in our sixth group commented on what they felt were important effects of the term's inherent subjectivity, noting that what might be *radical* in one place could be evidence of *radicalisation* in another:

It depends on the context it's being used … in a context around Prevent or something, you can see what is meant by saying someone has become radicalised and it's linked with more extremist views. But then I guess there's other contexts where you could refer to someone's radical ideas or radicalism in a way that doesn't mean those things. For me it has so many different meanings in different contexts. Some of them, for me, are not as clean-cut as others.

Focus Group 6, Participant 1

In the above, we see how students plainly recognise the ambiguity and subjectivity of radicalisation. However, there was also a view that – short of conversations such as those taking place in focus groups in which time is afforded for unpacking concepts, their implications and applications – radicalisation has an intuitiveness and powerful 'common sense'. Students recognised that radicalisation is a complicated and context-dependent phenomenon. Nevertheless, they also suggested that when it came to how the term was typically spoken of or acted upon, much of this subjectivity was black-boxed and what was left – the link between the signifier 'radicalisation' and what it signifies – was typically understood as a lot more concrete. The student below, for instance, notes how they talk about 'the radicalisation process' as a sort of linguistic shortcut, *despite* recognising what this conceals, including the problems that lie therein with regards to deradicalisation interventions:

> We sort of fall into using the term as if it means something specific, but it's really hard to pick apart what that actually means. Yeah, I don't know. I fall into the habit of saying, 'it's the radicalisation process', but then that looks different for every single person that it happens to so, it's really hard to then spot a specific sign.
>
> Focus Group 5, Participant 6

Radicalisation, then, is a powerful and risky signifier but one that links to an amorphous and subjective signified. Our seventh group were particularly vocal in approaching this ambiguity as a deliberate political strategy either because definitional alternatives such as typologies of more specific terms would offer little value:

> I would also agree that it is purposely vague, but then the alternative would potentially be trying to divide up something which can't be divided or labelling things which overlap. I don't know. It's not good that it's so vague, but then I'm not sure what the alternative would be.
>
> Focus Group 7, Participant 2

Or, because the ambiguity itself served as a useful means to apply the label wherever something emerged that was 'counter [to] what society is generally looking for':

> I would say it's too vague. Kind of purposely kept as an umbrella term so that whatever is considered to be counter to what society is generally looking for can be considered radicalisation. You can have political extremism and religious extremism and all these things, and they can come under this very loose term.
>
> Focus Group 7, Participant 4

These two students both view radicalisation as vague, yet there is an import-ant difference between the two. The former viewed this vagueness as a real-ity of trying to attach a label to an amorphous phenomenon, while the latter saw this as the outcome of instrumental decisions. The feedback from across all of our groups, however, was generally one of scepticism about efforts to define radicalisation and thereby escape these issues of subjectivity and power relations. Nevertheless, a small minority did speak about the possi-bility or desirability of maintaining radicalisation's distinctiveness in order to distinguish it from closely related but separate terms:

> I think it is a useful term because it creates a definition between other similar acts that are within the criminal world. So, we talk about grooming and it's a similar process, there's no doubt about it. It's about people of power influenc-ing the people who are vulnerable and seeking to exploit them for their own gains or their own cause, it's a very similar process. So [radicalisation is useful] to help people conceptualise the two different processes even though there's so much in a crossover there.
>
> Focus Group 3, Participant 2

From the analysis of this section, we can draw two primary conclusions. First, that students in our focus groups had a number of problems with radi-calisation as a label (the signifier) and with radicalisation as a phenomenon (the signified). The former focused on the radical/radicalisation distinction, while the latter concerned the ambiguity of that being signified and on the effects of power and subjectivity. Second, despite these issues, our partici-pants also had a 'common' or intuitive sense of what was typically meant by radicalisation. Or, put another way, when we asked about radicalisa-tion specifically, they 'knew what we were getting at'. Even in a context of scepticism, there was a willingness from most students to default back to something that looked like the dominant discourse on radicalisation when conversations required a stable common ground.

The first conclusion reflects something very familiar to that found within constructivist social sciences: radicalisation exists as a contested concept whose meaning is contingent, therefore impermanent and because of this, contestable. However, on the second conclusion, it seems noteworthy that radicalisation could be subjected to so much critique in our discussions and yet elsewhere – in the same discussions – enjoy a surprising degree of surface-level acceptance. On reflection, it seems that students were willing to accept radicalisation as a real and potentially risky phenomenon and therefore rarely had fundamental issues with the signifier 'radicalisation'. However, this came at the same time as tremendous uncertainty around what it signified. Perhaps this proves an illustrative microcosm of a wider critique, and how, in the absence of an alternative vision, the dominant discourse remains the placeholder. At the very least, it seems to speak to just how dominant the 'common sense' of radicalisation is that it can sustain this level of criticism and still emerge as a coherent idea. Despite this, as our final section illustrates, students were also attuned to the problems that could and do present when a phenomenon with dangerous connotations and poorly understood mechanics becomes operationalised.

Concerns

The confusion and criticism that students voiced about radicalisation led to several concerns around the term's application. At one level, we saw students speaking about what they perceived to be nefarious intentions behind the emergence and deployment of the concept. Others, though, spoke more about unintended harms that could stem from the use of this lexicon.

To continue with the preceding section's theme, students across several of our focus groups believed that radicalisation ultimately served as a powerful tool in a wider *political strategy* designed to conflate critical thought and radical action with the spectre of terrorism. Where governments saw opposition or challenge that they found unacceptable, in this reading, they could construe or construct those individuals or groups as 'being on the pathway to radicalisation or encouraging radicalisation' (Focus Group 7, Participant 4). The term, here, was sufficiently ambiguous that it could be deployed 'in different ways so to promote interventions where the Government thinks they're necessary' (Focus Group 7, Participant 4). 'The term has been weaponised', one student said, to 'condone certain strategies in response to terrorism' (Focus Group 8, Participant 5).

In this vein, Saul (2006: 2) writes that 'the more confused a concept, the more it lends itself to opportunistic appropriation.' One student, for instance, drew attention to the treatment of the Uighurs in Xinjiang to illustrate the deadly consequences that can occur when a term like radicalisation enters the lexicon of the powerful and is appropriated for political purposes:

> I think it's not that useful for similar reasons to what's been said, and it's because it's very subjective and political. Because for example, China … defend[s] what they're doing with Uighurs, as they're trying to stop radicalisation, whereas the rest of the world sees that by and large as crimes against a religion. So, you could say that one political view of radicalisation is completely different to what we would see it as in the UK.
>
> Focus Group 4, Participant 6

Here the student draws attention to the usage of the language of radicalisation as a mechanism for justifying human rights violations. Whether we accept that Chinese actions in Xinjiang – or, say, US-led actions in Iraq – are *really* about deradicalisation or security, there is a concern here with this rhetorical device's ability to *condemn the actions of the other* within a logic of securitisation. Thus, a subjective and confused, but powerful, concept has led, in this reading, to opportunistic appropriation that in the most extreme cases has cost lives.

Elsewhere, students remarked on how the fuzzy boundaries of radicalisation and its semantic relationship with being radical could have detrimental *depoliticising effects*:

> The symptom is what we're talking about, but there is a cause of a symptom. What this symptom is or how it is defined is not clear to me, but insofar as it's seen as a bad thing for people to be an oppositional force, for them to develop that opposition into some very active forms and potentially get to the point where they may not break the law, I mean, these are all steps that you could argue on a scale. Now you could certainly talk about somebody becoming either violent or committing criminal acts as being on that scale, somewhere, whether any of that constitutes terrorism, or whether you need to go a step further before you get there. I mean, was Sylvia Pankhurst a terrorist?
>
> Focus Group 3, Participant 1

Here the student describes a spectrum of political action in which the terroristic use of violence would represent a criminal act, yet other steps short of this may represent legitimate 'oppositional force'. The example of Sylvia Pankhurst illustrates, for this student, that forceful direct action is sometimes necessary to bring about progressive change such as, in this instance, women's suffrage. The implication the student makes is that the amorphous notion of radicalisation threatens to muddy the distinction between qualitatively discrete activities at the more radical end of established political spectrums. Such muddying could have additional negative effects, including dissuading others from making their voices heard, thus rendering it harder to hold governments to account, or to challenge the status quo for fear of having one's actions linked to terrorism and extremism.

Linked to this, but situated in the context of their university studies, students also spoke of radicalisation impacting on freedom of speech (Focus Group 5, Participant 5) and leaving them feeling 'a bit less secure' and 'a bit more exposed' in the classroom (Focus Group 3, Participant, 4). Because discussing controversial issues and ideas were now tied up with Prevent (see Chapter 1), some students expressed fears that a misspoken sentence or misunderstood contribution might end up being erroneously linked to radicalisation with the detrimental effect of limiting 'students' abilities to express their ideas' (Focus Group 3, Participant, 4).

Connected to radicalisation as a potentially depoliticising force was the impact it might have in *denying the agency* of individuals. The beginnings of this argument emerge from a conceptualisation of radicalisation we considered above; as a *process* that was *done to* (vulnerable) people. The pejorative connotations of radicalisation here strongly imply that the end point one arrives at is an inherently negative, irrational, one. The radicalised person has been manipulated into a point of view that stands in opposition to legitimate political views and contemporary moral sensibilities. Indeed, the power of the radicalisation discourse is partly evidenced in its ability to create a situation which militates against sustained investigation into the legitimacy of individual grievances. On the one hand, the radicalised individual has been manipulated and therefore does not need to be taken seriously. On the other, to try and distil rational politics from this process is folly and endangers the suggestion of terrorist sympathy. Of course, this is not to argue that there always exist legitimate arguments or grievances behind ideas or behaviours deemed 'extreme' or 'radical'. Nor is it to suggest that the means with which individuals want to achieve political objectives are always ethical or proportionate.

Students were particularly sceptical of the blanket way those deemed radicalised saw their line of thinking 'explained away' with reference to analogies such as mental illness. Others noted how those who had a history of mental illness were viewed as incapable of forming rational thoughts:

> If you treat it as like mental illness, then it's something that you have to treat by controlling that person's thinking without acknowledging where it's coming from or what could be the reasons for thinking in that particular manner. It takes away all agency from people who are treated as dealing with mental illness because they are deemed as incapable of forming thoughts. So, definitely it cannot lead to any meaningful advancement in dealing with this, you know.
>
> Focus Group 6, Participant 4

In this understanding, analogising radicalisation to mental illness, and giving that analogy comprehensive explanatory power, risked encouraging us to ignore 'the content of what someone [has] started to believe and why' (Focus Group 6, Participant 1). These students implied, then, that there was a reticence to look too closely at the politics of these ideologies, perhaps for fear of granting them a sort of legitimacy, or that there might be 'something there' for 'us' to reflect on. Moreover, presumably failing to look more closely at the agency of these individuals might lead to missing opportunities to intervene and prevent violence.

A final concern in our groups was with the *inconsistency* of how the term 'radicalisation' was applied, and the harmful effects this could have. In the first instance, this appeared to closely follow the 'suspect communities' critique (see Chapter 1). Using the case study of the US, for instance, one student remarked:

you might find someone that commits a white supremacist attack wouldn't necessarily be considered radicalised, whereas if you were to get a Muslim terrorist, they would be considered radicalised ... so that subjectivity. Even though two people might commit the same crime, one is seen as worse than the other.

Focus Group 4, Participant 4

Radicalisation was viewed here as something not only with internal ambiguities, but as suffering, too, from inconsistency of application. Who might be considered radicalised was seen to be linked to issues such as race and religion, as for instance in the case of Shamima Begum. Begum is a woman who left the UK for Syria at the age of 15 to join ISIS, and has since been the subject of significant press coverage on account of the British government's refusal to allow her return to the UK. We made no reference to Begum's case in the groups, but in two separate instances students raised what they perceived as a double standard around how radicalisation had been applied and understood in this context:

I don't know if this is really relevant, but it's just quite interesting when you look at the Begum case and with her and it's like the different perspectives people can have on it. It's either people saying she was groomed into the situation or she was radicalised and it's just interesting to see like from one case where like people can have really different views on, not only her status, but how she was brought into the environment, whether it was off her own bat and it was through her own research into it, or whether because she was at such a young age, whether you classify as like sexual grooming and things like that.

Focus Group 1, Participant 5

Another student similarly remarked:

But then that's not how people would necessarily have treated the Begum case. She's someone who was a teenager who was essentially groomed into joining a group, essentially brainwashed if we're using that analogy and was a very vulnerable person. And yet the way that she's been treated is not at all in keeping with the idea that someone has been kind of trafficked or groomed or brainwashed.

Focus Group 6, Participant 1

In both commentaries, we see a recognition that despite Begum being a minor at the point of her travel to Syria, there is a closing-off of any sympathetic reading of this as a case of child exploitation in which Begum is the victim. Rather, Begum is stigmatised on account of her association with terrorism and, despite her age, is portrayed as someone who acted with purpose and rationality; as someone who, 'knew what she was doing'.

There are inconsistencies on at least two levels here. First, in a continuation of the points made above by Participant 4 in Focus Group 4, there is a sense here that Begum has received harsher treatment on account of her identity as a Muslim woman that has gotten involved with a terrorist organisation. It is beyond the scope of this chapter to elaborate on this here, but there is considerable research on the stigmatisation of Muslims going back to the beginning of the Global War on Terror, and of course far beyond this (e.g., Pantazis and Pemberton 2009; Kundnani 2014). It seems unlikely that a child adhering to the ideal victim typology (Christie, 1986) would be viewed as responsible in the same way.

Second, this case also demonstrates the inconsistency with which radicalisation is operationalised or understood. Throughout this chapter, different conceptualisations of radicalisation have been considered, with the degree of agency afforded to the 'radicalised' representing one area of variability between them. Prevent speaks of radicalisation as something that affects vulnerable people and therefore requires safeguarding intervention. Prevent is the 'soft' part of the strategy that aims to identify and intervene where people are 'at risk'. Indeed, the justification for so much intervention within education reflects a consensus that young people are particularly susceptible to extremist ideologies, as they 'seek to uncover their own identity, look to bolster self-confidence and are in search of meaning in their lives' (Ghosh *et al.* 2017: 119). And yet in this real example of a child deciding to travel to Syria, the 'radicalisation as exploitation' narrative is notably lacking, and Begum's own agency is stressed. As the student remarked, 'the way that she's been treated is not at all in keeping with the idea that someone has been kind of trafficked or groomed or brainwashed' (Focus Group 6, Participant 1).

Conclusion

Radicalisation makes up the central logic and underpinning foundation of the UK government's counter-radicalisation strategy. Given this significance, it was important to ensure that our conversations with students gave this concept adequate coverage. What these conversations revealed is illuminating on several fronts. In the first instance, we witness rather different understandings of radicalisation at work within contemporary vernacular discourse. On some occasions, these understandings map very closely with official accounts. In other instances, we see participants in our groups working with very different conceptions that diverge some way from the model at the heart of Prevent. Metaphorical and analogous reasoning was also evident in how the students made sense of this phenomenon, although again with considerable heterogeneity here. For example, where some students likened radicalisation to practices of brainwashing or grooming in which a targeted individual is seen to have little to no agency, others articulated the decision to utilise violence as an act of purposeful political agency.

Conversations about what was said to cause radicalisation could be broadly broken down into two categories: dissatisfaction stemming from grievances, and the influence of wider communities. These factors were not seen to be mutually exclusive and we encountered a common argument that particular grievances may foster a desire to seek out a community of like-minded individuals capable of subsequently compounding these feelings to the point of a violent conclusion. Conversations began to adopt a more critical tone as participants in our groups started to unpack the term 'radicalisation', drawing attention to what they felt were ambiguities, contradictions, and hard-to-resolve tensions. For example, several students voiced how they felt much of the contemporary counter-terrorism vernacular was used interchangeably in a manner lacking precision. Moreover, our conversations took a particularly interesting turn when students reflected on the pejorative connotations of radicalisation in contrast to the often desirable idea of being a 'radical'. A final avenue explored here concerned the relationship between the contemporary radicalisation discourse and *power*. Among other things, students drew our attention to what they perceived to be prominent historical double standards, where an individual's categorisation as a radical terrorist gave way to their identity as an advocate for radical progressive change.

4

Knowing Prevent

In Chapter 3, we spent some time exploring vernacular constructions of the core conceptual frame underpinning the UK's Prevent Strategy: 'radicalisation'. We detailed different understandings of this phenomenon and its drivers, reflecting on their metaphorical and analytical construction in everyday discourse. We finished the chapter by turning to some more explicitly political concerns with radicalisation as a framework, including around its internal ambiguities and inconsistent external application.

In this chapter, we now explore vernacular understandings of Prevent as a high-profile example of counter-radicalisation policy. We begin the discussion by exploring heterogeneities in public conceptions of Prevent and its ambitions. Here, we argue that although there exists a general familiarity with the strategy, there is considerable disagreement and even confusion around the underpinning aspirations of Prevent. This includes, importantly, debate around the targets of Prevent, and how these have evolved over time, including the significance of designations of 'vulnerability' that we began exploring in the preceding chapter. Particularly pointed here, we show, are questions around Prevent's racialised logics and whether the strategy deliberately targets Muslim individuals and communities.

The chapter's second section then explores key sources of knowledge for understandings of Prevent. Although a small number of students participating in this research had not encountered the strategy before, we show here that most had some familiarity with Prevent prior to these focus groups. This knowledge came from a range of sources, four of which appear particularly important: family and friends, education, employment and training, and the media. Public concerns with the availability and reliability of information around Prevent raised in these discussions lead us to a final section which details a common argument in our focus groups that more needs to be done to raise awareness around the strategy. Greater awareness-raising activity, we show, is seen to have potential for addressing biases and distortions in how Prevent is communicated, especially for particular – potentially vulnerable – populations. The chapter's findings are summarised in Table 4.1.

Table 4.1 Vernacular discourse on Prevent

	Cases	Discussion	Example
Understandings of Prevent	(i) What is Prevent?	Prevent seeks to intervene at an early stage against the formation of extremist ideology.	'Prevent exists to prevent extremist and violent extremist ideologies from forming'
	(ii) At whom is Prevent targeted?	Prevent targets those who are vulnerable to radicalisation, in particular the young.	'Prevent is a scheme to get people away from terrorism … particularly vulnerable people who are quite easily fooled'
	(iii) Who 'does' Prevent?	A range of different organisations implement the Prevent Strategy, in particular public institutions such as educational establishments.	'it's falling on teachers to actually be responsible for trying to notice things that they are concerned about, and then that can be referred … If a teacher is worried that they can use the Prevent scheme'
Sources of knowledge about Prevent	(i) Family and friends	Whilst several had gained some knowledge of Prevent from family and/or friends, others commented on their friends' lack of knowledge of Prevent.	'I think having a group of friends who are quite like politically active. It's been through discussions with them … I've learned more about Prevent'

(*continued*)

Table 4.1 (Cont.)

Cases	Discussion	Example
(ii) Secondary education	Some recalled covering Prevent in lessons or pastoral sessions, and others had seen posters on the walls, but the majority said they had been told nothing about Prevent during their secondary education.	'It feels like it was ignored. I don't remember ever kind of talking about it other than you know, conversations after watching the news or something like that'
(iii) Higher education	Students tended to have learned about Prevent either from completing Prevent training as part of a leadership role or through having covered it as part of their studies.	'Aside from the academic stuff, I haven't heard about Prevent at university other than the module that I've done'
(iv) Employment/training	Several students had completed Prevent training as part of a university or extra-curricular role, or in the course of employment.	'Mandatory training is required every so often in the NHS. Unfortunately, quite a lot of which doesn't seem to be delivered to a particularly high quality, so people coming along tend to be fairly reluctant. But it's obligatory, so you have to turn up'

	(v) The media	For several, this was their primary source of knowledge, yet there were concerns about the tenor and accuracy of media coverage.	'You've also got this whole culture and kind of media discussion about these issues, which is often kind of heightened and a lot more emotional, emotive, and I think maybe the combination there I find a bit problematic'
Awareness raising	(i) The need to challenge bias and misperceptions	It is important that the public are aware of the number of referrals for far-right extremism.	'They need to change the perspectives of Prevent and try and change public perception of what a terrorist threat looks like. It's not always going to be a Muslim boy or Muslim girl just because they're wearing a headscarf stood at a train station'
	(ii) The need to raise awareness of the positive work done by Prevent	The lack of strategic communication around Prevent leads to an information vacuum that is filled by negative media coverage.	'increasing good press and actually making sure people understand what it is that Prevent does rather than kind of having their own ideas about it would probably be really useful'

What is Prevent?

We begin our discussion by exploring vernacular understandings of Prevent encountered in our focus groups, in response to three deliberately broad questions set out in the topic guide discussed in Chapter 2: First, what is Prevent? Second, at whom is Prevent targeted? And, third, who 'does' Prevent?

In response to the question 'What is Prevent?', some participants in our focus groups simply referred to the name of the strategy itself: 'the name is really quite like indicative of what it's trying to achieve' (Focus Group 1, Participant 1); 'it's kind of what it says on the tin, really' (Focus Group 8, Participant 1). Others, however, referenced its broad objectives, arguing, for instance, that 'it's just a kind of scheme to just get people away from terrorism' (Focus Group 3, Participant 3). Others still answered by positioning Prevent within the wider CONTEST strategy discussed in Chapter 1 (Focus Group 1, Participant 1; Focus Group 3, Participant 2). Whilst some of our participants were able to name the other three Ps in the strategy (Pursue, Protect, Prepare), and even to explain the differing objectives of each of these strands, we also encountered a tendency amongst some students to describe initiatives from other parts of CONTEST as elements of Prevent. For example, one student described Prevent as follows:

> It's an initiative to get as many people as they can on board to stop these actions [like 9/11 or 7/7] happening before they do. Whether that's through public involvement, noticing something suspicious happening, and reporting it through the likes of the ACT app [Action Counters Terrorism] or government initiatives involving the police and organisations.
>
> Focus Group 8, Participant 1

For other students in our groups, at its core Prevent is concerned with 'tackling the root causes of terrorism' (Focus Group 7, Participant 1). In discussions such as this, importantly, several participants expressed doubts about the efficacy of Prevent. In some instances, this was because of concerns about the discourse of radicalisation that were discussed in the previous chapter. For example, one student commented, 'I think my conception of this programme from several years ago was that it was specifically designed to prevent something called "radicalisation". But my particular view of that was that radicalisation was not at all clear in terms of what it meant' (Focus Group 3, Participant 1). Others, though, were concerned that Prevent focuses on specific root causes, to the exclusion of potentially relevant others: '[Prevent] aims to tackle root causes of problems but I don't know to what degree because I feel like it assumes that certain root causes are definitive, whereas other ones for example poverty are not as much' (Focus Group 3, Participant 5).

A recurring theme in students' descriptions of Prevent was an emphasis on ideology and early intervention. Prevent's *raison d'être* was frequently described in pre-emptive terms, such as 'Prevent exists to prevent extremist and violent extremist ideologies from forming' (Focus Group 5, Participant 4); 'Prevent to me is like preventing more vulnerable people from going down the route of getting into terrorism and all that kind of stuff' (Focus Group 5, Participant 5), and '[Prevent is] mainly getting to the root cause of things that [cause] radicalisation and stopping it right at the beginning before it becomes worse and harder to stop' (Focus Group 5, Participant 1). These depictions emphasise the role of ideology in leading people to commit acts of terrorism. Moreover, the emphasis of this framework is seen to lie not in dissuading those that have already adopted extremist beliefs, but in stopping those beliefs from taking hold in the first place. Hence some students used terms such as 'potential radicalisation' (Focus Group 7, Participant 4) and 'at risk of radicalisation' (Focus Group 8, Participant 3).

This leads neatly to the next question: at whom is Prevent targeted? If the rationale of Prevent is to stop the fomentation of extremist beliefs, at whom are these efforts directed? There were a number of different approaches to answering this question in our groups. At one extreme, some students stated that Prevent could be 'focused on anyone' (Focus Group 2, Participant 5), with no specific characteristics or factors used to identify where efforts should be targeted. Others suggested that Prevent is aimed at particular communities (Focus Group 7, Participant 1), including particular localities: '[Prevent is] targeting the at-risk groups and areas and environments where people are deemed most vulnerable and as a result more susceptible to picking up ideologies as part of communities and other factors' (Focus Group 1, Participant 1). This was frequently contested, however, with a number of participants saying that Prevent has moved away from a focus on communities towards a focus on individuals, for example: 'It's very different from how it initially was where I believe it was more community focused and has now moved to a more individual focus in terms of preventing extremism' (Focus Group 2, Participant 3).

In terms of individuals, the language of vulnerability discussed in the preceding chapter was most commonly used to describe those targeted by Prevent. According to one student, for example, the strategy seeks to prevent 'more vulnerable people from going down the route of getting into terrorism and all that kind of stuff' (Focus Group 5, Participant 5). Importantly, however, different understandings of the word 'vulnerable' were evident across our focus groups. For some, it seemed akin to gullibility. One student, for instance, suggested that Prevent is a scheme to 'get people away from terrorism … particularly vulnerable people who are quite easily fooled' (Focus Group 3, Participant 3). Another said that vulnerable people are those who, 'may not notice the signs that say they are being radicalised and then go along with it' (Focus Group 5, Participant 1). Other participants in our groups, however, focused instead on contextual vulnerabilities brought about by a person's broader life circumstances:

> Radicalisation is just one of the ways that vulnerability can manifest, but it could go in other directions as well ... I don't know the reasons for vulnerability. Could be all sorts of things, could be family breakdown or something, but something that happens to somebody that causes issues and trauma that then leaves them open to being kind of taken under someone's wing and this is the way that that manifests.
>
> Focus Group 5, Participant 6

One characteristic that several students associated with vulnerability was youth. In the words of one student, 'there are some kids who get brainwashed' (Focus Group 6, Participant 4). Others suggested that, because young people are more impressionable, the delivery of Prevent is focused specifically on the young. One stated that 'school children are sort of targeted because they are more vulnerable and susceptible to these types of things' (Focus Group 5, Participant 1), whilst another explained that Prevent

> allows for higher education institutions and people within the community that act as teachers or people that look after young children to intervene on the basis of potential radicalisation on the understanding of the language that they use or kind of, there's a big checklist, essentially of signs of children or young adults who are more likely to be sort of simulating attitudes that the Government construed as being conducive to terrorism.
>
> Focus Group 7, Participant 4

We also encountered repeated suggestions of the sort discussed in Chapter 1, around Prevent's especial targeting of Muslims. According to one student, Prevent is 'trying to counter like Islamic terrorism and that side of terrorism, trying to stop that' (Focus Group 5, Participant 5), whilst another commented, 'I would just say that the Prevent Strategy is targeted towards Muslims ... You can directly kind of compare terrorism in that sense to terrorism in Northern Ireland with Protestant Catholic that kind of thing' (Focus Group 7, Participant 4). Another student recounted their experience of watching a Home Office video on YouTube in which 'there were mothers telling stories about their children falling into this trap of radicalisation':

> I did not see any white people or any white children, white mothers telling their stories. It was just Muslim women and Muslim men and you could tell by their appearance ... that it was the Muslim community which it was targeted at.
>
> Focus Group 6, Participant 4

The suggestion that Muslims communities are the target of Prevent did not go unchallenged by other participants, however. Indeed, it was contested in three different ways. First, some students pointed to strategic evolution within Prevent, arguing that whilst it may once have been directed primarily at Muslims, this was no longer the case. According to one student arguing thus: 'when it first came in, in the 2000s, it was mainly focused on … jihadi terrorism and has now branched out to include the far right and also animal rights activists' (Focus Group 2, Participant 1). Second, some students drew a distinction between the policy itself and its implementation, stating that, whilst Prevent is not directed primarily at Muslims at the policy level, it does focus on them in its implementation and delivery. For example, one participant stated that Prevent is focused on jihadism and far-right terrorism, but in schools, 'the vast majority of the students that have been referred' have been referred 'in connection with concerns of links to Islamic terrorism rather than far right terrorism' (Focus Group 6, Participant 1). Third, other students drew a distinction between perceptions of Prevent and the reality. For these, even though Prevent is not focused specifically on Muslims, this perception remains widely held by others. For example:

> I had a conversation quite recently with somebody who said, 'Oh, you know? I thought maybe we didn't really need to do that round here, 'cause we haven't got that many Muslims' and I was kind of like 'oh God, okay.' And I was just surprised that that attitude was still there … I know that the policy focuses wider and Prevent says that it's about all forms of extremism. But then that idea is still there.
>
> Focus Group 5, Participant 6

These mistaken perceptions of Prevent were frequently said to be the result of distorted or partial news media coverage. One student, for instance, commented, 'at university, it sort of uncovered through various modules that referrals to Prevent are actually higher among right-wing terrorism, whereas I feel like a lot of the media focuses on Prevent to do with Islamist terrorism' (Focus Group 8, Participant 5). We turn more fully to the importance of different sources of knowledge about Prevent, such as higher education and news media, later in this chapter.

In the context of this discussion, students were also asked who 'does' Prevent, in order to encourage reflection on implementation and delivery of the Prevent Strategy at the local level. There were widely differing answers to this question in our focus groups. At one extreme, some participants said that responsibility for its delivery is universal, or at least covers as many people as possible. For one student, for instance, 'everyone sort of has a responsibility', including co-workers, family members and friends (Focus

Group 5, Participant 4). Several others emphasised that Prevent involves a multi-agency approach. In the words of one:

> Before my undergraduate [degree], I didn't actually quite realise how many different bodies or sectors within society are actually involved within Prevent. So, you know, it's not just people within government, but you're looking at like your local government … It moves a lot further beyond that, and so you know, schools, universities have this legal obligation to report any suspicious activity, also the health care sector.
>
> Focus Group 8, Participant 6

In fact, one student suggested that 'the burden of the work was primarily on public organisations which includes educational institutions and includes social and health care institutions' (Focus Group 3, Participant 1). In response to this suggestion, another student pointed out that, whilst public bodies have a statutory obligation to engage with Prevent, 'that doesn't apply to private sector organisations as such. But even still you'll start to see these organisations like third sector organisations, charities and stuff, they've kind of bought into the Prevent Strategy and they've sought Prevent training' (Focus Group 3, Participant 2).

There were other students whose answers to the question 'who does Prevent?' focused specifically on the education sector. This included reflection on the role of both universities and schools. In terms of universities, as well as mentioning lecturers (on which more below), some students stated that, by taking on student leadership roles, they themselves had been recruited as potential delivers of counter-radicalisation policy: 'I know there's online training that's offered up, for instance, like within our university for kind of student leaders. We were kind of signposted towards the online training. It wasn't mandatory, but it was highly recommended' (Focus Group 7, Participant 3). In respect of schools, the possibility of teachers referring pupils to Prevent was also mentioned by some. One student explained, 'it's falling on teachers to actually be responsible for trying to notice things that they are concerned about, and then that can be referred … If a teacher is worried they can use the Prevent scheme' (Focus Group 6, Participant 1). The students' personal experiences of Prevent during their secondary education are discussed later in the chapter.

The other sector that was regularly highlighted in our focus groups was social media companies. According to one student, for instance, such organisations have a responsibility for Prevent because 'a lot of radicalisation happens over social media' (Focus Group 5, Participant 1). This seems to blur the boundaries between a general responsibility for preventing violent extremism, on the one hand, and the formal statutory Prevent Duty discussed in Chapter 1, on the other. Indeed, one student picked up on the difficulties those tasked with the Prevent Duty may face in identifying possible indicators of radicalisation in online spaces:

> Social media pops into my head ... Terrorist kind of organisations that might have like Facebook groups and things like that and if you're sharing that kind of information, it might be a sign that you were kind of becoming radicalised. I'm not really sure how schools could monitor that, but maybe that's something that like families and more close-knit people to the individual would identify.
>
> Focus Group 7, Participant 1

Students also identified social media as a potential avenue to raise public awareness of Prevent. This suggestion leads us to the next section, which focuses on where knowledge about Prevent comes from in everyday life, and how different discursive resources are drawn upon to explain, clarify, and justify particular understandings.

Sources of knowledge

To begin this second part of the chapter, it is worth noting that three students in our focus groups said that they had never previously heard of the Prevent Strategy. After learning of the opportunity to take part in a focus group for this study, one of them 'read up about it a bit' (Focus Group 3, Participant 3), whilst another 'went to YouTube and searched "what is Prevent?" and that showed me this Home Office video about it' (Focus Group 6, Participant 4). This particular participant, who was an international student, expressed their annoyance at not having been informed of Prevent sooner: 'I was not told about Prevent at all or through any process during immigration or whatever and even during my university education. So, I was not aware of it' (Focus Group 6, Participant 4).

As the previous section showed, most of the students in the focus groups did have at least cursory knowledge of Prevent before learning of the opportunity to take part in this research. Four principal sources of knowledge emerged throughout our discussions: family and friends, education, employment and training, and the media. These are considered now in turn.

Family and friends

Several students said that they had gained some knowledge of Prevent from other family members. In some cases, this was because a parent worked in a school and so had received Prevent training. Others said that there had been conversations at home following high-profile terrorist attacks in which

Prevent had been discussed. Some students also noted that they had learned about Prevent from their peers. One participant, for instance, remarked, 'I think having a group of friends who are quite like politically active. It's been through discussions with them … I've learned more about Prevent' (Focus Group 8, Participant 7). In contrast, other students commented on their friends' lack of knowledge of Prevent. For one, this was in part due to age: 'Obviously, the age I am, I don't remember 9/11 … A lot of people who are a similar age to me, those who aren't actively politically engaged in this particular area, are relatively unaware of it' (Focus Group 2, Participant 3). This was echoed by another participant, who expressed surprise at how few of their peers were aware of Prevent:

> I mentioned this focus group with some friends being like, 'Oh, do you wanna do this thing about Prevent?' because they were students. And a lot of them said like 'What is Prevent?' And I was really surprised. So I've learned that maybe I'm in a minority knowing about it for so long.
>
> Focus Group 2, Participant 1

Secondary education

Students were asked what coverage, if any, there had been of Prevent during their secondary or further education. Some students did recall hearing about Prevent at secondary school, although the sources of this information varied. In some instances, the information was imparted in lesson time. This could have been as part of the syllabus for a particular subject – 'From my A-Levels. I did Business Studies and it kind of came up when we were studying social media because obviously they have a big thing in terms of like guidelines to do with terrorism, radicalisation, extremism, and that kind of thing' (Focus Group 4, Participant 3) – or in pastoral sessions, for instance: 'At college, in our tutor group once a week we used to have different topics and I think one of them was Prevent, well … broad counter-terrorism rather than just specifically on Prevent' (Focus Group 5, Participant 4), and 'an assembly on it where they would show you like a video and stuff' (Focus Group 5, Participant 1). Pastoral sessions on the Prevent Strategy were not always well-received, by pupils or teachers, however: 'in sixth form, being taught British values. We're all like "Why? Why are we being taught this?" And all the teachers said, "Ah, it's Prevent, we need to do this"' (Focus Group 7, Participant 2). Others that learned about the strategy at secondary school encountered it in less formal settings. As well as conversations with friends, including discussions of events in the news, some students recalled seeing posters about Prevent on the walls. One recounted: 'There was a poster in one of the bathrooms at my school, but was really explicitly, like, if you need to talk, you can come, you know, let's prevent things from happening and prevent was in bold and highlighted' (Focus Group 7, Participant 3).

By far the most common response, however, was for students to say that they had never been told anything about Prevent during their secondary or further education. Comments included: 'not a word' (Focus Group 5, Participant 6), 'I don't know whether it's maybe because I wasn't paying much attention, but I never really heard of it in secondary school' (Focus Group 7, Participant 1), and, 'It feels like it was ignored. I don't remember ever kind of talking about it other than you know, conversations after watching the news or something like that' (Focus Group 6, Participant 3). One student reflected:

> There was never really any discussion about terrorism or extremism in primary school or in secondary school from a sort of, these are the signs to look out for, these are the signs to spot. There was, of course, discussions about if you feel affected by this, come and talk to us or whatever … Looking back at it, I knew, I think, relatively little about terrorism or about what was really going on. Other than that these were bad guys who were bombing places. And, you know, I remember even up to when I was relatively old, not understanding that Al Qaeda and the Taliban were different things. I thought they were just different names for the same organisation.
>
> Focus Group 2, Participant 3

Some students attempted to offer explanations for why Prevent had not been covered at their school or college. These explanations tended to focus on geographical location. One participant, for instance, commented, 'I don't know whether it's because I grew up in Wales or I still live here, but I never got taught anything about Prevent at school ever. It was just not a thing' (Focus Group 7, Participant 4). In the words of another, similarly, 'I think it does depend on location because I've had friends from like schools from Cardiff, and stuff and they're really on it' (Focus Group 1, Participant 2). Another student, however, suggested that it might depend more on the type of school they had attended, rather than its geographical situation: 'I live in London and even then nothing. I think maybe that's to do with my schooling. I went to a faith school so I think that might have something to do with it, the absolute lack of teaching on quite a few subjects' (Focus Group 1, Participant 4).

Participants in the groups were also encouraged to reflect on what discussion, if any, there had been around (counter-)radicalisation in the aftermath of high-profile terrorist attacks, such as the 2017 Manchester Arena bombing or the London Bridge attack of the same year. According to some students, attacks such as these were simply not discussed at their school. For example, one student described their school's non-response to the

Manchester Arena bombing as 'really odd', especially considering its geographical 'proximity' to the attack:

> I don't think my school addressed any of these sort of recent terror attacks in the UK at all. I remember the Manchester Arena bombing happened I think a day before one of my exams. It was never mentioned in school and even other terror attacks that happened whilst I was at school that were relatively geographically close to where I went to school were very rarely mentioned.
>
> Focus Group 8, Participant 5

Another student stated that at their school, terrorism was 'never like introduced as a topic', partly because it was 'taboo' but also because of 'the triggers that it could have to some students'. As they continued: 'I think it was that worry because they always gave us like a consent thing before they brought it up to see if we were comfortable talking about it. Obviously, a couple of people knew people in the Manchester attacks and the London attacks in 2017, so it was upsetting for some students' (Focus Group 8, Participant 1).

For those participants that said their school had reacted to terrorist attacks, the response typically took one of three forms. First, some students recalled pastoral sessions or messages. Following the London Bridge attack, for instance, one student remembered an 'assembly where they spoke about the attack and I think they said things like if we had any concerns or if we wanted to just talk about it then we could go to members of staff and speak to them' (Focus Group 7, Participant 1). Another said that they too had experienced 'quite a lot of like seminars after [the London Bridge attack]. Kind of making sure everyone was okay. But other than that it wasn't really spoken about at my school, they just kind of said, you know, see a therapist if you need to' (Focus Group 4, Participant 4). Similarly, another student remembered an email, 'after the Manchester attack about if you've got concerns, here's where to go to, but other than that it wasn't ever really addressed in any way' (Focus Group 7, Participant 3).

Second, following some terrorist attacks, some of our participants recalled more specific discussion of whether school trips should go ahead as planned, particularly if the attack was within relatively close proximity to a planned trip. Some schools were reported as being particularly risk-averse here, either preparing the pupils for what to do if an attack occurred – 'they wanted to make sure everyone knew what to do in certain situations like that and how to keep safe' (Focus Group 5, Participant 1) – or cancelling trips altogether: 'They stopped us going on a photography trip which was planned another two days after the attack because they said, "Look, we don't know what's going on. It's too unsafe"' (Focus Group 4, Participant 5). Such precaution was not only to be found amongst school decision-makers, however, with another student describing their own decision to pull out of a school trip two weeks after the London Bridge attack because they did not think it was safe, to which their teachers, in this case, responded, 'Oh no, you're overreacting, we're going to be fine' (Focus Group 4, Participant 7).

Third, although not necessarily directly linked to Prevent, several participants in our focus groups recounted their memories of 'lockdown drills'. One student, for instance, explained: 'So aside from the fire alarm, we also had like terrorist alarm drills in our school where we'd have to like lockdown classrooms and pile desks up against the walls and hide under the tables' (Focus Group 8, Participant 6). In one school, drills like these were introduced following the London Bridge attack: 'After the attack, we had a massive whole school sit-down and we were told we're gonna do like lockdown drills because I think at the time the terror threat went up a level and we did about a week of lockdown drills specifically designed for a terrorist attack' (Focus Group 4, Participant 5) In another, it was in response to school shootings in the US: 'We started doing lockdowns. It must have been year 11. We had like a specific bell that would go off and we'd have to hide under the tables. This was in case somebody was gonna come into school and do a school shooting and this was around the time period of when America was experiencing a lot of school shootings' (Focus Group 8, Participant 1).

Higher education

Higher education appears to be a particularly prominent source of vernacular knowledge around counter-radicalisation, with many of our participants stating that they knew very little about the Prevent Strategy prior to starting university. Within the university context, students tended to have learned about Prevent from one of two sources. First, as mentioned above, some students had completed Prevent training as part of a student leadership role. More commonly, though, students had learned about Prevent as part of their degree programme. Some students explained that they had even chosen to write a dissertation on counter-terrorism, and researching this had led them to the Prevent Strategy. For others, Prevent formed part of the syllabus for a taught module they were taking.

As will be seen in Chapter 5, a small number of students also recalled lecturers making passing comments about the strategy. For example, one student recounted their lecturer telling them about Prevent and the training they had received and how the lecturer felt the Prevent Duty placed them in a 'very uncomfortable situation' (Focus Group 1, Participant 5). More broadly, however, several students expressed surprise that they had not been told about Prevent until they came across it in their studies. According to one, 'Aside from the academic stuff, I haven't heard about Prevent at university other than the module that I've done' (Focus Group 7, Participant 1), whilst another commented 'You don't get told at university that it is a part of university in the sense, like, universities are part of the programme and will be on the lookout for extremist tendencies' (Focus Group 7, Participant 2). For one international student – who hoped to remain in the UK following completion of their degree and was concerned about the possible future implications for any visa application of a Prevent referral – the failure to inform students of the Prevent Duty was especially concerning: 'I don't know why I was not told about this. I should be told about it. I think there should be the courtesy of telling people … "This is a strategy we have and it's a responsibility for professors to keep an eye"' (Focus Group 6, Participant 4).

Employment and training

A third source of knowledge about Prevent we encountered was education and training. Some students had completed Prevent training as part of a university internship or student leadership role (Focus Group 1, Participant 1; Focus Group 7, Participant 3), including one that had completed a placement in a school as part of their PhD research (Focus Group 6, Participant 1). Others had extra-curricular roles for which they had received Prevent training. These included volunteering for a Youth Offending Team (Focus Group 5, Participant 6) and working for a local police force (Focus Group 8, Participant 3). Others had completed Prevent training as part of a previous career. One had in fact worked as a Prevent practitioner (Focus Group 3, Participant 2). Another had worked for the NHS (Focus Group 3, Participant 1), whilst one other said that they had received Prevent training as part of a business administration apprenticeship (which they thought seemed 'a bit random') (Focus Group 4, Participant 1). There were others, still, that said that, whilst they had not completed Prevent training, they had received more generic counter-terrorism training. One had worked previously in a defence company and had been trained in what to do in the case of a terrorist attack (Focus Group 2, Participant 2). Another recounted training they had received as part of a supermarket job:

> A bog-standard video saying 'If they have a lot of contact lens solution, don't assume that they have bad eyes, they're probably a terrorist' and you're like, 'Okay, you know, a bit of a big step, but I can get that.' And then just loads of similar things like that like hair dye. Anything in ridiculously large volumes.
>
> Focus Group 1, Participant 2

Some commented positively on the training they had received. One described the Prevent Coordinator that took their training session as 'really good' (Focus Group 5, Participant 6), whilst the PhD student that had received training on placement said that 'it was taught quite well at the school I was at because they were trying to show that there is lots of different types of radicalisation and did put an emphasis as well on links to far-right groups' (Focus Group 6, Participant 1). However, the overall tenor of the feedback on experiences such as this was negative, as illustrated by the following comment:

> Mandatory training is required every so often in the NHS. Unfortunately, quite a lot of which doesn't seem to be delivered to a particularly high quality, so people coming along tend to be fairly reluctant. But it's obligatory, so you have to turn up. How much people get from it was definitely a question in my mind. Spoke to a couple of people afterwards. I don't think it was a positive experience for them.
>
> Focus Group 3, Participant 1

The students had two concerns in particular about the training they had received. First, some students said that there were aspects of the training that they 'didn't agree with' (Focus Group 1, Participant 1). One student recalled, 'I remember one of the first signs to look out for was if someone's growing a beard. That was a bit peculiar to me, because what if someone who doesn't grow a beard has been radicalised. It seemed a bit off' (Focus Group 4, Participant 1).

The second concern, which will be discussed further in the following chapter, was that many participants reporting finding the training vague and being subsequently left unsure what was expected of them. One student, for instance, described the online training platform as 'really interactive and good, but it didn't really leave a clear impression of what needed to be done, at least for me'. They continued:

> I was definitely left with the impression that kind of a lot of the people that I interact with on a daily basis showed one or two of the kind of warning signs, like disengagement or kind of apathy towards the democratic system, and so it was useful and interesting, especially given what I'm studying, but not particularly clear kind of where it applied. In a sense, it almost left me with more questions than answers.
>
> Focus Group 7, Participant 3

For this student, greater specificity was needed in the training so that it was more relevant and applicable to the particular context of those being trained.

In the face of these criticisms of Prevent training, the student that had worked previously as a Prevent practitioner offered two possible explanations. One was that the Home Office hadn't 'sought to have an active upgrade of the training … To sit on the same package for a decade is, you know, inexcusable, in my opinion', whilst the other was that 'there's a lot of people out there delivering training and, dare I say, it's become a bit of a cash cow for certain people – you know, perhaps in it for not the right reasons' (Focus Group 3, Participant 2).

The media

The final source of vernacular knowledge about Prevent we encountered in our groups was the media. There were several students that said that most – or all – of their knowledge about Prevent came from news media coverage, specifically, television news programmes or newspapers. Some students referred to general coverage or critiques of Prevent (Focus Group 2, Participant 5; Focus Group 3, Participant 1; Focus Group 8, Participant 7). Others talked about coverage of Prevent as part of news stories about recent incidents, including terrorist attacks (Focus Group 5, Participant 2), the 'Bethnal Green trio' that included Shamima Begum leaving the UK to travel to Syria (Focus Group 3, Participant 5) (see Chapter 3), and, more generally, instances 'where Prevent has kind of failed' (Focus Group 4, Participant 7), such as in the high-profile examples discussed in Chapter 1. There were also examples of intersection here with the sources of knowledge discussed previously, as news items often acted as a catalyst for conversation with family and friends (Focus Group 6, Participant 3) and formed the basis of class discussions in school (Focus Group 3, Participant 4). Aside from news media, one student said that they had gained some knowledge of Prevent from (fictional) television programmes and books (Focus Group 8, Participant 1), whilst one other said that they had seen a television advert that explained why you shouldn't leave the UK 'to join ISIS' (Focus Group 7, Participant 1).

Students expressed concern that news media coverage of Prevent offers 'a very skewed perspective of how effective it is' (Focus Group 4, Participant 4). It is normally talked about in a 'negative light' (Focus Group 2, Participant 3), focusing on 'where Prevent has kind of failed' (Focus Group 4, Participant 7). Participants commented that you 'very rarely see positive things' about Prevent (Focus Group 4, Participant 7), and 'we don't hear enough about the successes. We only hear about the failures' (Focus Group 4, Participant 6). For one student, this stood in marked contrast to conversations that they had had with Prevent practitioners: 'from speaking to people that actually work in Prevent, it is quite positive and a lot of the time it does succeed in what it aims to do' (Focus Group 4, Participant 4), a view shared by a student who had worked previously as a Prevent practitioner, who said that 'some good case stories' were needed to show that Prevent 'isn't all doom and gloom and failings' (Focus Group 3, Participant 2). In a similar vein, another student compared what they had learned about Prevent from the news media with what they had learned about Prevent during their PhD placement within a school:

> It's kind of an interesting like two-pronged thing where you're learning a school's policy for how to recognize extremism, for example, but then you've also got this whole culture and kind of media discussion about these issues, which is often kind of heightened and a lot more emotional, emotive, and I think maybe the combination there I find a bit problematic.
>
> Focus Group 6, Participant 1

At the same time, students felt that the tenor of news media coverage of Prevent was 'inevitable' (Focus Group 7, Participant 1). Often, media discussion of Prevent occurs in the aftermath of a terrorist attack. Such coverage tends to focus on failings and questions around whether attacks could, or should, have been prevented. To illustrate, one student offered the example of the 2017 London Bridge attack, following which there were reports that one of the attackers had been part of the Prevent programme (Focus Group 5, Participant 2). Another student observed that terrorism 'is a really hot topic and sells a lot' (Focus Group 7, Participant 4). In fact, this student suggested, the amount of news media coverage terrorism receives is out of proportion to the number of people that die in terrorist attacks (when compared to other causes of death). This was echoed by another participant in an earlier focus group, who recounted a terrorism-related incident near a relative's home. When the incident was reported on the national news, the relative's response was 'That's not what really happened there. They're sensationalising how bad it actually was' (Focus Group 1, Participant 2). Upon hearing this, another student commented, 'Ultimately, fear sells, right?' (Focus Group 1, Participant 1).

Another concern that participants in our groups raised was the anecdotal reporting of misplaced referrals to Prevent. For example, shortly before the focus groups took place, a number of national newspapers reported the case discussed in Chapter 1 of an eleven-year-old primary school pupil being referred to Prevent after he told his class that he wanted to 'give alms to the oppressed'. His teacher mistook the word 'alms' for 'arms' (Taylor 2021). This example was cited by students in several focus groups, who questioned whether an exclusive focus on such instances 'misses the point' and means that 'the public wouldn't know [Prevent] is being effective because they never see the benefits of it' (Focus Group 4, Participant 6).

Concern was also expressed at the potential for such reporting to 'create divides and splits between communities' (Focus Group 1, Participant 1). According to one student, news media 'play on the race and religious element when it comes to counterterrorism measures and Prevent a lot more than they would in any other news story. So, although someone in one story might just be described as a male, when it comes to counter-terrorism it's like an Asian male' (Focus Group 1, Participant 5). A similar bias is present in popular culture, several students opined. One said, 'Think about how terrorism is portrayed in film and TV. It's predominantly Muslims that are terrorists in a lot of Western films' (Focus Group 4, Participant 6). For a student from the Global South, this is symptomatic of a wider failure in Western culture to explore terrorism in a meaningful way:

> I don't think like [in] popular media level or even in friends or in families, the causes of terrorism are explored, or looked at in like a more nuanced way. It's usually like, okay, it's causing violence, it's leading to people's loss of life, so it is a taboo bad thing. If you're talking about it, it seems like something is wrong with you because why do you want to explore it? Because it's cost so much loss of life. And I think that also has to do with Global North, Global South and how the West has been so protected that now they think that, 'Oh, this is the most violence that we have ever seen', but in the Global South, we've seen more violence on a day-to-day basis, which is not just coming from bombs by some people.
>
> Focus Group 6, Participant 4

The impact on minority communities of ostensibly biased media coverage is considered further in the following chapter.

Awareness-raising

The previous sections examined the different sources of students' knowledge about Prevent. As we have seen, news media coverage was an important source of knowledge regarding the UK's approach to countering radicalisation, but there were widespread concerns about the tenor and selectivity of this coverage. Family and friends offered another important resource here, though this tended to be limited to those whose relatives worked in professions subject to the Prevent Duty or whose friends were politically active. A number of students also reported receiving Prevent training in the course of employment or other roles, such as internships or student leadership. In terms of the students' education, there was a feeling that there should have been greater coverage of Prevent at secondary school, particularly in the aftermath of high-profile terrorist incidents. Similar concerns applied to the students' university education. Most students who had learned about Prevent at university did so as part of their degree programme. There was, in this sense, some frustration that universities did not inform their students of the Prevent Duty as a pastoral matter at the start of their studies. In the words of one student, 'I should have been told that my lecturers might be spying on me' (Focus Group 6, Participant 4).

In light of this, it is unsurprising that a number of students argued that more needs to be done to raise public awareness and understanding of Prevent. Several suggested that there is a lack of strategic communication around Prevent. According to one student, 'A lot still needs to be done to communicate the ideas better about Prevent's aims and what it does and what it's actually treating' (Focus Group 3, Participant 4). This comment was echoed by others, who remarked that 'it's not something that's well communicated' (Focus Group 3, Participant 3) and 'the way this strategy is portrayed to the general public, you know, there's no media strategy around it' (Focus Group 3, Participant 2). This results in an 'information vacuum' (Reed *et al.* 2017: 30), which is filled by news media coverage. One student accordingly emphasised the importance of 'increasing general awareness for the general population who don't have any interest in it, rather than just leaving it kind of more with normal media sensationalisation' (Focus Group 1, Participant 5).

Participants in our groups identified two key potential contributions of a public information campaign. The first would be to challenge bias and mis-perceptions. Several students said that the public should be made aware of the prevalence of referrals for far-right extremism. This would challenge the perception that Prevent is concerned primarily with violent jihadism: 'They need to change the perspectives of Prevent and try and change public per-ception of what a terrorist threat looks like. It's not always going to be a Muslim boy or Muslim girl just because they're wearing a headscarf stood at a train station' (Focus Group 8, Participant 1). The second potential con-tribution would be to raise awareness of the positive work that is done by Prevent. According to one student, 'increasing good press and actually making sure people understand what it is that Prevent does rather than kind of having their own ideas about it would probably be really useful' (Focus Group 4, Participant 4).

In keeping with their association of youth with vulnerability, a number of participants felt that better awareness and understanding was particu-larly important in the case of young people. Here, students pointed to the importance of social media. Referring to their younger siblings, one student described the influence of content on platforms such as TikTok and Instagram as 'quite daunting', saying, 'they see things ... and that immediately becomes their view' (Focus Group 1, Participant 4). Some warned that, 'a lot of radicalisation does occur on social media' (Focus Group 5, Participant 1), with online echo chambers and personalisation algorithms identified as playing an important role. This was contrasted with the perceived absence of information about Prevent on social media. Several students suggested that information campaigns on social media would be worthwhile. As well as ensuring a wide reach – 'Social media adverts could be a good thing to do because everyone uses social media' (Focus Group 5, Participant 1) – there was a feeling that individuals would be more likely to engage with social media content as opposed to, for example, 'ads on webpages: who looks at those?' (Focus Group 1, Participant 2). However, it would be important to use the platforms that 'the younger generation are actually using', such as TikTok and Snapchat (Focus Group 1, Participant 2).

Students also felt that greater coverage of Prevent is needed in secondary schools and sixth form colleges. This was rooted in their sense that they had not received enough information themselves when they had been pupils, particularly following high-profile terrorist incidents. One student commented, 'I feel like you should be more active in schools, especially after a terrorist attack … In our college nothing was said, it was like nothing happened' (Focus Group 5, Participant 4). Some students urged the importance of regular sessions on Prevent, as opposed to one-off assemblies. This would help ensure that pupils know 'how to recognise if one of their friends is vulnerable or being manipulated by someone online' (Focus Group 5, Participant 2). Some of these sessions should be delivered by Prevent practitioners, who would have greater credibility and be more engaging for the pupils: 'someone who's actively involved in Prevent on a day-to-day basis would interest people a lot more because they can give their experiences and stories' (Focus Group 5, Participant 1). More generally, there was a feeling that schools need to do more to increase understanding of different religions and cultures, especially in areas that are not very diverse. According to one student:

> The school I went to was a Welsh language school in the valleys in South Wales, so needless to say diversity was not a feature in my school. You're not really exposed to different cultures when you go to a school like that and when you live in an area like that. When something like a terror attack happens, I think a lot of stereotypes and the kind of racist attitudes come out.
>
> Focus Group 5, Participant 6

Conclusion

This chapter has explored some of the ways in which counter-radicalisation initiatives such as Prevent are understood and experienced at the level of the everyday. Building on the vernacular constructions of radicalisation discussed in Chapter 3, we have attempted to demonstrate the existence of considerable heterogeneity in how 'ordinary' citizens understand the UK's Prevent Strategy, its ambitions, and mechanics. These understandings, we showed, have diverse roots, from direct and vernacular experiences through to more formalised encounters with Prevent, such as training sessions in employment contexts. In the following chapter, we now expand on this discussion by exploring public *evaluations* of counter-radicalisation initiatives and the political and moral implications of these for everyday life. Here, the focus is less on what is known about (counter-)radicalisation at the level of the vernacular, but rather on how strategies such as Prevent are appraised and valued within everyday discourse.

5

Evaluating Prevent

First introduced as a standalone strategy in 2007, Prevent has now enjoyed a longevity spanning over fifteen years and seven Prime Ministers. As outlined in Chapter 1, the strategy has been repositioned, reframed, and reformed over this period, but retains its fundamental objectives. Indeed, a recent report published by the Tony Blair Institute for Global Change, whose founder was Prime Minister at the strategy's first deployment, refers to Prevent as 'world leading' (Ahmed and Alvis 2020: 7). Claims such as this resonate with the strategy's global influence explored in Chapter 1. Yet, as we have also seen in the preceding chapters, the work of (counter-)radicalisation in the UK remains controversial and loaded with ambiguities at the level of the vernacular as much as within media and activist discourse.

The understandings of students within UK Higher Education Institutions in this context are important, in part, because – along with school pupils, NHS patients and others – they became a particular focus of counter-radicalisation initiatives when the Prevent Duty came into effect in 2015. In keeping with the vernacular approach set out in Chapter 2, this chapter now elaborates upon *evaluations* of Prevent offered by participants in our focus groups as a population of non-elites subject to the government's counter-radicalisation strategy. Talking to these students about their experiences and assessments of Prevent provides, we suggest, novel insight into the strategy's everyday functioning within UKHE, and incorporates non-traditional voices into the evaluation of security policies that directly affect the public.

The chapter progresses in three sections, summarised in Table 5.1. The first addresses what was a majority perspective among the students with whom we spoke: that Prevent (or at least something like it) was necessary. Students, here, recognised the risks posed by radicalisation both to the individual and the nation and therefore saw a preventative, 'soft' option as both pragmatic and preferable to more invasive alternatives. However, this majority position came alongside a slew of criticisms that our students also voiced and that are covered in the second section. Here, participants in our groups

Table 5.1 Vernacular discourse on evaluations of Prevent

	Cases	Discussion	Example
Whether a deradicalisation strategy is necessary	(i) Arguments in favour of a deradicalisation strategy	Radicalisation poses a threat, since there are people who are vulnerable to radicalisation, particularly the young.	Prevent 'actually deals with this sort of thing proactively, rather than reactively, so having something like that in place is always going to be worthwhile'
	(ii) It is difficult to assess the necessity of Prevent	It is difficult to measure the successes of Prevent and its negative impacts; it is also difficult to assess it without information on its cost and in isolation from the other parts of CONTEST.	'I really want to ask the individuals who were contacted by Prevent, "Do you think that you were on a path like with hindsight that was unhelpful, was dangerous or was damaging and do you think the intervention that you've got was actually useful for you?"'
	(iii) Misgivings about Prevent	Prevent is simultaneously necessary and counter-productive.	'I think that it's good that something is there … You know, it's better than having nothing at all, but at the same time it could be counter-productive'
Concerns about Prevent	(i) Empirical and theoretical underpinning	There is a lack of empirical evidence on the effectiveness of Prevent, coupled with too much emphasis on ideology to the exclusion of other factors and individual agency.	'I would like to raise the question as to whether there's any evidence about efficacy … I don't think I have heard anything that says that this is proven to be an effective approach'

(continued)

Table 5.1 (Cont.)

	Cases	Discussion	Example
	(ii) Training and vulnerability indicators	Whilst training is necessary, current offerings are vague and do not equip people to identify individuals who are vulnerable to radicalisation.	'It's actually far more complex and it has so much more variety and different experiences than you could possibly ever explain just in a small bit of training for someone in education, or to put in a poster like an advert'
	(iii) Freedom of expression and suspect communities	The Prevent Duty has a chilling effect on the right to freedom of expression – including in the higher education setting, and particularly for those from ethnic minorities – which is potentially counter-productive.	'I think that it would change my behaviour and it would make me more conscious as a person and less confident of expressing my thoughts, which would be so counter-productive for my learning in the university'
Proposals for reform	(i) Public information campaigns	There needs to be greater coverage of the positive work done by Prevent, to challenge widely held misperceptions.	'Increasing general awareness for the general population who don't have any interest in it, rather than just leaving it kind of more with normal media sensationalisation'
	(ii) Definitional clarity	Specificity is important, although the dangers of identifying specific groups or ideologies were also emphasised.	'The language of policy is obviously extremely difficult to perfect. A question that I asked myself a lot when researching was "How would I have put this?"'

(iii) Tackling root causes other than ideology	Socio-economic conditions can also result in individuals being vulnerable to radicalisation.	'I think it's looking at root causes … focusing on unemployment, lack of education, etc. … I think a lot of ethnic minorities and youth, in fact, are disengaged, they're deprived, and they're sitting at society's margins'
(iv) Locating Prevent outside of a counter-terrorism strategy	Engaging individuals who are at risk of radicalisation should be a safeguarding issue that sits outside the realm of counter-terrorism.	'You can't just tell someone they're wrong. You need to recognise them and value them as a person and then be like "This is wrong"'
(v) Avoiding gendered assumptions	Videos that appeal to mothers to safeguard their sons are based on problematic gendered constructions.	'There's definitely a kind of gender perspective imbalance in the Prevent Strategy which needs to be addressed'
(vi) Whether Prevent should be rebranded	Whether the Prevent Strategy is irreparably tarnished and so requires a new label.	'There's an argument to be made for rebranding it. There's a lot of negative connotations that come with the term Prevent now …It's met with a lot of resistance'

both drew on their own experiences of Prevent or recounted concerns they had heard reported elsewhere. This sense that a counter-radicalisation strategy like Prevent might be needed in spite of considerable concerns with its practical manifestation points to a tension between how our participants thought Prevent *should* operate and how they thought *it did*. The final section of this chapter therefore bridges this gap, by exploring suggestions for reforming the strategy and reflecting on the insights of others for whom Prevent was simply beyond repair.

The need for a deradicalisation strategy

Perhaps surprisingly, given the controversy that has surrounded Prevent, we encountered little suggestion from students in our focus groups that the UK should not have a deradicalisation strategy. The general feeling was that Prevent – or something similar – was needed. Students commented that 'there is a place for a counter-radicalisation strategy' (Focus Group 7, Participant 3) and 'I do definitely think that Prevent is the right direction to be going in' (Focus Group 5, Participant 1). The value of an engagement, as opposed to enforcement, approach to tackling the fomentation of violent extremist beliefs was often emphasised here. One student, for instance, stated that 'it's good in the sense that, when it comes to tackling terrorism and violent extremism, there should be a soft power response rather than just purely hard power like, you know, arresting people and that kind of thing' (Focus Group 4, Participant 3), whilst another said that Prevent 'actually deals with this sort of thing proactively, rather than reactively, so having something like that in place is always going to be worthwhile' (Focus Group 4, Participant 4). Whilst 'it's not perfect,' said one student, 'there's enough people trying to make it work' (Focus Group 3, Participant 2). In fact, some even regarded Prevent as pioneering and world-leading, using language similar to that of the Tony Blair Institute with which this chapter began. One student stated that 'On a global scale, it was a first. Prevent was really quite ground-breaking ... Fundamentally I'd say it was a good thing and it's possibly led to more good things on a global scale' (Focus Group 1, Participant 1). Another suggested that Prevent is 'better than what other countries are doing' (Focus Group 3, Participant 3).

As seen in the previous chapter, a number of participants were concerned that young people are particularly impressionable and, as a result, vulnerable to dynamics of radicalisation. This was one of the reasons why a deradicalisation strategy such as Prevent was felt to be important:

I definitely think Prevent's a good thing and it should be in society. It's important that we have something to look for signs of radicalisation in young people because I think that's an important stage where they can perhaps be changed on a different path or be, you know, rehabilitated.

Focus Group 7, Participant 1

Others also pointed to what was seen to be the very real threat of radicalisation. One described radicalisation as 'a problem that needs to be addressed', adding that the number of attacks that the Government states it has prevented each year is only 'the tip of the iceberg' (Focus Group 5, Participant 6). Another suggested that attacks such as the Manchester Arena bombing demonstrate there is 'definitely' a threat (Focus Group 7, Participant 1). Others agreed, stating that the UK 'will always be under threat because there's always gonna be somebody or a group of people that have an extremist view about something and want to enforce it' (Focus Group 8, Participant 1) and that the UK is a 'melting pot of different cultures and histories. There's some real, like, legitimate grievances, and there's still things going on with British foreign policy that are causing a whole load of anger and hate' (Focus Group 2, Participant 5). These concerns were often deemed to be exacerbated by the emergence of the internet and social media. One student, for instance, expressed concern at the number of 'younger kids now using social media … a lot more than they did a few years ago, which is also a very easy way for radicalisation to occur' (Focus Group 5, Participant 1). Another pointed to the greater reach afforded by the internet and the role of algorithms in structuring access to particular content:

Obviously, the internet is great and everything, but you know it's allowed for people to reach more specific communities than ever before. And it's allowed algorithms specifically tailored for optimising what someone wants and that can end up in an indoctrination pipeline.

Focus Group 2, Participant 3

A further reason that was offered for the importance of a deradicalisation strategy was the need to tackle extremism, both as a potential precursor to violent extremism ('you still want to prevent people from getting to that point') and as something that is 'inherently damaging' in its own right (Focus Group 2, Participant 3).

Whilst the general view amongst participants in our groups was that Prevent is needed, there were some students who were reluctant to express an opinion. These students identified four issues that, in their view, made it difficult to reach a conclusion. The first was the difficulty in measuring the success of Prevent. One student stated that 'you don't ever see' statistics on positive outcomes, such as the number of terrorist attacks Prevent has thwarted (Focus Group 5, Participant 2). Another pointed out that the successes of Prevent are not visible, commenting that 'by definition you only see the system failing. You never see the system working because when the system works you don't see anything' (Focus Group 2, Participant 3). Attempting to measure success based on whether a high or low number of terrorist attacks have occurred would also be difficult because of the small sample size, according to another student: 'it is really difficult to measure success in this area because terrorist attacks are Black Swan events anyway, so it's kind of hard to get a baseline of what would be normal and then figure out whether or not you're winning or losing, so to speak' (Focus Group 2, Participant 5).

The second issue complicating evaluation of Prevent's necessity was one of cost. One student here stated that the difficulty in measuring Prevent's success, coupled with a lack of information on how much Prevent costs annually, means that it is hard to determine whether the amount of money spent on Prevent is 'proportionate' (Focus Group 2, Participant 2). Another student – echoing the work of prominent critics such as John Mueller and Mark Stewart (2016, 2021) – wondered whether more lives might be saved if the money spent on countering the threat of radicalisation was instead spent on other dangers such as road safety (Focus Group 2, Participant 5).

The third issue was the difficulty in assessing Prevent without also considering the wider counter-terrorism strategy. One student stated, 'I don't think you can look at it in isolation. It's just a piece of the overall strategy' (Focus Group 2, Participant 2). Another student observed that 'Prevent can only be as good as the wider system' (Focus Group 4, Participant 4). This student discussed the attacks that occurred in the UK in 2017 and commented that any failings within Prevent had to be viewed alongside other failings (e.g., within the intelligence services) that had also taken place in the build-up to these attacks.

A fourth issue we encountered was the difficulty in measuring the negative impacts of Prevent. One student here referred to the impact of negative media coverage of Prevent, particularly on members of minority ethnic communities, and stated, 'You can't quantify failure' (Focus Group 1, Participant 1). Another pointed out the difficulty in those unaffected by Prevent seeking to assess its impact on those more likely to be targeted: 'it doesn't affect us and the kind of disproportionate impact it has on ethnic minorities of people of colour, particularly men, or young black men' (Focus Group 7, Participant 4). This was echoed by another student, who said that they would need to speak to people that have been referred to Prevent to be able to evaluate the strategy's effectiveness:

I really want to ask the individuals who were contacted by Prevent, 'Do you think that you were on a path like with hindsight that was unhelpful, was dangerous or was damaging and do you think the intervention that you've got was actually useful for you?' … What if people are vulnerable and scared and they're looking for extremist narratives to help them make sense of the world? Is being contacted by Prevent the best way to go about it? How is it making you feel? Do you feel safer in the UK as a result of this?

Focus Group 2, Participant 1

There were other students that accepted the need for a deradicalisation strategy, yet simultaneously expressed some misgivings. On occasion, this resulted in equivocal – or, even, contradictory – statements, such as the following suggestions that Prevent is counter-productive yet necessary:

I think that it's good that something is there … You know, it's better than having nothing at all, but at the same time it could be counter-productive … But yeah, but no, I think it is good that something is in place.

Focus Group 3, Participant 3

And:

I mean obviously these kinds of things have to be in place, but it's just the right way to go about it. I mean, I was trying to think myself, 'How would I correct this?' … I did come to the conclusion that it could potentially do more harm than good.

Focus Group 8, Participant 6

For some of these students, Prevent's counter-productivity lies in its focus on Muslim communities. One student commented that, whilst they 'agree with the implementation of Prevent and the necessity for countering terrorism and radicalisation … you can't deny the inherent focus on ethnic minorities and kind of subsequent racism that comes out of that. I think they're interlinked' (Focus Group 7, Participant 4). Another student also highlighted the focus on Muslim communities, but weighed this against the increased sense of security they themselves felt knowing that Prevent exists:

Ultimately, I think it's a good idea. I know it's used in the wrong way and I know it's used to target the wrong people and I don't like that. And if I could change that 100 per cent I would. But knowing that the Government is trying to do something and has finally realised how much of an issue terrorism is and how it does need to be addressed is a good thing and does make me feel a bit happier.

Focus Group 8, Participant 1

Given the significance of these concerns, the following section examines the students' misgivings about Prevent in greater detail.

Concerns about Prevent

The various concerns that students raised about Prevent are discussed in this section under three headings: empirical and theoretical underpinnings, training and vulnerability indicators, and freedom of expression and suspect communities.

Empirical and theoretical underpinnings

As discussed in the previous section, some participants in our groups identified various issues that they felt make it difficult to assess the effectiveness of Prevent empirically. These included the difficulties in measuring Prevent's successes and in quantifying its failures. One student questioned whether public bodies should be co-opted into the Prevent Strategy in the absence of a proven evidence base:

> I would like to raise the question as to whether there's any evidence about efficacy ... I don't think I have heard anything that says that this is proven to be an effective approach. Therefore, there's got to be a question mark as to why it's an effective thing for public bodies to be required to participate in. If you see it as a good thing, great. If you see it as a questionable thing, then there's to be an element of coercion.
>
> Focus Group 3, Participant 1

Other students questioned Prevent's theoretical underpinning, in two respects. First, as noted in the previous chapter, some specified that Prevent places too much emphasis on ideology as a root cause of terrorism, to the exclusion of other factors. One student suggested that Prevent 'assumes that certain root causes are definitive, whereas other ones for example poverty are not as much' (Focus Group 3, Participant 5). Other students made similar comments. One suggested that the money spent on Prevent would be better spent tackling poverty, which they said is also a cause of terrorism (Focus Group 3, Participant 4). Another stated that it would be better to provide community initiatives for those individuals identified as being socially excluded (Focus Group 4, Participant 3).

Second, some participants questioned the extent to which violent extremism is in fact driven by ideology. According to one student, 'you can get a lot of people that do have these extremist ideologies that would never commit a violent crime because of them', whilst conversely 'people can act on extremist ideologies without fully believing them' (Focus Group 4, Participant 4). This observation is in keeping with academic critiques of Prevent discussed in Chapter 1, which argue that the notion that an extremist ideology is a necessary precondition for terrorist activity does not withstand empirical scrutiny

(Schuurman and Taylor 2018; Venhaus 2010). Academics have also argued that to assert that terrorism emanates from the exposure of vulnerable individuals to extremist ideology diminishes individual agency (Thomas 2016). The students in our focus groups made a similar point, with reference to the case of Shamima Begum. To return to excerpts we referenced in Chapter 3, one student pointed out the 'different perspectives' people have on this case. Some say she was 'groomed into the situation', whilst others say it was 'off her own bat' (Focus Group 1, Participant 5). Another student opined, 'the way that she's been treated is not at all in keeping with the idea that someone has been trafficked or groomed or brainwashed. It's very much that she is culpable for her own actions … It's almost inconsistent (Focus Group 6, Participant 1).

Training and vulnerability indicators

The students emphasised the importance of training, to help those working in professions subject to the Prevent Duty to know how to recognise vulnerability to radicalisation. Such training, in this view, will help ensure that referrals are made when they are required and are not made when they are not. As one student explained, 'you need a very specific checklist of … the things you should be looking out for' (Focus Group 2, Participant 3). There was concern that the twenty-two factors listed in the Vulnerability Assessment Framework (HM Government 2020) do not provide this level of specificity. For example, one student claimed that 'there's a lot of confusion around what kind of behaviours are actually expected' before a referral is made (Focus Group 8, Participant 3). Moreover, as noted in the previous chapter, several of the students had completed Prevent training themselves. They felt that the training they had received had not adequately equipped them to identify individuals vulnerable to radicalisation. According to one, the training is 'very vague and kind of almost anything can be pointed to as a sign … Personally, I'm not entirely sure if the training is enough to provide that determination' (Focus Group 7, Participant 3). Another student doubted whether it is possible to impart the required expertise within the time allotted for Prevent training:

> It kind of blankets all these different kinds of cases. So, it seems that it's actually far more complex and it has so much more variety and different experiences than you could possibly ever explain just in a small bit of training for someone in education, or to put in a poster like an advert.
>
> Focus Group 6, Participant 1

A number of participants warned that, as a result of this vagueness, professionals subject to the Prevent Duty may fall back on stereotypical views and opinions. In particular, they might focus more on violent jihadism, with less emphasis placed on the far right and far left. This could lead to non-referrals in some cases where intervention would be justified. One student stated, 'How do you identify somebody that's not the typical terrorist? ... Unfortunately, [Prevent] doesn't really work because it pinpoints a specific area of society [Muslims] and half the time they're not even responsible' (Focus Group 8, Participant 1). Conversely, the vagueness of the vulnerability indicators could result in unjustified referrals based around false positives (Focus Group 5, Participant 5). A particular concern here was the potential influence of media and public discourse on individuals' application of the vulnerability indicators:

> There is such a kind of heightened atmosphere around that more generally I think that as soon as you start having a sort of checklist of things, that could be a cause for concern. Certain people are just going to start seeing those things, and I think that's because of our wider climate and media coverage of this.
>
> Focus Group 6, Participant 1

This concern was echoed by others, who expressed sympathy for schoolteachers tasked with performing the Prevent Duty. As the following quotes illustrate, there was a feeling that teachers have to tread a fine line between, on the one hand, potential accusations of bias or insensitivity should they make a referral that later turns out to have been misplaced. And, on the other, possible blame for not having referred an individual who later engages in terrorism-related activity:

> It's a bit of a rock and a hard place kind of thing because, if you don't intervene, an attack could be carried out but, at the same time, if [the pupil] genuinely [doesn't] have any intent of that then they've been labelled as a terrorist.
>
> Focus Group 5, Participant 5

> It just seems unfair because if you create a work environment where that teacher doesn't report it, because they don't want to be accused of being racist or bigoted, and you miss that opportunity to get in and in three or four years' time you've got a 15-year-old travelling to Somalia or Nigeria to join Boko Haram, then people will turn around and criticise the school and the agencies for not doing enough at the start.
>
> Focus Group 3, Participant 2

Within these conversations, it was felt that the Prevent training teachers receive is inadequate to equip them for this task. One student said that their mother, a schoolteacher, received Prevent training that consisted of little more than being told 'if you think a child is becoming radicalised or is a potential threat you fill out this form or you contact this number. That's pretty much all there is that's actually given to the people that are meant to be making these referrals' (Focus Group 4, Participant 4). More generally, some students recalled their schoolteachers making 'offhand comments about not being happy with the Prevent Strategy' (Focus Group 3, Participant 4). Others shifted the focus a little to question the impact of the Prevent Duty on the relationship between teacher and pupil. One described Prevent as a fear-breeding policy, commenting that 'It puts this pressure on teachers to be on the lookout for these radicals who are among us, particularly among high school children, like, how can that be? And what sort of environment does that create?' (Focus Group 8, Participant 7).

Similar concerns were expressed about other professions. With reference to health care and education, for example, one student explained that the Prevent Duty requires those 'whose role in public life is one of supporting clients' to 'take a role in which they are taking a very different relationship to clients and certain aspects of their lives. And that's necessarily going to change their relationship' (Focus Group 3, Participant 1). Some students recalled their university lecturers making informal or provocative comments about Prevent, such as one lecturer who told his students that Prevent prohibited him from asking them whether they had ever attended a protest (Focus Group 7, Participant 3). Another lecturer told a class that, whilst he 'understood the need' for Prevent, it nonetheless placed him in a 'very uncomfortable situation' (Focus Group 1, Participant 5). There was also some scepticism around whether university educators are well-placed to identify individuals vulnerable to radicalisation:

> I struggle to see how Prevent could make an impact in the university context in the sense that if it's lecturers that are doing the training and learning about this and then you see them for two hours a week, I feel like it isn't likely to be picked up on. Even then I feel like the period of time when people go to university is a period of time where people question what's going on around them. It is the time when you learn to question what's happening in society. It will be very difficult to pick up on extremist views.
>
> Focus Group 7, Participant 2

This suggestion that Prevent has the effect of stifling open discussion and freedom of expression is considered further in the next section.

Freedom of expression and suspect communities

The right to freedom of expression is enshrined in Article 19 of the International Covenant on Civil and Political Rights and Article 10 of the European Convention on Human Rights. In *Handyside v United Kingdom*, the European Court of Human Rights described freedom of expression as 'one of the essential foundations of [a democratic] society, one of the basic conditions for its progress and for the development of every man'. The Court added that the right 'is applicable not only to "information" or "ideas" that are favourably received or regarded as inoffensive or as a matter of indifference, but also to those that offend, shock or disturb the State or any sector of the population. Such are the demands of that pluralism, tolerance and broadmindedness without which there is no "democratic society"'.[1]

Freedom of expression and ideological debate have an important role in countering extremism. As Barendt has stated, 'We can only respond intelligently to undesirable extremist attitudes, and remove or reduce the reasons why they are held, if we allow them, to some extent, to be disseminated' (Barendt 2009: 453). Similarly, the CONTEST Strategy states that 'Encouraging free speech and open debate is one of our most powerful tools in promoting critical thinking and preventing terrorist and extremist narratives taking hold' (HM Government 2018: 37). This line of argument was echoed by a number of students in the focus groups. According to one, 'Diversity of opinion and open discourse can really do a lot of wonders ... Pulling people outside of these ideas of echo chambers is, in my opinion, possibly the best thing you can do for anyone, and humanising people that aren't of the same opinion of you is one of the better things that you could do' (Focus Group 1, Participant 1). For another student, such debate and discussion are a hallmark of higher education: 'in the university environment you are meant to be exposed to things' (Focus Group 2, Participant 1). Indeed, according to the CONTEST Strategy, the Prevent Duty 'does not restrict debate or free speech in schools, colleges and universities ... Our schools, colleges and universities should be places in which children and young people can understand and discuss sensitive topics' (HM Government 2018: 37).

The importance that the CONTEST Strategy appears to attach to freedom of expression and open discussion stands in marked contrast to the experiences of at least some of the students in our focus groups. The observations of several students offered evidence of a chilling effect on their freedom of expression. An important concept in the jurisprudence of the European Court of Human Rights, a chilling effect exists where state action has the effect of pre-emptively dissuading individuals from exercising their rights, such as the right to freedom of expression (Pech 2021). Students described how their awareness of the Prevent Duty sometimes made them reluctant to talk openly. For example, one stated that the Prevent Duty 'makes me feel a bit more on edge, having to consider that there are people surveilling your thoughts and ideas as you express them' (Focus Group 3, Participant 4). Students also warned each other to be circumspect when expressing their opinions. One participant recalled a discussion with their peers concerning an essay they were writing. The topic of the essay was theories of radicalisation and whether terrorist attacks can be explained in strategic terms. One student advised the others that 'the strategic argument sounds very much like an opinion that's sympathetic to terrorism. You want to be careful that that kind of opinion isn't reported' (Focus Group 8, Participant 5). On occasion, teachers also issued similar warnings. As well as the university lecturer mentioned previously, who declined to ask his students whether they had ever participated in a protest, one student remembered their politics A-Level class giving presentations on topics such as drones and suicide bombings. At the start of the class, the teacher warned the pupils 'Obviously, if you mention anything odd in your presentation, I will have to report you' (Focus Group 8, Participant 5).

The starkest evidence of a chilling effect, though, came from students from ethnic minorities. One student described a class discussion about Shamima Begum. The student said that because they are a Muslim, they felt they had to keep their opinions in 'check':

> Could it be because of my race or my religion that people think that I'm taking her side? Whereas I'm not, I'm just trying to say 'What are civil liberties and what is citizenship?' Like, these are questions that are normal. And if it was me with white skin and not a Muslim, I think it would be much easier to say that and not have to verify myself.
>
> Focus Group 3, Participant 5

Similar feelings were expressed by the international student who, as explained in the previous chapter, hoped to remain in the UK following their degree and was concerned about the possible future implications for any visa application of a Prevent referral. This student explained that 'the problem is that anything you say could be taken out of context in such a securitised environment' (Focus Group 6, Participant 4). As a result, they said they 'would be more conscious of what I am saying and how I'm expressing myself … I can't even imagine if I was Muslim, how I would be feeling in this environment.' As well as their future visa application, this student expressed concern at the impact of the Prevent Duty on their intellectual development:

> I think that it would change my behaviour and it would make me more conscious as a person and less confident of expressing my thoughts, which would be so counter-productive for my learning in the university … [I]f you're doing a politics course and you don't critique the state or its policies and you don't find nuance in these things and you're not able to express yourself like that anymore, it's so restricting and it could curtail your development as a scholar.
>
> Focus Group 6, Participant 4

As these comments indicate, there was a feeling amongst students in our focus groups that the Prevent Strategy impacts Muslims in particular. A recurring theme in every group was that being a Muslim is, in itself, something that gives rise to suspicion. A number of students explicitly used the term 'suspect community' to capture this differential treatment. A suspect community exists where members of a sub-group (which may be defined by a range of factors, such as race, ethnicity, religion, class, or gender) are targeted, not necessarily as a result of suspected wrongdoing, but simply because of their membership of the sub-group (Pantazis and Pemberton 2009: 649). The concept of a suspect community was first developed by Hillyard (1993) to describe the experiences of Irish people during The Troubles. More recently, it has been argued that Muslims are the 'new suspect community' (Pantazis and Pemberton 2009: 646). In this context, several participants referred to the focus of the 2007 Prevent Strategy on Muslim communities. According to one, Prevent 'got into a bit of controversy around racial profiling at the beginning when it first came out because they were focusing exclusively on Islamic extremists and so people felt like they were a suspect community' (Focus Group 2, Participant 5). Others described the 'targeting of specifically Muslim communities' as 'not a great strategy to have' (Focus Group 2, Participant 1), and stated that their 'biggest concern is the fact that it was targeted at Muslims specifically for quite a long time' (Focus Group 5, Participant 6). Another student described how Prevent was 'perceived by those communities as outright targeting them as possibly the only source of radicalisation and extremism, and a lot of social and community backlash came as a result' (Focus Group 1, Participant 1).

Some participants warned of the potentially counter-productive effects of the widespread perception that Muslims are a suspect community. One prominent concern here was that Prevent is divisive. For one student, for instance, counter-terrorism is a national security issue that should be the province of the state, and asking citizens to 'become spies for the government' erodes trust and generates separation (Focus Group 6, Participant 4). Another warned of the 'hostile environment that's been created in the UK', pointing to 'oppositional politics' that draws connections between distinct policy issues such as counter-terrorism and immigration (Focus Group 3, Participant 1). Others stated that Prevent 'aggravates cultural and community differences' (Focus Group 7, Participant 4), and leaves those communities that it targets feeling 'not really welcome or part of a wider society and that is just gonna cause bigger fractures' (Focus Group 6, Participant 1). According to one student, the effect is to 'reinforce those in- and out-group dynamics … I think the risk is really in people's views and building up walls instead of knocking them down, and the repercussions that come as a result' (Focus Group 1, Participant 1).

Connected to this was the concern that in some instances Prevent could itself be counter-productive and actually increase the risk of radicalisation. One student warned that 'Actually, Prevent is potentially a threat to UK security. How, if we're sort of profiling certain people, we're potentially alienating particular communities' (Focus Group 8, Participant 5). Another explained that the focus on Muslim communities 'inevitably creates a stigma and actually increases the risk of hardening a defensive kind of identification within young Muslim people. If they feel like they're being targeted, they would actively try to defend their own identity, which is going to be counter-productive' (Focus Group 8, Participant 3). It was suggested that feelings such as these could be exploited by radicalisers: 'extremist groups could make the argument that we are being picked on because of our demographics, you know, the Government's against us type thing ... They could play into that' (Focus Group 6, Participant 3). And, moreover, that the experience of being stigmatised might leave some vulnerable to such a message:

[P]eople who are potentially more vulnerable, who experienced the negative effects of Prevent strategies, could then be tipped into more radicalising behaviour than they would have been if a suspect community hadn't been created or they didn't feel like they were being targeted just because of something so simple as their race and religion.

Focus Group 1, Participant 5

These concerns were especially acute in respect of children and young people. It was suggested that Prevent 'might actually demonise Muslim schoolchildren' (Focus Group 4, Participant 1). To illustrate, one student recounted a story involving two schoolchildren in a physics class, one Muslim and the other white:

Both questioned something to do with nuclear fission and the construction of a bomb. The Muslim boy was reported to Prevent, but the other child wasn't. So, if you're looking at the way in which these things are being applied on the ground, that's obviously clearly discriminatory. And then you have the issue as that child starts to grow up and understand things, is this going to cause further alienation and then fuel further terror threats because of the way in which they've been targeted?

Focus Group 8, Participant 6

Other students pointed to the importance of the teacher–pupil relationship, arguing that being referred to Prevent by one's teacher could be potentially harmful. Stressing the challenges of adolescence, one student suggested that Prevent is 'just adding on to all of those worries which every child goes through. It's like creating another level of trauma and targeting, especially when it's coming from a position of power, which is teachers. It could be very alienating for people to be targeted like that' (Focus Group 6, Participant 4). Another student agreed, saying 'it's just so traumatising the idea that you could find out that your teacher has just reported you to a government agency.' For this student, there was a fundamental tension in tasking school-teachers with the Prevent Duty: 'the idea of a teacher being someone who's in the role of care and education provider being given also that task of spying on kids for me feels so wrong' (Focus Group 6, Participant 1).

Proposals for reform

The previous sections have shown that while many students in our groups felt that a deradicalisation strategy is necessary, a number of concerns about the specific assumptions and working of Prevent remain in vernacular understandings. For this reason, a number of students felt that it was important to discuss potential reform proposals. One commented that 'I mean, it's easy for us to sit here and criticise and say, "Prevent is rubbish"' (Focus Group 8, Participant 1), whilst another stated, 'You need something, so it's a case of, if you can't come up with anything better, be quiet' (Focus Group 3, Participant 2). As part of any process of reform, the students also emphasised the importance of ensuring that those targeted by Prevent are given a voice. One student urged that relevant communities are 'more involved rather than organising a policy at arm's length' (Focus Group 4, Participant 6), whilst another stressed that 'you've got to talk to the right people' (Focus Group 5, Participant 6).

As discussed in the previous chapter, the students in our focus groups regarded improved public information campaigns as important for raising awareness and understanding of Prevent. Such campaigns would challenge misperceptions of Prevent and engender a greater appreciation of the positive work that is done. As part of this wider effort, some students felt that greater coverage of Prevent is needed in secondary schools. As well as learning more about the 'signs of radicalisation' (Focus Group 4, Participant 7), the importance of self-awareness and digital literacy was also stressed in this context. One student explained that they are a vegan and then described their experience of joining animal rights groups online:

> I do think that radicalisation is a problem. I left all the animal rights groups I was on on Facebook because they were so racist. It was racist daily. It's people talking about Yulin and people talking about halal meats and people talking about kosher meats ... and not realising that you are just talking about communities of colour ... I just ended up getting fed up with having to report so much racist abuse on these Facebook pages. I don't think people have the

tools to recognise what these things are ... People don't have the tools to pick these things apart and not end up doing things that are quite racist.

Focus Group 2, Participant 1

This same student also emphasised the importance of improving understanding (of all age groups) of personalised recommendations and adverts online, as well as the ability to fact-check and identify misinformation: 'I want people to learn how to use the internet better. I would have education on how the internet works at every age group. I remember being in primary and secondary school and learning how ads work on Google. So I know how this works online. A lot of people don't' (Focus Group 2, Participant 1).

The next set of suggestions concerned definitions. There were calls for clearer definitions of such terms as radicalisation, extremism and British values (Focus Group 7, Participant 4). According to one student, for example, it is necessary to be 'really specific as to what Prevent is trying to combat' (Focus Group 7, Participant 2). At the same time, other students recognised the complexity of this definitional task. One student reflected, 'the language of policy is obviously extremely difficult to perfect. A question that I asked myself a lot when researching was "How would I have put this?"' In this student's opinion, 'the counter-productivity lies in this specification of religion and race ... Maybe being less specific and open to extremism, more broadly, is possibly a good thing' (Focus Group 1, Participant 1). Others echoed this suggestion that the naming of specific groups and ideologies should be avoided. One student suggested 'focusing more on actions rather than looking at specific ideologies' (Focus Group 4, Participant 4), whilst another said, 'you could use environmental extremism, political extremism, social, religious, etc., like whole demographics instead of individually naming Greenpeace or ISIS, etc.' (Focus Group 1, Participant 4). One of the difficulties here is reconciling these calls for greater generality with the students' criticisms of the vagueness of the discourse surrounding Prevent that were identified in Chapter 3.

Building on the sense that Prevent places too much emphasis on ideology as a root cause of terrorism, some participants said that Prevent needs to do more to address other factors. One student summarised this by saying that Prevent should be 'about improving people's lives' (Focus Group 8, Participant 4). Others talked specifically about socio-economic conditions, including employment, education, and inclusivity:

I think it's looking at root causes ... focusing on unemployment, lack of education, etc. ... I think a lot of ethnic minorities and youth, in fact, are disengaged, they're deprived, and they're sitting at society's margins. So, it's letting them in, it's creating an inclusive environment.

Focus Group 3, Participant 5

Another student emphasised the importance of 'equal opportunities for everyone to prevent them from even getting close to getting radicalised and turning to violence … It's important to be open, have an open society and acknowledge different experiences and also consider them when we're talking about counter-terrorism strategy' (Focus Group 2, Participant 4). Given this emphasis on inclusivity, there were a number of students that questioned the decision, in the 2011 version of Prevent, to separate Prevent from community cohesion – a shift described as a move towards 'community-targeted over community-focused methods' (Taylor 2020: 854). One argued that, if people feel that 'they are not considered the Other, then there is less room for indoctrinating them in the first place … and so I would put the money into developing communities, and not even specifically focused on particular communities, but just communities that haven't been developed' (Focus Group 2, Participant 3). Others emphasised the importance of youth services. For one student, the 'destruction' of provision for young people in recent decades has 'had a huge impact' (Focus Group 3, Participant 1). Another called for

> a nationwide youth service running youth clubs with professional mentors in there. And where they have a diverse ethnic population, those youth clubs reflect the diversity of that area. I think if you have that in process and, dare I say, not have the Government have anything to do with it … we would really see some benefits in the generations to come.
>
> Focus Group 3, Participant 2

Other students, who were also concerned that Prevent places too much emphasis on ideology, proposed a different remedy: to position engagement with individuals that are at risk of engaging in terrorism-related activity as a safeguarding issue that sits outside the realm of counter-terrorism. These students urged the importance of personal engagement, in order to understand individuals' welfare and support needs (Focus Group 2, Participant 2; Focus Group 3, Participant 5). This requires the development of a relationship of trust with the affected individual. One student stated that it 'requires sensitivity and awareness to counteract these thoughts or views. You can't just tell someone they're wrong. You need to recognise them and value them as a person and then be like "This is wrong"' (Focus Group 6, Participant 3). According to another student, in a health care or educational setting, identifying the support needs of a patient or pupil should be a welfare or child protection matter. Positioning the provision of welfare support as part of a counter-terrorism strategy is neither 'proportionate' nor 'helpful' (Focus Group 6, Participant 1). This student suggested that, with the system that is in place at the moment, referrals to Prevent should be avoided wherever possible and should never be made without the knowledge of the individual involved. Instead, schools, universities and health care providers should attempt to support individuals via other safeguarding mechanisms. This was echoed by another student, who said that a 'much softer' approach is needed, that allows service providers to try and address a person's welfare needs before making a referral to Prevent (Focus Group 2, Participant 3).

Concern was also expressed about gender constructions, in particular the depiction of women in communication around (counter-)radicalisation. As mentioned in the previous chapter, one student said that they had watched a Home Office YouTube video about Prevent. As well as questioning the video's exclusive focus on Muslims, this student also had misgivings from a gender perspective:

> When it talked about these women, these mothers losing their children, I think it was trying to appeal to the emotions of women who are considered emotional and overprotective of their children. So, it's trying to appeal to them to safeguard their children because of the notions associated with motherhood. There were no fathers in it, and even the children who were being talked about were all boys. No girls were talked about.
>
> Focus Group 6, Participant 4

A student in a different group offered similar comments:

> I think women are definitely viewed as passive agents that don't really get involved with terrorist organisations. And that's not the case. They are often used as suicide bombers and things like that ... There was another issue that I found where Muslim mothers were asked to look for signs of radicalisation in their children ... There was no mention of the father doing the same thing. Although the Government has tried to rectify some of these issues, I personally think that they're still there. There's definitely a kind of gender perspective imbalance in the Prevent Strategy which needs to be addressed.
>
> Focus Group 7, Participant 1

This student added that there is a lack of female mentors within Prevent, yet females that are identified as vulnerable and at risk of radicalisation are 'much more likely to be able to open up and talk to a female mentor'.

Finally, there was some discussion of whether Prevent itself is beyond repair. For some students, the Prevent Strategy is irreparably tarnished because it will always be associated with the targeting and stigmatisation of Muslim communities. Given the counter-productivity of this, it is necessary to change the public's perception – and the only way to do so, according to these students, is to re-label – or rebrand – Prevent. One stated that 'you have to re-label it for people to have a different perception of it' (Focus Group 8, Participant 1), whilst another said that 'there's an argument to be made for rebranding it. There's a lot of negative connotations that come with the term Prevent now ... It's met with a lot of resistance' (Focus Group 1, Participant

1). Others were sceptical of whether a rebranding would be sufficient. These students suggested going further, essentially starting afresh. For one student, this was because the Prevent Strategy is ill-equipped to address the challenges posed by far-right extremism and so a fundamental rethink is needed:

> Prevent came from a sort of reactionary anti-Muslim feeling post-9/11 moral panic. I don't think we can get it to a place where it's going to be working efficiently against far-right terrorism from the place where it started. I think you would need a completely different organisation and policy for that.
>
> Focus Group 8, Participant 7

This student accordingly called for 'a complete overhaul of the whole thing', with a replacement strategy focused on investment in communities and welfare services (Focus Group 8, Participant 7). Another student reiterated that, in their view, a deradicalisation strategy is needed, but said that Prevent should be rewritten from scratch: 'it's supposed to be community-based ... and it's supposed to promote cohesion and togetherness, but I think it actually achieves the very opposite" (Focus Group 7, Participant 4).

Conclusion

From the findings included in this chapter, it is apparent that the students with whom we spoke were, in the main, supportive of the existence of some form of counter-radicalisation strategy. Rationales for this obviously varied, but recent examples of terrorist attacks in the UK and the perceived increase of extremism within society seemed to serve as important indicators of the severity and seriousness of the threat posed by radicalisation. Consequently, a 'soft', preventative strategy that could help mitigate against the prevalence of terrorist violence was viewed by many as attractive and pragmatic. However, it should also be re-stated that we encountered two important exceptions to this majority position. First, a number of students felt they could not properly evaluate the impact or success of Prevent and therefore were unable to assess whether it was necessary or valuable. And, second, a smaller proportion still that believed the strategy was so flawed and/or counter-productive that it should be scrapped.

Given the consensus amongst our population that having a counter-radicalisation strategy was a good idea, it was striking how critical many also were of Prevent in its current manifestation. Criticisms of the strategy were extensive, and voiced frequently across every group. They ranged from those arguments that the strategy was theoretically and/or empirically unsound, through to suggestions of it having counter-productive effects, including a chilling effect on particular forms of speech, and the stigmatising of specific communities.

Of course, arguing that such a strategy is a good idea but criticising the one *we have* is by no means contradictory. However, it does perhaps speak to a conceptualisation of security in which security is accumulated and 'balanced' against insecurities. In this context, 'I' might be willing to accept the known insecurities and shortcomings that are a feature of Prevent because I calculate that *on balance*, I am more secure than if it were not to exist (perhaps because I do not feel targeted by the strategy in its current form). Here, it is important to note the precarity of the 'we' and 'I' in these sorts of calculations, not least because what might, for one person, represent an 'acceptable cost' of counter-radicalisation capable of mitigation over time, may be a traumatic lived experience for another individual, *right now*. This speaks further to the importance of continued vernacular investigations into security with diverse populations and in particular, those that have historically been overpoliced or the subjects of disproportionate and invasive security practices. In Chapter 6, we turn now to considerations such as this by linking the findings of our empirical chapters to wider conversations around the nature, meaning, and functions of security.

Note

1 *Handyside v United Kingdom*, application no. 5493/72, 7 December 1976, paragraph 49.

6

Theorising (counter-)radicalisation in the vernacular

In the preceding chapters, we offered a descriptively rich exploration of public understandings – or, better, constructions – of radicalisation, counter-radicalisation, and the UK Prevent Strategy more specifically. Read collectively, these chapters investigate the discursive terrain through which the everyday politics of (in)security play out in the vernacular. Such a politics, in this context at least, is – as we have seen – multiple and contested, and underpinned by local experiences, interpretations, memories, and values. That the methodological design of our research militates against any claim to have exhaustively mapped this terrain, indeed, hints at the potential for still greater multiplicities here. It would be unlikely that speaking to other people, in other contexts, at other times, would fail to generate additional understandings or impressions.

In this chapter, we push a little harder on the conceptual importance of these empirical findings, by situating them within wider contemporary literatures on security. Doing so, we suggest, achieves two goals. First, it allows us to further demonstrate the value of a vernacular approach to the most pressing of contemporary security challenges by explicitly connecting the empirical findings just charted to the book's opening chapters. Second, and as importantly, it allows us to engage with absolutely fundamental debates on security's meaning and functions (see Jarvis and Holland 2015). These debates are ontological – for instance, what is security, and what counts as a security threat; epistemological – what can we know about security, and political – who gets to speak or construct security in particular contexts? These two ambitions are, moreover, connected. Highlighting the capacity of everyday perspectives to think about the politics of security differently – perhaps, even, to think the politics of security anew – has capacity as argued in Chapter 2, to open up new 'ways of seeing' the world (Parker in Rogers 2020: 109).

This chapter begins by arguing that the perspectives and experiences discussed in the preceding chapters should be approached as theorisations of (in)security. A second section then explores the ostensibly surprising prominence of 'radicalisation' as an interpretive framework in the vernacular discourse explored in this book. Here, we inquire into this terminology's regular invocation in everyday understandings of violence and extremism, including by people with profound scepticisms about the term's explanatory utility and political desirability. In the chapter's third section, we explore the value of vernacular security research for shedding light on the contexts and creators of security discourse, highlighting the importance of quotidian spaces and relationships in the reproduction and negotiation of this particular politics of (in)security. Although feminist and other scholarship has pointed us toward the significance of such spaces in the generation of global politics (see Chapter 2), vernacular security research, we argue, provides concrete, detailed illustration of the implication of, say, supermarket training rooms and familial relationships in productions of (counter-)radicalisation. We finish the chapter by pointing to the significance of our research for fundamental questions relating to security's meaning, exceptionality, and referents. Vernacular research, we argue, helps shed new light on security's ambiguities and pluralities as these are made meaningful in the context of concrete everyday experiences.

Theorising in the vernacular

Theoretical knowledge has a precarious standing today. On the one hand, the theoretical is often juxtaposed to that which is applied, that which is practical, perhaps even that which is useful. At the same time, theory retains connotations of epistemological depth: a rarefied understanding of something that goes beneath or beyond superficial surface appearances. Theory, here, is the work of specialists: the arrival, perhaps, at a privileged knowledge of the underpinning properties and working of some realm of reality be that subatomic particles, the composition of music, or the forces that structure economic outcomes. These connotations of abstractness and specialism are not unconnected, of course, and speak to a wider disquiet about experts and expertise that is particularly pronounced in the UK. Even if his remarks were taken out of context, Michael Gove's suggestion during the 2016 Brexit Referendum that 'people in this country have had enough of experts … saying that they know what is best and getting it consistently wrong' rather neatly encapsulates this disparagement (Steerpike 2021).

Theory, however, should not be thought of as the preserve of experts or elites. Theory is something that all of us do, all the time, in the context of our everyday lives. As Marysia Zalewski (1996: 346) argues, theory is a verb not a noun; it is a practice, rather than a tool waiting to be picked up and used by the ivory-tower dwelling expert: 'We theorise about how to make cups of tea, about washing clothes, about using the word processor, about driving a car, about collecting water, about joking, about what counts as relevant to international politics and about how we relate to colleagues, students, families, friends or strangers.' As this implies, theory is inseparable from everyday activities or experiences and the practical knowledge on which they rely. In Rowley and Weldes's (2012: 526) terms:

> Theorizing is both a form of practice and an inescapable component of practice. As scholars, we therefore need to stop talking about – and very occasionally at (a very small, elite portion of) – the world and start listening to its inhabitants, in order to discover the wealth of what we do not know about how in/securities are theorized and, crucially, how these are theorized in and through everyday practices.

The vernacular perspectives explored in the preceding chapters may be seen as theorisations – of (counter-)radicalisation, of (in)security, of politics, and more – in at least two ways. In the first instance, they are *constitutive* rather than descriptive of that which is being spoken about. By depicting, or, better, by constructing the politics of (counter-)radicalisation in particular ways – as necessary for national security, as inevitable, as flawed, as racist, and so forth – they contribute to the production of that politics in specific ways because 'ways of thinking and acting in the world will be (re)produced as reality' (Zalewski 1996: 351). This is not to say that other participants inevitably agree with, or internalise any particular perspective articulated in our groups. Nor, of course, is it to argue that readers of this book will not refuse or take umbrage with our treatment of these perspectives in the preceding chapters. Rather, our claim is that individual perspectives (and their reproduction in books such as this) form part of, and contribute to, wider conversations through which – in this instance – (counter-)radicalisation becomes meaningful. As argued in Chapter 2, the value of the focus group method used in this book is, in part, the inter-subjective emphasis it places upon knowledge, viewing this as something constructed collaboratively.

The contributions to vernacular discourse explored in this book may be seen as theorisations in a second sense, too: as efforts to interrogate, disrupt, or unmake established ways of understanding and doing security (via, in this instance, counter-radicalisation initiatives). As we have seen, many of the participants in our focus groups expressed disquiet or even anger at the UK's Prevent Strategy and its implementation. In so doing, they highlight and reflect upon potentially hidden assumptions, exclusions, and implications of counter-radicalisation practice, even going so far, at times, as to offer alternatives. The vernacular perspectives with which we have been working, in short, have both a constructive and deconstructive energy: generating insight into, helping to make meaningful, and at the same time critically interrogating, the workings of (counter-)radicalisation. For these reasons, as well as the wider claims we make in the book's conclusion, they merit serious reflection.

Radicalisation, sedimentation, and critique

As we have seen in the previous three chapters, the discussions in our focus groups were rich, in-depth, and revealed a variety of different insights and perspectives. As might be expected, given the politically contentious focus, we encountered instances of conflicting opinions between students within particular groups. We also encountered examples of individuals migrating between ostensibly contradictory opinions – and sometimes explicitly recognising this. Yet, despite this plurality, there were some issues around which a consensus appeared to emerge in our groups. In the first instance, we encountered a widely shared belief in the existence of a phenomenon known as 'radicalisation' posing a very real threat to lives in the UK. There was near unanimity, too, on the connected point that the UK needs a counter-radicalisation strategy to counter this threat, with many participants in our research praising the value of a proactive, engagement-led, soft power approach, as opposed to sole reliance on a reactive, enforcement-led, hard power framework. Perhaps more surprisingly, we also encountered a widespread argument – often framed around personal experience or the recounting of conversations with practitioners – that a lot of good work has been done as part of the Prevent Strategy, even if this is rarely publicised.

Throughout the discussions, it was evident that our participants not only understood the policy-level discourse of Prevent, but also that this discourse resonated with vernacular efforts to make sense of concrete and contemporary socio-political dynamics and challenges. And yet, as we saw in Chapter 3, the term 'radicalisation' was not uniformly understood across our focus groups, with two prominent conceptualisations evident. In the first, radicalisation was understood as a process, one in which vulnerable people lacking agency are led by external influences away from the political centre (the normal) towards the fringes (the radicalised). In the second understanding, radicalisation existed more as an intolerant attitude that underpins support for, or a willingness to use, violence. Key differences between the two, we argued, included the latter model's enhanced scope for agency on the part of the radicalised individual, and attenuated emphasis on the passage of time as an intervening factor.

Although these heterogeneous conceptualisations were both offered by participants in our groups as objective descriptions of radicalisation, the significant differences between them sheds some light on the term's ambiguities, and therefore contestability, in vernacular understandings and deployment. This contestability, of course, echoes – and may even be driven by – established concerns relating to the term and its usage that have been discussed at length by academics, policymakers, and others, as explored in Chapter 1 (e.g., Hörnqvist and Flyghed 2012; Neumann 2003). Perhaps more interesting here, though, is the term's discursive *resilience* within our focus group discussions and the continuing willingness of our participants to use it – including with fidelity to governmental understandings – even where there was real scepticism about the concept's value and implications. Although numerous adjacent concepts and frameworks (see Buzan and Hansen 2009: 13–16) might have been called upon as replacements for this (relatively new) terminology, we encountered very little sense of any active, intentional, substitution going on at the vernacular level. The widespread use of this lexicon, moreover, is particularly important, given pronounced epistemological concerns of participants relating to this concept. It is to these concerns that we now turn.

First, a number of people with whom we spoke queried the evidence base around the phenomenon of 'radicalisation', and the effectiveness of Prevent for countering this threat. As we have seen, some pointed to, or posited, a lack of robust, empirically grounded research into the Prevent Strategy itself, whilst others identified multiple impediments to meaningful evaluation of the strategy, including a lack of information on the programme's financial costs, the fact that Prevent's failures generate more attention than its successes, and the difficulty in quantifying any negative impacts of Prevent. More generally, there was a feeling amongst some of our participants that terrorism is a taboo topic, one that is rarely discussed in depth or with any nuance. In particular, these contributors to our groups felt there is a reluctance to try to understand what causes people to commit acts of terrorism, lest efforts at explanation be construed as attempts to exonerate – or even justify – such acts (see Butler 2004: 8–9). This was felt to be true of the media (mainstream and otherwise; factual and fictive), as well as of education in schools, where concerns around exposing pupils to potentially upsetting or distressing subjects (at least, without prior parental consent) could present a further obstacle for understanding here.

Second, we also encountered profound concerns around the obfuscatory effects of what arguably remains the dominant discourse on radicalisation and Prevent. Dubbed the 'conveyor belt' theory of radicalisation (Thomas 2016), this discourse

> promotes a view of radicalisation and terrorism as the product of professional, charming, extremist recruiters lurking among individuals and (in particular Muslim) communities, invading and contaminating the minds of innocent vulnerable children and young adults with a contagious virus, such as a religious ideology.
>
> Qurashi 2017: 204

For the participants in our focus groups, the emphasis placed on ideology within accounts such as this obscures the importance of other factors that potentially contribute to, or cause extremism. Such factors may be structural and material – rather than individual and ideational – and include socio-economic dynamics such as poverty, social exclusion, and entrenched inequalities. The dominant discourse – and its use of a raft of different metaphors to depict the radicalisation process – brainwashing, grooming, contagion, mental illness, and so forth – moreover, was also questioned for its diminishment of individual agency. Some participants used the example of Shamima Begum to problematise this, pointing out that, whilst Begum's story could have been – and was frequently – narrated as that of a vulnerable child being groomed, many retained a strong urge to hold her fully responsible and accountable for her actions.[1]

Building on this sense that there exists a reluctance to understand what causes people to commit acts of terrorism, some participants also suggested that one effect of the dominant discourse's diminution of individual agency was a downplaying of individual grievances as potential motives for violence. Such grievances, for a number of our participants, might play a very significant causal role as precipitants for terrorism (see Crenshaw 1981: 381). They might also, even, have legitimacy. The possibility to reflect on terrorism's micro-level causes or ethics, though, is obscured by the language of brainwashing and grooming which reduces its protagonists to simple dupes. As Ramsay (2017: 154) explains, 'Prevent depoliticises the encounter between students and "extremist" ideas, and in the process discounts students' ability to make reasoned judgements and to pursue them'. This depoliticisation discounts 'the possibility that the students' own rational agency could not only protect them from any psychological harm that might result from exposure to hostile ideas but actually strengthen them and undermine the credibility of those ideas' (Ramsay 2017: 154).

A third concern with dominant understandings of radicalisation here surrounded the gendered nature of this discourse. A number of participants highlighted a widespread media and political tendency to story radicalisation around a binary in which vulnerable, passive, and feminised victims fall prey to the interests and actions of powerful, active, and masculinised proselytisers such as hate preachers. Other participants expressed frustration at Countering Violent Extremism (CVE) training materials urging mothers to protect their sons from extremist messaging. This was seen not only as neglecting the responsibility of male fathers and carers for childcare, well-being and the management of home life, but, in addition, as at risk of overlooking the participation of (young) women in terrorist activities. Such concerns speak to longstanding feminist engagements with the marginalisation and misrepresentation of the complex and multiple imbrications that exist between women and political violence (Sjoberg *et al.* 2011).

The fourth set of epistemological concerns centred on terminological vagueness and ambiguity. As we saw in the preceding chapters, terms such as 'radicalisation', 'extremism', and 'British values' were frequently criticised as unclear or opaque, with discussion across the focus groups also demonstrating divergent understandings of related concepts, such as 'vulnerability'. These concerns extended beyond the definitional to encompass the operational. Those individuals that had completed Prevent training, for instance, were generally critical of its content, stating that a failure to clarify expectations of employees encountering suspicious circumstances often left them uncertain on how to fulfil their responsibilities. Other participants, who had not completed Prevent training, recounted conversations with family members and friends who had done so in order to voice similar concerns.

Concerns such as these were frequently scaffolded by wider political understandings and commitments. For some individuals, the inadequacy of Prevent training reflected a lack of commitment on the part of government to the practical implementation of the strategy. Others, however, doubted whether it would ever be possible to impart the necessary knowledge and expertise within the limited time available in person or during online Prevent training sessions. And, even if the necessary know-how could be adequately transferred to Prevent trainees, other participants still expressed doubts about the efficacy of attempts to implement the Prevent Duty in the context of educational settings, in particular: the focus of much of our discussion. At the level of Higher Education, this was linked to the limited contact between university tutors and their students, as well as the emphasis in universities on open debate and enquiry. At the level of secondary education, this was at times connected to teachers' lack of access to important sites of radicalisation, especially online spaces.

It is important, here, not to overstate the prominence of such concerns around conceptual and operational ambiguities. Indeed, in our focus groups, we also encountered acceptance that some degree of definitional ambiguity was likely, perhaps even inevitable or necessary in this context. On the one hand, participants recognised the complexity of the definitional task confronting those charged with countering radicalisation and related threats. Moreover, when asked to suggest proposals for reform, some participants expressly recommended a level of definitional generality in order to avoid singling out – and thereby stigmatising – specific ideologies or groups. Others argued that one potentially overlooked advantage of a lack of specificity is the resultant flexibility it affords practitioners, facilitating intervention against emergent or unforeseen behaviours that might fall beyond the scope of more tightly drawn definitional frameworks. This claim around the desirability of definitional flexibility, though, was also perceived by others in more nefarious terms, as part of a deliberate political strategy to augment the discretion and therefore authority of powerful figures and institutions. On this view, subjectivity in definition is inescapably linked to the possibility of abuse, with these individuals warning that confused but powerful concepts, such as radicalisation, are prone to opportunistic appropriation.

This leads to a fifth set of concerns, which focus on what the dominant discourse around radicalisation *does*. Students emphasised that the term 'radicalisation' has inherently pejorative connotations and powerful delegitimising and depoliticising effects. While in some contexts the status of 'a radical' might be regarded as desirable, the semantic relationship between radical and radicalisation carries with it potential for 'the good kind of radical' to be regarded as a threat – something that is both facilitated and exacerbated by the definitional ambiguities described above. One likely effect of the state's increasing control over who gets labelled 'radical' is that citizens will be dissuaded from making their voices heard, from holding governments to account for their wrongdoings, and from challenging the status quo, its inequalities, and prejudices. Our focus groups also provided evidence of a wider 'chilling effect', with some participants explaining that their own awareness of the Prevent Duty made them reluctant to talk openly and express their opinions in educational settings. Such apprehensions were sometimes amplified through direct encounter with warnings issued by teachers and lecturers, and – as might be expected, the starkest evidence of a chilling effect came from individuals from minority ethnic groups and, in particular, from Muslim students. As related research has found, students from diverse ethnic and religious backgrounds all argued that being Muslim, in itself, is today often seen as grounds for suspicion in relation to radicalisation, extremism, and terrorism. So, for example, a Muslim student felt unable to question the government's handling of the Shamima Begum case, in case this was misconstrued as an expression of support for Begum's decision to travel to Syria to join the Islamic State. As this illustrates, the power to delegitimise and depoliticise that is conferred on the state by its own discursive construction of the dominant discourse around radicalisation and Prevent is experienced with varying degrees of intensity, and fundamentally related to wider experiences of identity and citizenship (see also Jarvis and Lister 2013a)

These epistemological concerns with the conceptual precision, functions, and implications of terms such as 'radicalisation' are clearly profound and relate to fundamental understandings and expectations of the state, of government, and of life in established democracies such as the United Kingdom. How, then, do we make sense of the resilience of the term 'radicalisation' – and the continuing, often unreflexive, resort to this discourse – within our focus groups, *even amongst those most sceptical of this language?*

One explanation is a simple methodological one. The focus groups from which our analysis derives were set up as an opportunity for participants to discuss and debate the Prevent Strategy in light of Lord Shawcross's impending Independent Review (an immediate setting for our research, to which we return in the book's Conclusion). It is, therefore, potentially understandable that participants fell back upon language associated with the Prevent Strategy in their discussion, perhaps through expectation of what was contextually expected and appropriate. Moreover, even if such expectations were not universal, the possibility of 'norming' within such groups – for instance, through deference to particular speakers – might help to explain the prominence with which this language was used, often in a manner faithful to that found within official discourse.

An alternative explanation would be to place emphasis on the hegemony enjoyed by Prevent and its surrounding discourse in the UK today. As Amna Kaleem (2021) has argued, drawing on research with practitioners, Prevent has increasingly become a 'common-sense' approach to the policing of ideas and behaviour; one that is grudgingly accepted by those with responsibility for its delivery. In such a context, it may be that vernacular discourse tends toward dominant framings because the latter are so entrenched that to think otherwise is increasingly difficult. Despite the criticisms and ambiguities explored above, 'radicalisation' is not a totally empty signifier (see also Huysmans 1998). It is loaded with political, normative and other connotations that serve to constrain everyday understandings and usage, notwithstanding the capacity of individuals to resist or reflect on these. As Kaleem (2021: 272) summarises, drawing on her Gramscian approach:

> common sense denotes a system of beliefs and ideas commonly held by a group of people. These are neither concrete nor uniform and do not necessarily belong to the intelligentsia or the opinion makers. These thought processes are embedded within the collective psyche in a way that they are taken as a given, such as being a good neighbour or a patriotic citizen. People know they have to follow them without thinking too much about it. Their ideas on what it takes to be a good neighbour or a patriotic citizen may vary, but there is an unspoken consensus on the primary fact that one should be neighbourly and patriotic.

Approached thus, the widespread turn to this language in our groups may reflect – or may offer evidence of – a wider socio-political context in which 'It does not matter whether people experience a process of radicalisation or not, because the discursive apparatus of academia, media and state have already decided that radicalisation always precedes violence. It has become impossible to explain violence otherwise' (Heath-Kelly *et al.* 2015: 1).

One way to think about the implications of a movement of 'radicalisation' into common sense is through Ernesto Laclau's notion of sedimentation. For Laclau, as for many other poststructural theorists, society and its constituent identities, interests, and so forth is not determined by any fundamental truth or logic. Social entities and processes become recognisable because political projects are able to stabilise and therefore make them meaningful, if only temporarily and contingently. Sedimentation, for Laclau, occurs when 'people apply social practices through the forgetting of the moment of original constitution' (in Hansen and Sonnichsen 2014: 260). In his example: 'when you are using a mathematical instrument to apply automatically some formula, your original theorem, through which that original formula was established, is entirely forgotten. So, sedimentation is the moment in which there is a forgetting of the origin' (in Hansen and Sonnichsen 2014: 260).

Something similar may plausibly be the case for radicalisation today. So widespread is the term in academic and media use, that it may be turned to in order to make sense of, or explain, political violences without any real engagement with the concept's social and political origins, or the thinness of its underpinning evidence base, or its problematic association with assumptions around race and religion. Radicalisation may serve, simply, as a sort of shorthand interpretive framework that appears to make sense of the individual journey toward the political extreme. That may be the case in our focus groups. It may also, perhaps more importantly, be the case beyond them. Although such an observation takes us beyond the scope of this book, it highlights, we hope, how active engagement with vernacular securities of the sort explored here provides real opportunity to explore the resonance, embeddedness, and resilience of 'top-down' security discourses and paradigms through the prism of everyday life.

The contexts and construction of (in)security

Despite the considerable and widespread concerns around Prevent documented in the preceding pages, we also encountered a feeling across our focus groups that more needs to be done to raise public awareness and understanding of the strategy. Aside from news media coverage – which was reported as being one of the primary sources of information for most contributors to the groups – our participants tended to learn about Prevent in one or more of three ways. First, several had completed Prevent training, either in the course of employment, or through other roles such as an internship or a student leader. Second, perhaps unsurprisingly given the context of our study, a number of the participants had studied Prevent as part of their university education either on taught modules or in their own research. And, third, some students had learned about Prevent from family members or friends who had themselves completed Prevent training or who were politically active, or had especial interest in the strategy and its consequences.

Something that is striking about these sources of knowledge is that these participants did not report learning about Prevent simply by virtue of being a pupil or student whose education provider was under a duty to have 'due regard to the need to prevent [them] from being drawn into terrorism'.[2] And, perhaps surprisingly, this was a cause of significant frustration amongst those in our groups. In relation to higher education, the students often expressed both surprise and disappointment that they had not been routinely informed of the Prevent Duty at the commencement of their studies, not least because of its implications for their own contributions in class discussion and the like. In terms of secondary education – and notwithstanding some sympathy for the predicament of teachers, including the perceived lack of adequate training, the political sensitivity of the topic, and the potential impact of Prevent on the teacher-pupil relationship – a number of our participants also felt that there should have been greater coverage of Prevent and terrorism more generally. This was particularly the case in the aftermath of major terrorist attacks. Whilst some schools took precautionary measures relating to the threat of terrorism, such as cancellation of trips or lockdown drills, and some also appear to have encouraged pupils to contact staff if advice or support was needed, many of the students in our focus groups were bemused by the lack of discussion of high-profile acts of terrorism, especially where these were geographically proximate to their place of education.

For many of the participants, it was news media coverage that plugged this information gap. Yet there was widespread concern at both the tone and the content of this coverage. Whilst students suggested that a focus on Prevent's failings – ranging from anecdotal examples of misplaced referrals to its failure to intervene and prevent major terrorist attacks – was inevitable, there was also concern at the effects of sustained negative coverage. As well as obscuring the positive work done by Prevent practitioners, participants in our groups felt that media coverage often has a racial or religious bias, contributing to the demonisation of individuals or communities already deemed suspect. For those students that had completed Prevent training and found it to be vague and of little assistance, there was the added concern that exaggerated and biased media coverage would influence how others tasked with implementing the Prevent Duty would try to identify at-risk individuals, exacerbating tensions between communities.

It was also apparent that many students felt digital technology companies – in particular, the major social media platforms – have an important role to play here, in three respects. First, such platforms may not only play host to terrorist content, but could even promote and amplify it. Students expressed concern about the possibility of algorithms recommending such content – a concern that is not without empirical support (Whittaker *et al.* 2021) – and of vulnerable people ending up in an echo chamber. Second, it was suggested that online spaces such as social media are where one is most likely to find indicators that a person is at risk of being radicalised. Third, in terms of promoting awareness, understanding, and positive coverage of Prevent, particularly amongst young people, social media were also seen to be key. Against this backdrop, it was striking that – with the exception of a Home Office video that one student had found on YouTube and which was regarded as being both highly gendered and targeted specifically at Muslims – social media were not mentioned as a source of knowledge about Prevent.

The range of social sites and spaces within which Prevent is constructed or known is, in some ways, unsurprising. There exists a vast literature now on the role played by media organisations, and even popular culture, in communicating – and thereby – producing security threats from migration, to terrorism, nuclear weapons, and beyond (see, amongst many others, Weldes 1999; Fey *et al.* 2016; Innes and Topinka 2017). Even if governments have a privileged position in setting the tone and tenor of public debate on specific issues, other actors including formal forms of political opposition, activist groups, and cultural producers contribute to the shaping of security discourse through reproducing, contesting, or negotiating dominant understandings of threat and danger. And audiences or recipients of security discourse are crucial, too, not only because they must decode and respond to particular constructions of (in)security. But, in addition, because they play an active contribution in the co-constitution of such constructions through practices such as repetition or the asking of questions (Oren and Solomon 2015; Jarvis and Legrand 2017).

Understood thus, the vernacular discourse explored in the preceding chapters sheds, we argue, important new light on some of the specificities of security's production in everyday contexts. As we have seen, 'security' is constructed and produced in all manner of everyday or banal spaces, from the training rooms of supermarkets in which Prevent training is delivered, to the school assembly hall, to the kitchen table in the family home. In this sense, our research speaks, especially, to feminist work which has long encouraged us to take such spaces seriously as sites in the (re)production of global political dynamics (e.g., Enloe 2000). The vernacular discourse with which we have been working shows, in the first instance, how such spaces contribute in very concrete ways to the (re)production and negotiation of (counter-)radicalisation knowledge and practice, by providing rich, descriptive detail on who gets to speak or do security, as well as how, where, and when. What concrete examples of suspicious or 'risky' behaviour, for instance, are identified by those implementing Prevent training? How are those examples received by their recipients? It also points us toward what 'little security nothings' (Huysmans 2011) get remembered as important, instructive, or perhaps even problematic in everyday understanding of this specific politics of (in)security.

Related to this is the highlighting, in the preceding chapters, of the importance of a range of securitising actors – those who attempt to convince others that something constitutes a security problem (see Buzan *et al.* 1998: 35–38) – that remain relatively neglected in scholarship on the construction of (in)security. As we saw in Chapter 4, a wide range of institutions and individuals contribute to the shaping of radicalisation as a security issue within the contemporary UK: employers, educators, the mainstream media, and so forth. It might be tempting to explain these away as part of a passive conveyance of 'top-down' security discourse to individual citizens: as stages through which that discourse must pass to reach 'ordinary' people. Such actors, however, unquestionably play a mediating role in shaping *how* that discourse is communicated and therefore understood at the level of the everyday. They do so, for instance through possession of authority for the introduction, framing, and discussion of training materials, say, or through responsibility for the timing of and priority afforded to Prevent-related discussions in classrooms, workspaces, the family home, and beyond.

Of particular interest here is the role of family and friends in explaining and conveying security knowledge to individuals. As one participant in our focus groups put it: 'My dad used to be in the police and my mum works in schools. I only actually became aware of [Prevent] because I know mum's done some training with it before, and so I sort of just take an interest in it' (Focus Group 5, Participant 5). This recollection, in itself, falls short of what would typically be assumed to constitute a (successful or otherwise) securitising act: there is no evidence, for instance, of this individual's parents invoking radicalisation as a genuine, even existential, threat. It does, though, provide a sense of kith and kin as loci of security knowledge – as potentially important places in which security and insecurity are spoken. And, as the following suggests, we did encounter evidence, too, of such encounters serving to confirm or reinforce other discursive contact with (counter-)radicalisation:

> my mum works in the school and she goes to quite a lot of training and stuff like that that I know of and I worked as part of an educational charity and

I remember doing a bit on [Prevent] in terms of like what to lookout for and stuff like that. And so I've got experience in that way of it, yeah.

Focus Group 3, Participant 5

Vernacular security discourse, in short, has capacity to both extend and nuance our understanding of the politics of (in)security. This includes identification of potentially hidden social contexts within which security is (re)produced, negotiated, or contested, and illustration of the agency and authority of otherwise neglected actors to speak on security. In this sense, work such as this contributes to the contemporary shift *away* from political and other elites that have hitherto dominated epistemologically constructivist work on (in)security, and a pulling of attention *toward* the implication of a range of everyday security dynamics.

Prevent as security threat or response?

Although the ostensible purpose of Prevent is to enhance (national) security by tackling radicalisation, the participants in our focus groups also raised important questions about whether the strategy might itself present a security *threat*. These questions took two different forms. First, in terms of providing security against the threat of terrorism, it was suggested by some that Prevent may be ineffectual and does little to reduce the risk of terrorism. Others, in stronger tenor, argued that Prevent may actually be counterproductive and *increase* the likelihood of terrorist activity. Second, some participants also pointed to other referents beyond the state – including individuals and communities – that may be threatened by the UK's counter-radicalisation activities, including those widely deemed risky, suspicious, or suspect.

In terms of individual security, as noted above, students expressed concern that the dominant discourse surrounding radicalisation and Prevent serves to legitimate potentially intrusive forms of state intervention. The language of vulnerability, in this analysis, 'produces (discursively) the threats it claims to identify for the performance of governance' (Heath-Kelly 2013: 408) and thus 'serves to legitimise interventions in the lives of individuals, which would not otherwise be normatively and legally possible within liberal structures of governance' (Elshimi 2017: 172). Such interventions, as we saw in Chapter 1, may have significant and longstanding impacts upon their targets, many of whom may be young and vulnerable. On top of this, we encountered considerable concerns, too, that the UK's Prevent Strategy may have important and multiple depoliticising effects. These included: diminishing individual agency to contest or resist government actions or narratives; downplaying individuals' grievances; placing 'good radicals' in danger of being rendered dangerous others; a chilling effect on individuals' exercise of their right to free speech; a risk that Muslim students, in particular, will fear engaging in open and honest political discussion, and finally, the impacts on immigration status and planned future visa applications of particular individuals such as international students (see also Winter *et al.* 2022: 88–89).

In terms of the security of communities, whilst several of our participants emphasised that the number of referrals to Prevent for far-right extremism has grown significantly, there was a widespread feeling that Muslims remain a 'suspect community' within the UK (and potentially beyond) (on this, see, for example, Ragazzi 2016). This positioning was seen as divisive, stigmatising, and likely to generate feelings of alienation and resentment amongst communities that may already be or feel unjustly treated. When asked for proposals to address such risks through reform of the Prevent Strategy, several students stressed the importance of community cohesion projects and of giving those most impacted by Prevent a meaningful voice in such processes.

Although such concerns were widespread in our groups, they were not universally articulated. Indeed, reflecting on these themes, a couple of participants felt that, for them, the impact of Prevent on certain communities was outweighed by a personal sense of reassurance that derived from knowing that the government had a counter-radicalisation strategy in place (see also Jarvis and Lister 2015a: 89–93). As well as reinforcing community divides, this juxtaposition of the impact on others with one's own reassurance rests on the 'weight of numbers' to favour the 'aggregate us' (Zedner 2005: 513). In this sense, as Jeremy Waldron (2010: 33–39) has shown, the key distributive question here may not be one of balancing liberty and security, that is, the typical framing through which the impacts of counter-terrorism policies are debated. It may rather (or, perhaps, also) be a balance between justice and utility that is being invoked: between that which is normatively desirable, and that which is politically expedient. Other students, however, performed a different calculus, explaining that feelings of stigmatisation and resentment could increase individuals' vulnerability to radicalisation, particularly amongst young people. On this view, Prevent is seen as potentially counter-productive as a means toward its own proclaimed ends. Far from offering greater security against the threat posed by terrorism, it could in fact contribute to individuals choosing to engage in terrorist activity by creating or perpetuating the kind of grievances that lie beneath 'radicalisation'.

Reflections such as these speak directly to absolutely fundamental debates within the study of security. In the first instance, they caution us against assuming that security and insecurity are binary opposites: that increasing the former, say, inevitably leads to reducing the latter. Attempts to enhance security through counter-radicalisation may increase, rather than decrease security, in the same way that efforts to reduce street crime or terrorism through armed police or CCTV cameras may generate insecurity rather than reassurance in everyday life (see C.A.S.E. Collective 2006: 457; Bigo 2014: 221). Vernacular discussion of highly contentious security dynamics, put otherwise, encourages us to reflect again on the meaning of fundamental terms like 'security' and 'insecurity'. And, in the process, to question dominant framings of such terms and their relations within privileged sites from elite political discourse to academic debate. At a very fundamental level, is security most helpfully viewed in negative terms: as the absence of threat, danger, or risk, perhaps? Or, should security be viewed positively: as the capacity to do or achieve certain things, or to (choose to) live in particular ways (see Booth 2007)?

Second, in doing the above, vernacular engagements of counter-radicalisation as a form of (in)securitisation also encourage us to ask the obvious subsidiary question: what counts as a security threat? Is it useful to view incursions on freedoms of speech as questions of security? Or would these more productively be viewed otherwise: as part of a pervasive attenuation of citizenship and its protections, for instance? Is alienation a problem of security or of integration? Are community tensions security challenges, or failures of, say, multiculturalism? Part of one's answer to such questions will be a matter of bar-setting. Do we (or should we) limit 'security' to the most serious threats that challenge the very existence of something or someone? Such, famously, was the Copenhagen School's formula in the earliest articulation of securitisation theory, wherein 'security is about survival. It is when an issue is presented as posing an existential threat to a designated referent object ... that justifies the use of extraordinary measures' (Buzan *et al.* 1998: 21). Many others, of course, have subsequently questioned this logic (e.g., Huysmans 2011; Roe 2012: 252), exploring less dramatic and more quotidian productions of (in)security that appear redolent more of a politics of unease, than of existential challenges.

A final issue, already alluded to in the above, is the question of security's appropriate referent: put simply, whose security should we prioritise (Booth 1991: 319–321; Jarvis and Holland 2015: 94–97)? The vernacular knowledge explored in the preceding chapters contains numerous efforts to question or decentre the traditional answer to this question: the state. Reflections on the individual or community costs of security policies such as the UK's Prevent Strategy highlight how (in)security can be lived or experienced in very different ways that tend to be occluded by the instinctive turn to frameworks of 'national security'. And, viewed thus, security appears far more heterogeneous or plural: something that cuts across ostensibly discrete 'levels of analysis' (see Singer 1961), but not necessarily in predictable or foreseeable ways. This is why work around vernacular security tends to highlight issues of multi-scalarity (Bubandt 2005: 279; Mac Ginty 2019), because such a focus enables interrogation of the connections between ostensibly discrete sites of security: the global, the national, the local, and so forth.

Questions such as these are all fundamental to any understanding of security and insecurity. A research project such as this cannot definitively answer any of these, nor, in our view, should it seek to do so. The important thing is the capacity of vernacular research to flesh out how such questions are answered in concrete ways relating to everyday life and experiences of (for want of a better term) 'ordinary individuals'. As explored further in the concluding chapter, such research can tell us how non-elites think, or better, talk about such issues, offering insight into how security and insecurity are constituted in specific contexts, and potentially also providing resources for the critique or destabilisation of dominant understandings and discourse. Doing so, 'facilitates a diversifying – and therefore broadening – of knowledge around (counter-)terrorism: telling dominant truths differently [through] engaging with the vernacular, the mundane, the everyday and the local' (Jarvis 2019b: 351).

Conclusion

The analysis of security has always been an evolving one, shaped by developments in the 'real world' of global politics – the ostensible object of analysis for disciplines such as Security Studies – and internal developments within academic debates, approaches, norms, and so forth. As we argued in Chapter 2, the focus and techniques of security research have changed dramatically since a Cold War preoccupation with nuclear strategy and great power politics (Walt 1991). And yet, at the same time, the ongoing conflict in Ukraine stands as a vivid reminder of the future's unpredictability as much as of the past's continuing importance. The point, here, is that today's security challenges, threats, discourses, and technologies may not be tomorrow's. And security research will always need to engage with new theoretical approaches, new methods, new case studies, and so forth, in order to maintain its relevance, irrespective of whether we see such research as a problem-solving, story-telling, or, indeed, critical, exercise (Jarvis 2013).

In this chapter, we have attempted to demonstrate some of the ways in which the vernacular perspectives documented in the previous chapters might add insight to understandings and debates within security research. These perspectives, to reiterate, were generated through application of a novel conceptual framework – vernacular security – put into practice via a relatively recent methodological approach to the study of security – focus groups – in order to investigate a particularly prominent and contested set of security issues relating to radicalisation and counter-radicalisation. As we have seen, the perspectives of participants in our research have importance not only for pushing forward studies of vernacular security, but also for studies of security more generally given their relevance to longstanding and fundamental debates on this topic. It is to this wider importance and resonance that we turn now in concluding the book.

Notes

1 Recent allegations that an intelligence agent working for Canada facilitated Begum's journey to Syria serve as a vivid – if unusual – illustration of the wider geopolitical and security contexts within which such processes are located (see Baker 2022).
2 CTSA 2015, section 26(1).

Conclusion

Our argument throughout this book has been for greater attention to, and engagement with, the seemingly mundane workings of security politics. Understanding the social life of initiatives such as the UK Prevent Strategy, we suggested, involves looking beyond the decisions, speeches and actions of politicians and practitioners on whom researchers have typically focused. We need also to unpack how such initiatives function at a far more mundane, everyday, level, in order to investigate how policies are understood, experienced and, ultimately, constructed, by citizens who may find themselves subject to them. Doing so, we have shown, helps shed light on the complexity, ambiguities, and contradictions of security frameworks that are neither monolithic in their construction, nor uniform in their implementation.

To make this argument, we began the book with a discussion of the UK Prevent Strategy as one of the world's most prominent and influential counter-radicalisation frameworks. Following a brief introduction to the strategy's conceptual moorings, implementation, outcomes, and failings, we turned our attention to existing scholarship in this area. Our argument, here, was that there now exists considerable academic debate around (counter-)radicalisation as a political discourse and policy arena. Unlike many other areas of terrorism research, this work is often marked by an explicitly critical approach to its subject material. It benefits, moreover, from considerable conceptual and methodological pluralism, a pluralism that includes expositions of the conceptual ambiguities and aporias of terms such as 'radicalisation' and 'extremism', as well as more empirically oriented engagements with the perspectives of practitioners such as educators who are responsible for delivering counter-radicalisation in practice. We finished this scene-setting effort by noting a lack of existing engagement with individuals and communities potentially subject to Prevent initiatives – especially students at Higher Education Institutions – the voices and experiences of which populate this book.

In the second chapter, we introduced the meta-theoretical framework underpinning our research. We began this discussion by retracing quite profound transformations within the study of security that have taken place since the 1990s. This work, we argued, opened considerable space for two important analytical manoeuvres. The first, was a rethinking of security as a constructed rather than objective phenomenon: something that is given, not made. The second move we highlighted here was an increased willingness to take seriously the ostensibly trivial, banal, or everyday within the politics of security. As Jonna Nyman (2021: 314) puts it in a recent article, 'Security shapes everyday life. It filters down into mundane spaces, where it is made and remade in routine practices and feelings, shaping the lived experience and lifeworlds of ordinary people.' Against this background, we introduced the notion of 'vernacular security' as a relatively recent framework of growing prominence that encourages analysts to access and analyse 'bottom-up' constructions of security threats and responses. This approach, we argued, enables us to centre everyday experiences and their framing, refusing the temptation to abstract or generalise around the consequences of security politics. We then spent some time outlining the focus group method on which we have drawn in this book as a productive way of co-creating knowledge of (in)security. In so doing, we reflected on practical issues of recruitment and representation within our own groups, before outlining the framework we employed for our coding and analysis of the conversations these generated.

Chapters 3 to 5 contained the book's empirical findings. In Chapter 3, we introduced distinct vernacular understandings of the meaning and causes of 'radicalisation', before exploring concerns with this terminology that were raised by contributors to our groups. Chapter 4 turned to vernacular understandings of the Prevent Strategy and its workings, before introducing the various sources of knowledge underpinning these. In Chapter 5, we then looked at public evaluations of Prevent as a framework for countering radicalisation as expressed and discussed by participants in our groups. Here we moved from generally supportive accounts of Prevent as a necessary response to a set of genuine and significant problems, on the one hand, to, on the other, more critical assessments of the framework's failings and injustices. We concluded Chapter 5 by engaging with suggestions for counter-radicalisation reform, approaching our focus group discussions as an opportunity for, and exercise in, political imagination as much as (or, better, rather than) a site for accessing pre-existing knowledge. In Chapter 6, finally, we connected our empirical analysis to some of the wider debates on security hinted at in the book's outset. In it, we argue that vernacular constructions of security threats and responses, open new insight into significant and longstanding questions, including around security's meaning, referents, processes, and consequences.

To bring our discussion to a conclusion now, the remainder of this chapter is organised in three parts. We begin by saying a few words about the book's origins and background, highlighting its emergence at the intersection of academic and policy contexts. Doing this here is important, we argue, in order to situate the analysis of the preceding chapters within the conditions of its production – knowledge, after all, is always 'for someone and for some purpose' (Cox 1996: 87) – *and* for reflecting on those wider social and political environments more broadly. A second section then offers a more detailed exploration of the value of vernacular security research such as that offered here. We finish this Conclusion, finally, by setting out some areas which seem to us potentially very productive for future research building on our framework and findings.

Academic and policy contexts

In the preceding chapter, we spent some time thinking about the importance of the vernacular perspectives with which we have been engaging for longstanding debates within the academic study of security. By taking a broader look, now, at the socio-political importance of these perspectives, we build on existing work on the 'vernacular turn' within Security Studies (Croft and Vaughan-Williams 2017), while reflecting as explicitly as possible on our own motivations and interests as researchers.

It is in this spirit of reflexivity that we share a few words now on the book's origins, and its connection to the very policy contexts we have been interrogating in the preceding pages. That is, the material on which we have been drawing – our focus group 'data', if you like – was initially collected (or, better, co-produced) at the request of the team responsible for the Independent Review of Prevent that had been re-launched under the leadership of Lord Shawcross in January 2021 (see Chapter 1). As a result of prior connections with counter-terrorism practitioners and reviewers, we were invited to organise and run a series of focus groups with students in Higher Education settings to feed into this exercise: a population of especial interest to the review team. Students recruited to our groups were, of course, explicitly informed about the ambitions of the research, and that their involvement would, effectively, contribute to this high-profile, and controversial, policy discussion. It is, therefore, plausible that some of our participants shaped their contributions according to their expectations and beliefs about what would constitute appropriate engagement in this context. For some, this may have involved some element of self-censorship: withholding experiences, or opinions, perhaps, out of a desire to avoid attracting the security state's attention. (Although, those most concerned by this prospect may simply have decided not to participate in the research, so our findings here may be self-selecting.) Other participants may have contributed to the focus groups out of a determination *to be heard* precisely because of the chance to shape public policy and, perhaps, to 'speak truth to power' (see Jarvis and Lister 2016).

There will be some readers for whom these origins raise questions about the independence, or the criticality, of the preceding discussion. Some may even go further and believe these connections with policymakers taint our analysis, perhaps irrevocably. There was a high-profile boycotting of the independent review of Prevent amongst some academics, civil society organisations, and community groups, not least because of ongoing concerns with the review's independence (see Chapter 1). Concerns such as these – of researchers being somehow contaminated by proximity to political elites – are not new, and find illustration in discussion, amongst other things, of the 'terrorism industry' which posits a revolving door of self-serving expertise between academia, think tanks, lobby groups, and the government (see Herman and O'Sullivan 1989). Richard Jackson (2016: 120), for instance, identifies a 'potential contradiction, or point of tension' within academic research that aspires for both 'critical distance' and 'policy relevance'. In his words:

> it can be argued that scholars who work with the state in either designing or enacting its counterterrorism practices – through advising practitioners working on the implementation of counter-radicalisation programmes, for example – may result in reducing harms to some potential victims. However, the overall primary effect is the legitimisation and perpetuation of the broader system of counterterrorism, rather than its dismantling or destruction.
>
> Jackson 2016: 122

Concerns such as this merit serious reflection, not least in a book that aims to speak critically to counter-radicalisation programmes such as Prevent. And our response to them is three-fold.

First, at a very practical level, we enjoyed near-complete independence in the construction of this research project. To be clear, as the three of us set about the process of research design via a series of conversations which led, amongst other things, to the topic guide for our focus groups, we were, of course, conscious of the types of finding likely to interest the independent review team. We had also committed ourselves to reporting directly back to the team via a research report that set out our findings in a presentational style more appropriate or useful to policymakers. Nevertheless, we encountered no interference in the content of our questions, or in their framing, ordering, and analysis, and we had no engagement with the review team in the writing of this book. We have not presented our findings in a way that deliberately sought to legitimise – or, indeed, to delegitimise – counter-radicalisation knowledge or practice either in this book or in the accompanying report. And, although the boundaries between policy practitioners and reviewers may be more fluid than they initially appear, it is worth reiterating that this research was initiated at the request of an independent team tasked with evaluating the UK's Prevent Strategy, and not at the behest of the strategy's authors or practitioners. It might also be worth noting here that we received no funding or financial incentive for completing this piece of research.

Second, our research was also designed, *from the start*, with two purposes in mind: a policy-relevant one, and a more straightforwardly academic one. In setting up the project, our intention was always to write academic publications as well as a report for the review team, with the former as important as the latter to us in formulating our research questions and ambitions. Such a strategy is not unusual in the contemporary academic community, which valorises – for better or worse, depending on your standpoint – engagement with and impact on the wider world. And the research design therefore builds directly upon prior work we have undertaken, which demonstrates a similar effort to bring forward non-elite understandings of security politics (e.g., Jarvis and Lister 2016). In this sense, one might argue that our contribution to the independent review is as much at risk of being tainted by our academic commitments – ontological, epistemological, methodological, normative, political – as our scholarship is by our agreement to also contribute to the review process.

Finally, as academics we should be clear that we share a willingness, even a commitment, to attempt to influence policy and policymakers through our research. Running through this book, and through much of our prior work – both individually and collectively – is a curiosity about the formulation, communication, implementation, and consequences of security politics, whether in relation to anti-social behaviour (Macdonald 2006), counter-terrorism policy (Jarvis and Lister 2015a), cybersecurity (Whiting 2020), or the COVID-19 pandemic (Jarvis 2022b). At a fundamental level, this curiosity incorporates a belief that the construction of security threats – such as, in this instance, radicalisation and extremism – is neither objective nor neutral. And, therefore, that responses to threats – counter-radicalisation policy, counter-extremism policy, and so forth – should not be taken as inevitable, either. Approached thus, two questions present themselves. First, what analytical strategies do we bring to our critical engagement with entities such as (counter-)radicalisation (see Jarvis 2019b)? And, second, what are the purposes of, or ambitions for, the critical work we want to do in deconstructing or otherwise challenging security dynamics? Here, although we should be cautious of the risk that our research may be co-opted by policy elites and their interests, we should also be wary of seeing those actors and interests as fixed, unchanging, or monolithic (Toros 2016). In the case of this book, it would be a mistake to see either the review team, or, indeed, Prevent practitioners as anything other than multiple actors with likely diverse interests/ aspirations. And, although we cannot know in advance what impact our research will have, we fully endorse Marieke de Goede's (2020: 112) argument that, 'engagement with the world of practice and policy advice – however dangerous and flawed – is part of the uncertain, fallible, speculative experimentations that we could engage in.' Even if our critical engagements are doomed to failure – however failure is understood (see Sjoberg 2019) – our view, in short, is that we should continue with them nonetheless.

Revisiting the vernacular

In Chapter 2, we introduced a number of relatively recent studies foregrounding vernacular perspectives on the politics of security in different thematic and geographical contexts. Having now spent several chapters tracing these in the context of UK (counter-)radicalisation, it may be useful to reflect a little further about the wider social and political importance of engagements such as these.

In the first instance, vernacular research into non-elite constructions of security problems and policies significantly broadens our understanding of the ways in which initiatives such as Prevent percolate through and across social life. It is, we suggest, naïve to assume that such initiatives are experienced uniformly or comparably – even amongst individuals who may be similarly structurally located. Policies do not simply 'wash over' citizens; they are interpreted, discussed, negotiated, contested, and resisted in the spaces, practices, and engagements of everyday life (Jarvis and Lister 2013a: 661). Accessing these experiences, however obliquely, through encouraging 'ordinary' individuals to speak on (their own understandings of) such initiatives, in their own words, therefore enriches our knowledge of security's heterogeneities. It does so, as set out in Chapter 2, by offering 'a significantly broader tapestry of (in)security stories for researchers to hear (or co-construct)' (Jarvis 2019a: 118). This matters, because as Vaughan-Williams and Stevens (2016: 41) note:

> relatively little is known about how citizens conceptualize and experience 'threat' and '(in)security', whether they are aware of, engage with and/or refuse governmental attempts to enlist them in building societal resilience, and what the implications of these initiatives might be for [amongst other things] social interaction among multi-ethnic publics.

Second, as indicated in Chapter 2, vernacular research such as that pursued in this book opens new opportunity for political contestation and critique precisely because of the space it provides for knowledges and perspectives that may be marginal or subjugated. Security, historically, has been something of an elite sport. Despite significant recent work on security's 'bottom-up' manifestations (see Jarvis 2019a), the term still conjures up images of high politics, of guns and bombs, of war and strategy, of secretive decision-making by (white, male) executive authority, of urgency, of drama, and of exceptionalism (see Hansen 2019: 37; Wæver 1995). Research like that pursued here, in the first instance, allows individuals to partake directly in discourse on security issues and threats, providing opportunity for publics to engage with scholars and scholarship as well as policymakers and practitioners in conversations on, in this case (counter-)radicalisation. In so doing, of course, vernacular or non-elite contributions to these discussions may raise hitherto unconsidered lines of argument or contestation around security politics and their manifestation. Such concerns – situated in the intricacies and particularities of everyday life – may, in turn, provide opportunity for rethinking how security operates in practice. Vernacular research, in other words, might be thought of as an opportunity for a very grounded form of immanent critique in which the tensions, contradictions, and violences of security may be documented and exposed *by those who have lived them.*

We need be wary here of pushing this claim too far. There is no reason, of course, to assume that non-elite voices are any more critical of dominant forms of security knowledge and practice than elites – such as, for instance, found in parliamentary oppositions or in academia. Moreover, the engagement of publics in these discussions through research projects such as this is limited in various ways. Such engagements are indirect – taking place across a temporal and spatial distance. They may never reach the ears of those in positions of privilege or influence, perhaps because of editorial decisions made by researchers such as us. And they may, of course, be ignored, disregarded, or dismissed even if ever encountered by others. And, yet, we must not lose sight of the *potential* of everyday and vernacular forms of knowledge to disrupt that which is taken for granted as objective, automatic, or necessary in the politics of security (Vaughan-Williams and Stevens 2016). It is hard to over-emphasise that possibility – of speaking or knowing security otherwise – as part of the motivation for this book.

Third, as we have attempted to demonstrate throughout the book, vernacular research also provides scope for wider insight on social and political imaginaries that extend beyond the parameters of the particular security context being immediately discussed. Vernacular conversations of policy areas – such as Prevent – inevitably draw in, draw on, refer to, or dance around other issues, topics, ideas, and assumptions. People's responses might, for instance, highlight assumptions about race, gender, class, or sexuality. People may sketch perceived differences or equivalences with other political initiatives or thematic areas, allowing insight into their understanding of, say, the workings of public policy on education or migration. We may glimpse, in these discussions, reflections on the power of ideas in social life, or – as we saw in Chapter 3 – on the relationship between structures and their agents in specific contexts. To paraphrase an earlier piece of research, in short:

> Public debate over what we should do about terrorism, then, may reveal considerably more than public attitudes towards counter-terrorism (important though this is), permitting us also to glimpse into public conceptions of religion, politics, multiculturalism, 'Britishness', liberalism, democracy, security, and so on.
>
> Jarvis and Lister 2016: 280

Fourth, vernacular research also facilitates reflection on the ways in which elite or hegemonic forms of security discourse resonate more widely. Do publics draw upon the vocabularies, idioms and examples favoured by politicians on a particular topic? Do they do so deliberately, with reflection, or unconsciously, as if they constituted common-sense understanding? Or, is there evidence of a critical distance, in which people remain wary of government framings of problems and threats? As we demonstrate in Chapter 3, the concept of radicalisation appears now so ingrained in everyday discourse, that even those most sceptical toward the term in our research fell back upon it in debating the causes of terrorism. Such a finding is only possible, we suggest, through qualitatively rich work such as this, in which individuals are afforded the space to think, discuss, and reflect on such topics at length and in their own vocabularies.

Going forwards

Given the value of a vernacular approach to security discourse and practice sketched in the above section, there is considerable scope for future work, building on the analysis presented in this book. Most obviously, there is rich opportunity for work on other (counter-)radicalisation contexts to explore potentially significant similarities and differences across national boundaries. Do citizens in Denmark or Nigeria, say, demonstrate similar understandings as those explored in this book? Do they draw upon similar discursive resources to explain and justify their interpretations and evaluations? If there are significant differences, what might this tell us about the implementation and communication of security policies across national contexts? Indeed, what might such differences tell us about citizenship and social life, more broadly, as these are lived by non-elite individuals?

Our focus in this book has been upon the understandings of one particular – albeit variegated – population: students at Higher Education Institutions in England and Wales. In the UK context, there therefore remains considerable scope for expanding this analysis geographically – perhaps to communities in Scotland and Northern Ireland, but also demographically – to other cohorts whose lives might be touched by (counter-) radicalisation in similar or different ways to the experiences recounted in this book. This might include, most obviously, communities disproportionately targeted by Prevent, but could expand, of course, beyond this. Are there differences, for instance, between communities of students, here? Do older populations with different historical memories and experiences situate counter-radicalisation in other contexts? What knowledge do schoolchildren have, and so forth? Cutting into this field with a different thematic focus, moreover, could add additional depth to the analysis that we have offered in the preceding pages. Are there, for instance, gendered differences within citizen understandings and experiences of (counter-)radicalisation? Do other structural dynamics such as race or social class make significant interpretive differences, here? Experientially, do understandings vary with greater or lesser exposure to Prevent? How do one's ideological or political leanings influence perceptions here?

Finally, to pick up on the argument developed in Chapter 2, there remains vast scope for exploring vernacular securities in other contexts unrelated to extremism, radicalisation, or terrorism. How, for instance, do citizens conceptualise security in the context of pandemics such as COVID-19 or HIV/AIDS? How is cybersecurity constructed and experienced in everyday life and encounters? And, of course, the list goes on: climate change, war, organised crime, gender-based violences, homophobia, racism, hate crimes, and so on. One advantage of the vernacular approach mobilised here is in its openness to multiple issues and contexts. This book, we hope, therefore stands both as an illustration of its analytical productivity, as well as an example upon which future research might build.

Bibliography

Abbas, M. S. (2019) 'Producing "internal suspect bodies": divisive effects of UK counter-terrorism measures on Muslim communities in Leeds and Bradford', *The British Journal of Sociology*, 70:1, 261–282.

Abbas, T., Awan, I. and Marsden, J. (2021) 'Pushed to the edge: the consequences of the "Prevent Duty" in de-radicalising pre-crime thought among Muslim university students', *Race, Ethnicity and Education*, early access, 1–16. https://doi.org/10.1080/13613324.2021.2019002

Addley, E. and Topping, A. (2017) 'Council admits racially discriminating against two boys over Prevent toy gun referral', *Guardian*, 27 January. Available online at: www.theguardian.com/uk-news/2017/jan/27/bedfordshire-local-education-authority-admits-racial-discrimination-brothers-toy-gun-school-police Last accessed 29 November 2021.

Åhäll, L. (2016) 'The dance of militarisation: a feminist security studies take on "the political"', *Critical Studies on Security*, 4:2, 154–168.

Ahmed, M. and Alvis, S. (2020) *Past, Prevent and Future: Improving Prevent for a New Generation*. London: Tony Blair Institute for Global Change. Available online at: https://institute.global/sites/default/files/2020–09/Tony%20Blair%20Institute%2C%20Past%2C%20Prevent%20and%20Future%20FINAL.pdf Last accessed 22 November 2022.

Aistrope, T. (2016) 'The Muslim paranoia narrative in counter-radicalisation policy', *Critical Studies on Terrorism*, 9:2, 182–204.

Aked, H. (2022) '"Mad", bad or Muslim? The UK's vulnerable support hubs and the nexus of mental health, counterterrorism and racism', *Bioethics*, 36:3, 290–297.

Alkopher, D. T. (2016) 'From Kosovo to Syria: the transformation of NATO Secretaries General's discourse on military humanitarian intervention', *European Security*, 25:1, 49–71.

Aradau, C. (2004) 'Security and the democratic scene: desecuritization and emancipation', *Journal of International Relations and Development*, 7:4, 388–413.

Aradau, C. (2006) 'Limits of security, limits of politics? A response', *Journal of International Relations and Development*, 9:1, 81–90.

Aradau, C. (2008) *Rethinking Trafficking in Women: Politics Out of Security*. Basingstoke: Palgrave.

Aradau, C. (2018) 'From securitization theory to critical approaches to (in) security', *European Journal of International Security*, 3:3, 300–305.

Aradau, C. and van Munster, R. (2007) 'Governing terrorism through risk: taking precautions, (un) knowing the future', *European Journal of International Relations*, 13:1, 89–115.

Aradau, C. and van Munster, R. (2012) 'The time/space of preparedness: anticipating the "next terrorist attack"', *Space and Culture*, 15:2, 98–109.

Archer, T. (2009) 'Welcome to the Umma: the British state and its Muslim citizens since 9/11', *Cooperation and Conflict*, 44:3, 329–347.

Atakav, E., Jarvis, L. and Marsden, L. (2020) 'Researching "British [Muslim] Values": vernacular politics, digital storytelling, and participant researchers', *International Journal of Qualitative Methods*, 19. https://journals.sagepub.com/doi/10.1177/1609406920938281

Awan, I. (2012) '"I am a Muslim not an extremist": how the Prevent Strategy has constructed a "suspect" community', *Politics & Policy*, 40:6, 1158–1185

Baele, S. J. and Jalea, D. (2022) 'Twenty-five years of securitization theory: a corpus-based review', *Political Studies Review*, 1–14. https://journals.sagepub.com/doi/10.1177/14789299211069499

Baker, B. and Lekunze, M. (2019) 'The character and value of vernacular security: the case of South West Cameroon', *Journal of Contemporary African Studies*, 37:2–3, 208–224.

Baker, C., Hutton, G., Christie, L. and Wright, S. (2020) 'COVID-19 and the digital divide', *UK Parliament Post*, 17 December. Available online at: https://post.parliament.uk/covid-19-and-the-digital-divide/ Last accessed 29 November 2022.

Baker, J. (2022) 'Shamima Begum: spy for Canada smuggled schoolgirl to Syria', *BBC Online*, 31 August. Available online at: www.bbc.co.uk/news/uk-62726954 Last accessed 29 November 2022.

Baldwin, D. A. (1997) 'The concept of security', *Review of International Studies*, 23:1, 5–26.

Balzacq, T. (2011) 'A theory of securitization: origins, core assumptions, and variants', in: Balzacq, T. (ed.) *Securitization Theory: How Security Problems Emerge and Dissolve*. Abingdon: Routledge, 1–30.

Barbour, R. (2007) *Doing Focus Groups*. London: Sage.

Barendt, E. (2009) 'Incitement to, and glorification of, terrorism', in Hare, I. and Weinstein, J. (eds.) *Extreme Speech and Democracy*. Oxford: Oxford University Press, 445–462.

Barnett, J. (2003) 'Security and climate change', *Global Environmental Change*, 13:1, 7–17.

Barrett, D. (2018) 'Tackling radicalisation: the limitations of the anti-radicalisation Prevent Duty', *European Human Rights Law Review*, 5, 430–541.

Bauer, M. W. (2000) 'Classical content analysis: a review', in Bauer, M. W. and Gaskell, G. (eds.) *Qualitative Research with Text, Image and Sound*. London: Sage, 131–151.

BBC (2015) 'Muslim ex-police officer criticises Prevent anti-terror strategy', *BBC Online*, 9 March. Available online at: www.bbc.co.uk/news/uk-31792238 Last accessed 29 November 2022.

BBC (2016) 'Lancashire "terrorist house" row "not a spelling mistake"', *BBC Online*, 20 January. Available online at: www.bbc.co.uk/news/uk-england-lancashire-35354061 Last accessed 29 November 2022.

BBC (2017) 'Reality check: what is the Prevent strategy?', *BBC Online*, 4 June 2017. www.bbc.co.uk/news/election-2017-40151991 Last accessed 29 November 2022.

Beighton, C. and Revell, L. (2020) 'Implementing the "*Prevent Duty*" in England: the semiotisation of discourse and practice in further education', *Discourse: Studies in the Cultural Politics of Education*, 41:4, 516–531.

Benzing, B. (2020) 'Whom you don't know, you don't trust: vernacular security, distrust, and its exclusionary effects in post-conflict societies', *Journal of Global Security Studies*, 5:1, 97–109.

Bertrand, S. (2018) 'Can the subaltern securitize? Postcolonial perspectives on securitization theory and its critics', *European Journal of International Security*, 3:3, 281–299.

Bigo, D. (2011) 'Security: a field left fallow', in Dillon, M. and Neal, A. W. (eds.) *Foucault on Politics, Security and War*. Basingstoke: Palgrave Macmillan, 93–114.

Bigo, D. (2014) 'The (in)securitization practices of the three universes of EU border control: Military/Navy – border guards/police – database analysts', *Security Dialogue*, 45:3, 209–225.

Bloor, M., Frankland, J., Thomas, M., Stewart, K. and Robson, K. (2000) *Focus Groups in Social Research*. London: Sage.

Bogardus, E. S. (1926) 'The group interview', *Journal of Applied Sociology*, 10, 372–382.

Booth, K. (1991) 'Security and emancipation', *Review of International Studies*, 17:4, 313–326.

Booth, K. (2007) *Theory of World Security*. Cambridge: Cambridge University Press.

Boucek, C. (2008) 'Counter-terrorism from within: assessing Saudi Arabia's religious rehabilitation and disengagement programme', *The RUSI Journal*, 153:6, 60–65.

Bowcott, O. (2019) 'Lord Carlile removed from Prevent review after legal challenge', *Guardian*, 20 December. Available online at: www.theguardian.com/uk-news/2019/dec/19/lord-carlile-prevent-review-legal-challenge Last accessed 29 November 2022.

Breen-Smyth, M. (2014) 'Theorising the "suspect community": counterterrorism, security practices and the public imagination', *Critical Studies on Terrorism*, 7:2, 223–240.

Brighton, S. (2007) 'British Muslims, multiculturalism and UK foreign policy: "integration" and "cohesion" in and beyond the state', *International Affairs*, 83:1, 1–17.

Brown, K. E. (2021) 'Gendered reflections on the "Event" narrative of 9/11', *Critical Studies on Terrorism*, 14:4, 479–483.

Brown, K. E. and Saeed, T. (2015) 'Radicalisation and counter-radicalisation at British Universities: Muslim encounters and alternatives', *Ethnic Racial Studies*, 38:11, 1952–1968.

Bubandt, N. (2005) 'Vernacular security: the politics of feeling safe in global, national and local worlds', *Security Dialogue*, 36:3, 275–296.

Busher, J., Choudhury, T. and Thomas, P. (2019) 'The enactment of the counter-terrorism "Prevent duty" in British schools and colleges: beyond reluctant accommodation or straightforward policy acceptance', *Critical Studies on Terrorism*, 12:3, 440–462.

Butler, J. (2002) 'Explanation and exoneration, or what we can hear', *Grey Room*, 7, 56–67.

Butler, J. (2004) *Precarious Life: The Powers of Mourning and Violence*. London: Verso.

Buzan, B. (2007) *People, States and Fear: An Agenda for International Security Studies in the Post-Cold War Era (Revised Edition)*. Colchester: ECPR Press.

Buzan, B. and Hansen, L. (2009) *The Evolution of International Security Studies*. Cambridge: Cambridge University Press.

Buzan, B., Wæver, O. and De Wilde, J. (1998) *Security: A New Framework for Analysis*. London: Lynne Rienner.

C.A.S.E. Collective (2006) 'Critical approaches to security in Europe: a networked manifesto', *Security Dialogue*, 37:4, 443–487.

Cage Advocacy (2015) *Failing Our Communities: A Case Study Approach to Understanding Prevent*. Cage Advocacy: London. Available online at: www.cage.ngo/wp-content/uploads/2015/07/failing_our_communities.pdf Last accessed 29 November 2022.

Carter, D. M. (2017) '(De)constructing difference: a qualitative review of the "othering" of UK Muslim communities, extremism, soft harms, and Twitter analytics', *Behavioral Sciences of Terrorism and Political Aggression*, 9:1, 21–36.

Casciani, D. (2022) 'Sir David Amess: how MP's killer was a textbook radicalisation', *BBC Online*, 11 April. Available online at: www.bbc.co.uk/news/uk-61062285 Last accessed 29 November 2022.

Cassam, Q. (2018) 'The epistemology of terrorism and radicalisation', *Royal Institute of Philosophy Supplements*, 84, 187–209.

Chandler, D. (2008) 'Review essay: human security: the dog that didn't bark', *Security Dialogue*, 39:4, 427–438.

Chaudhary, V. and Tingle, R. (2022) 'From football-loving aspiring doctor to terrorist who murdered David Amess: how Ali Harbi Ali descended down spiral of self-radicalisation after watching videos of ISIS and Bashar al-Assad's brutal Syrian regime', *Mail Online*, 11 April. Available online at: www.dailymail.co.uk/news/article-10707833/How-David-Amess-killer-descended-spiral-self-radicalisation.html Last accessed 29 November 2022.

Cherney, A., Belton, E., Norham, S. A. B. and Milts, J. (2022) 'Understanding youth radicalisation: an analysis of Australian data', *Behavioral Sciences of Terrorism and Political Aggression*, 14:2, 97–119.

Christie, N. (1986) 'Ideal victim', in Fattah, E. A. (ed.) *From Crime Policy to Victim Policy: Reorienting the Justice System*. London: Macmillan, 17–30.

Ciută, F. (2009) 'Security and the problem of context: a hermeneutical critique of securitisation theory', *Review of International Studies*, 35:2, 301–326.

Clubb, G. and McDaid, S. (2019) 'The causal role of ideology and cultural systems in radicalisation and de-radicalisation', *Journal of Critical Realism*, 18:5, 513–528.

Collins, A. (2013) *Contemporary Security Studies*, 3rd Edition. Oxford: Oxford University Press.

Coolsaet, R. (2016) '"All radicalisation is local": the genesis and drawbacks of an elusive concept', *Egmont-Royal Institute for International Relations*, 84, 1–48.

Coppock, V. (2014) '"Can you spot a terrorist in your classroom?" Problematising the recruitment of schools to the "War on Terror" in the United Kingdom', *Global Studies of Childhood*, 4:2, 115–125.

Coppock, V. and McGovern, M. (2014) '"Dangerous minds"? Deconstructing counter-terrorism discourse, radicalisation and the "psychological vulnerability" of Muslim children and young people in Britain', *Children & Society*, 28:3, 242–256.

Cox, R. (with Timothy J. Sinclair) (1996) *Approaches to World Order*. Cambridge: Cambridge University Press.

Cram, I. and Fenwick, H. (2018) 'Protecting free speech and academic freedom in universities', *Modern Law Review*, 81:5, 825–873.

Crawford, A. and Hutchinson, S. (2016) 'Mapping the contours of "everyday security": time, space and emotion', *British Journal of Criminology*, 56:6, 1184–1202.

Crenshaw, M. (1981) 'The causes of terrorism', *Comparative Politics*, 13:4, 379–399.

Croft, S. and Vaughan-Williams, N. (2017) 'Fit for purpose? Fitting ontological security studies "into" the discipline of international relations: towards a vernacular turn', *Cooperation and Conflict*, 52:1, 12–30.

De Goede, M. (2020) 'Engagement all the way down', *Critical Studies on Security*, 8:2, 101–115.

De Goede, M. and Simon, S. (2013) 'Governing future radicals in Europe', *Antipode*, 45:2, 315–335.

Department for Education (2015) *The Prevent Duty: Departmental Advice for Schools and Childcare Providers*. Available online at: https://assets.publishing. service.gov.uk/government/uploads/system/uploads/attachment_data/file/ 439598/prevent-duty-departmental-advice-v6.pdf Last accessed 29 November 2022.

Department of Health and Social Care (2022) *Guidance: NHS Prevent Training and Competencies Framework*. Available online at: www.gov.uk/government/ publications/nhs-prevent-training-and-competencies-framework/nhs-prevent-training-and-competencies-framework Last accessed 29 November 2022.

Dodd, V. (2022a) '"I've killed him": David Amess murder was last act of two-year plot', *The Guardian*, 11 April. Available online at: www.theguardian.com/uk-news/2022/apr/11/david-amess-last-act-two-year-plot-ali-harbi-ali Last accessed 29 November 2022.

Dodd, V. (2022b) 'Ali Harbi Ali guilty of murdering MP David Amess in terrorist attack', *The Guardian*, 11 April. Available online at: www.theguardian.com/ uk-news/2022/apr/11/david-amess-verdict-terrorist-attack-ali-harbi-ali-guilty Last accessed 29 November 2022.

Downing, J. (2021) 'Memeing and speaking vernacular security on social media: YouTube and Twitter resistance to an ISIS Islamist terror threat to Marseille, France', *Journal of Global Security Studies*, 6:2, 1–17.

Downing, J. and Dron, R. (2020) 'Theorising the "Security Influencer": speaking security, terror and Muslims on social media during the Manchester bombings', *New Media & Society*. https://journals.sagepub.com/doi/pdf/10.1177/ 1461444820971786

Downing, J., Gerwens, S. and Dron, R. (2022) 'Tweeting terrorism: vernacular conceptions of Muslims and terror in the wake of the Manchester Bombing on Twitter', *Critical Studies on Terrorism*, 15:2, 239–266.

Drezner, D. W. (2014) *Theories of International Politics and Zombies (revised edition)*. Princeton, NJ: Princeton University Press.

Edkins, J. (2002) 'After the subject of international security', in Finlayson, A. and Valentine, J. (eds.) *Politics and Post-structuralism: An Introduction*. Edinburgh: Edinburgh University Press, 66–82.

Edmiston, V. (1944) 'The group interview', *Journal of Educational Research*, 37, 593–601.

Elgot, J. and Dodd, V. (2022) 'Leaked Prevent review attacks "double standards" on far right and Islamists', *The Guardian*, 16 May. Available online at: www. theguardian.com/uk-news/2022/may/16/leaked-prevent-review-attacks-double-standards-on-rightwingers-and-islamists Last accessed 29 November 2022.

Elshimi, M. S. (2015) 'De-radicalisation interventions as technologies of the self: a Foucauldian analysis', *Critical Studies on Terrorism*, 8:1, 110–129.

Elshimi, M. S. (2017) *De-Radicalistion in the UK Prevent Strategy*. London Routledge.

Elshtain, J. B. (1987) *Women and War*. New York, NY: Basic Books.

Elwick, A. and Jerome, L. (2019) 'Balancing securitisation and education in schools: teachers' agency in implementing the Prevent duty', *Journal of Beliefs and Values*, 40:3, 338–353.

Enloe, C. (2000) *Bananas, Beaches and Bases: Making Feminist Sense of International Politics*. Berkley, CA: University of California Press.

Enloe, C. (2011) 'The mundane matters', *International Political Sociology*, 5:4, 447–450.

Eroukhmanoff, C. (2015) 'The remote securitisation of Islam in the US post-9/11: euphemisation, metaphors and the "logic of expected consequences" in counter-radicalisation discourse', *Critical Studies on Terrorism*, 8:2, 246–265.

Ezaydi, S. (2022) 'Muslims already feel targeted by Prevent, the Shawcross review leak will make things worse', *i Online*, 18 May. Available online at: https://inews.co.uk/opinion/muslims-targeted-prevent-shawcross-review-leak-1635470   Last accessed 29 November 2022.

Farquhar, C. and Das, R. (1999) 'Introduction: the challenges and promise of focus groups', in Kitzinger, J. and Barbour, R. S. (eds.) *Developing Focus Group Research*. London: Sage, 47–62.

Farrell, F. (2016) '"Why all of a sudden do we need to teach fundamental British values?" A critical investigation of religious education student teacher positioning within a policy discourse of discipline and control', *Journal of Education for Teaching: International Research and Pedagogy*, 42:3, 280–297.

Farrell, F. and Lander, V. (2019) '"We're not British values teachers are we?": Muslim teachers' subjectivity and the governmentality of unease', *Educational Review*, 71:4, 466–482.

Farrell, T. (2002) 'Constructivist security studies: portrait of a research program', *International Studies Review*, 4:1, 49–72.

Federal Republic of Nigeria (2017) *Policy Framework and National Action Plan for Preventing and Countering Violent Extremism*. Available online at: https://ctc.gov.ng/wp-content/uploads/2020/03/PCVE-NSA-BOOK-1.pdf Last accessed 29 November 2022.

Fern, E. F. (2001) *Advanced Focus Groups Research*. London: Sage.

Fey, M., Poppe, A. E. and Rauch, C. (2016) 'The nuclear taboo, Battlestar Galactica, and the real world: illustrations from a science-fiction universe', *Security Dialogue*, 47:4, 348–365.

Fisher, J. and Leonardi, C. (2021) 'Insecurity and the invisible: the challenge of spiritual (in) security', *Security Dialogue*, 52:5, 383–400.

Floyd, R. (2011) 'Can securitization theory be used in normative analysis? Towards a just securitization theory', *Security Dialogue*, 42:4–5, 427–439.

Foret, F. and Markoviti, M. (2020) 'The EU counter-radicalisation strategy as "business as usual"? How European political routine resists radical religion', *Journal of European Integration*, 42:4, 547–563.

George, N. (2017) 'Policing "conjugal order": gender, hybridity and vernacular security in Fiji', *International Feminist Journal of Politics*, 19:1, 55–70.

George, N. (2018) 'Liberal–local peacebuilding in Solomon Islands and Bougainville: advancing a gender-just peace?', *International Affairs*, 94:6, 1329–1348.

Ghosh, R., Chan, Alice W. Y., Manuel, A. and Dilimulati, M. (2017) 'Can education counter violent religious extremism?', *Canadian Foreign Policy Journal*, 23:3, 117–133.

Gillespie, M. and O'Loughlin, B. (2009) 'News media, threats and insecurities: an ethnographic approach', *Cambridge Review of International Affairs*, 22:4: 667–85.

Gomes, M. S. and Marques, R. R. (2021) 'Can securitization theory be saved from itself? A decolonial and feminist intervention', *Security Dialogue*, 52:2, 78–87.

Gray, J. (2003) *Al Qaeda and What it Means to be Modern*. London: Faber and Faber.

Greenbaum, T. L. (1998) *The Handbook for Focus Group Research*. London: Sage.

Greer, S. (2010) 'Anti-terrorist laws and the United Kingdom's "suspect Muslim community": a reply to Pantazis and Pemberton', *The British Journal of Criminology*, 50:6, 1171–1190.

Greer, S. and Bell, L. C. (2018) 'Counter-terrorist law in British universities: a review of the "Prevent" debate', *Public Law*, 2018:1, 84–104.

Grierson, J. (2019) '"My son was terrified": how Prevent alienates UK Muslims', *Guardian*, 27 January. Available online at: www.theguardian.com/uk-news/2019/jan/27/prevent-muslim-community-discrimination Last accessed 29 November 2022.

Grierson, J. (2020) 'Revealed: how teachers could unwittingly trigger counter-terror inquiries', *Guardian*, 21 February. Available online at: www.theguardian.com/uk-news/2020/feb/21/public-sector-teachers-doctors-prevent-inquiries-trigger-referrals Last accessed 29 November 2022.

Grierson, J. (2021) 'Human rights groups to boycott government's Prevent review', *Guardian*, 16 February. Available online at: www.theguardian.com/uk-news/2021/feb/16/human-rights-groups-to-boycott-government-prevent-review Last accessed 29 November 2022.

Halliday, M., Mill, D., Johnson, J. and Lee, K. (2021) 'Let's talk virtual! Online group facilitation for the modern researcher', *Research in Social Administrative Pharmacy*, 17(12): 2145–2150.

Hammond, M. and Wellington, J. (2020) *Research Methods: The Key Concepts*. London: Routledge.

Hannah, E. and Wilkinson, R. (2016) 'Zombies and IR: a critical reading', *Politics*, 36:1, 5–18.

Hansard HL Debate. Vol. 7933 col. 1737, 12 November 2018. Available online at: https://hansard.parliament.uk/Lords/2018–11–12/debates/6777BAC0-F7EB-410C-A2F8-D8B6B77E9EE2/Counter-TerrorismAndBorderSecurityBill?highlight=%22prevent%20strategy%22%20%22toxic%22#main-content Last accessed 29 November 2022.

Hansen, A. D. and Sonnichsen, A. (2014) 'Discourse, the political and the ontological dimension: an interview with Ernesto Laclau', *Distinktion: Scandinavian Journal of Social Theory*, 15:3, 255–262.

Hansen, L. (2000) 'The Little Mermaid's silent security dilemma and the absence of gender in the Copenhagen School', *Millennium*, 29:2, 285–306.

Hansen, L. (2019) 'What is constantly changing? The concept of security', *Security Dialogue* 50:4(Suppl), 36–37.

Hardy, K. (2018) 'Comparing theories of radicalisation with countering violent extremism policy', *Journal for Deradicalization,* 15:1, 76–110.

Hay, C. (2002) *Political Analysis: A Critical Introduction*. Basingstoke: Palgrave.

Heath-Kelly, C. (2013) 'Counter-terrorism and the counterfactual: producing the "radicalisation" discourse and the UK PREVENT strategy', *The British Journal of Politics and International Relations*, 15:3, 394–415.

Heath-Kelly, C. (2017a) 'The geography of pre-criminal space: epidemiological imaginations of radicalisation risk in the UK Prevent Strategy, 2007–2017', *Critical Studies on Terrorism*, 10:2, 297–319.

Heath-Kelly, C. (2017b) 'Algorithmic autoimmunity in the NHS: radicalisation and the clinic', *Security Dialogue*, 48:1, 29–45.

Heath-Kelly, C. and Strausz, E. (2019) 'The banality of counterterrorism "after, after 9/11"? Perspectives on the Prevent duty from the UK health care sector', *Critical Studies on Terrorism*, 12:1, 89–109.

Heath-Kelly, C., Baker-Beall, C. and Jarvis, L. (2015) 'Introduction', in Heath-Kelly, C., Baker-Beall, C. and Jarvis, L. (eds.) *Counter-Radicalisation: Critical Perspectives*. Abingdon: Routledge, 1–13.

Herman, E. S. and O'Sullivan, G. (1989) *The Terrorism Industry: The Experts and Institutions That Shape Our View of Terror*. New York, NY: Pantheon.

Hillyard, P. (1993) *Suspect Community: People's Experience of the Prevention of Terrorism Acts in Britain*. London: Pluto.

HM Government (2011) *Prevent Strategy*. Available online at: https://assets. publishing.service.gov.uk/government/uploads/system/uploads/attachment_data/ file/97976/prevent-strategy-review.pdf Last accessed 29 November 2022.

HM Government (2018) *CONTEST: The United Kingdom's Strategy for Countering Terrorism*. Available online at: https://assets.publishing.service.gov.uk/government/ uploads/system/uploads/attachment_data/file/716907/140618_CCS207_ CCS0218929798–1_CONTEST_3.0_WEB.pdf Last accessed 29 November 2022.

HM Government (2020) *Channel Duty Guidance: Protecting People Vulnerable to Being Drawn Into Terrorism*. Available online at: https://assets.publishing. service.gov.uk/government/uploads/system/uploads/attachment_data/file/ 964567/6.6271_HO_HMG_Channel_Duty_Guidance_v14_Web.pdf Last accessed 29 November 2022.

HM Government (2021a) *Revised Prevent Duty Guidance: For England and Wales*. Available online at: www.gov.uk/government/publications/prevent-duty-guidance/ revised-prevent-duty-guidance-for-england-and-wales Last accessed 29 November 2022.

HM Government (2021b) *Prevent Duty Guidance: For Higher Education Institutions in England and Wales*. Available online at: www.gov.uk/government/ publications/prevent-duty-guidance/prevent-duty-guidance-for-higher-education-institutions-in-england-and-wales Last accessed 29 November 2022.

Holland, J. (2013) 'Foreign policy and political possibility', *European Journal of International Relations*, 19:1, 49–68.

Holmwood, J. and Aitlhadj, L. (2022) *The People's Review of Prevent*. Available online at: https://peoplesreviewofprevent.org/wp-content/uploads/2022/02/ mainreportlatest.pdf Last accessed 29 November 2022.

Homolar, A. and Löfflmann, G. (2021) 'Populism and the affective politics of humiliation narratives', *Global Studies Quarterly*. https://journals.sagepub.com/ doi/10.1177/14789299211069499

Horder, J. (2019) *Ashworth's Principles of Criminal Law*, 9th edition. Oxford: Oxford University Press.

Hörnqvist, M. and Flyghed, J. (2012) 'Exclusion or culture? The rise and the ambiguity of the radicalisation debate' *Critical Studies on Terrorism*, 5:3, 319–334.

House of Commons Home Affairs Committee (2016) *Radicalisation: The Counter-Narrative and Identifying the Tipping Point. Eighth Report of Session 2016–17*. Available online at: https://publications.parliament.uk/pa/cm201617/cmselect/ cmhaff/135/135.pdf Last accessed 29 November 2022.

Howell, A. and Richter-Montpetit, M. (2020) 'Is securitization theory racist? Civilizationism, methodological whiteness, and antiblack thought in the Copenhagen School', *Security Dialogue*, 51:1, 3–22.

Hultin, N. (2010) 'Repositioning the front lines? Reflections on the ethnography of African securityscapes', *African Security*, 3:2, 104–125.

Husband, C. and Alam, Y. (2011) S*ocial Cohesion and Counter-Terrorism: A Policy Contradiction?* Bristol: Policy Press.

Huysmans, J. (1998) 'Security! What do you mean? From concept to thick signifier', *European Journal of International Relations*, 4:2, 226–255.

Huysmans, J. (2011) 'What's in an act? On security speech acts and little security nothings', *Security Dialogue*, 42:4–5, 371–383.

Innes, A. J. (2014) 'Performing security absent the state: encounters with a failed asylum seeker in the UK', *Security Dialogue*, 45:6, 565–581.

Innes, A. J. and Topinka, R. J. (2017) 'The politics of a "Poncy Pillowcase": migration and borders in Coronation Street', *Politics*, 37:3, 273–287.

Innes, M., Roberts, C. and Lowe, T. (2017) 'A disruptive influence? "Prevent-ing" problems and countering violent extremism policy in practice', *Law and Society Review*, 51:2, 252–281.

Jackson, R. (2016) 'To be or not to be policy relevant? Power, emancipation and resistance in CTS research', *Critical Studies on Terrorism*, 9:1, 120–125.

Jackson, R., Jarvis, L., Gunning, J. and Breen Smyth, M. (2011) *Terrorism: A Critical Introduction*. Basingstoke: Palgrave.

James, N. (2022) 'Countering far-right threat through Britishness: the Prevent duty in further education', *Critical Studies on Terrorism*, 15:1, 121–142.

Jarvis, L. (2009) *Times of Terror: Discourse, Temporality and the War on Terror.* Basingstoke: Palgrave.

Jarvis, L. (2013) 'Conclusion: the process, practice and ethics of research', in Shepherd, L. J. (ed.) *Critical Approaches to Security: An Introduction to Theory and Methods*. Abingdon: Routledge, 236–247.

Jarvis, L. (2019a) 'Toward a vernacular security studies: origins, interlocutors, contributions, and challenges', *International Studies Review*, 21:1, 107–126.

Jarvis, L. (2019b). 'Terrorism, counter-terrorism, and critique: opportunities, examples, and implications', *Critical Studies on Terrorism*, 12:2, 339–358.

Jarvis, L. (2022a) 'Counting coronavirus: mathematical language in the UK response to COVID-19', in Musolff, A., Breeze, R., Kondo, K. and Vilar-Lluch, S. (eds.) *Pandemic and Crisis Discourse*. London: Bloomsbury, 79–93.

Jarvis, L. (2022b) 'Constructing the coronavirus crisis: narratives of time in British political discourse on COVID-19', *British Politics*, 17:1, 24–43.

Jarvis, L. (2023). 'Counting security in the vernacular: quantification rhetoric in "everyday" (in) security discourse', International Political Sociology, 17:3, olad013.

Jarvis, L. and Holland, J. (2015) *Security: A Critical Introduction*. Basingstoke: Palgrave.

Jarvis, L. and Legrand, T. (2017) '"I am somewhat puzzled": questions, audiences and securitization in the proscription of terrorist organizations', *Security Dialogue*, 48:2, 149–167.

Jarvis, L. and Lister, M. (2010) 'Stakeholder security: the new western way of counter-terrorism?', *Contemporary Politics*, 16:2, 173–188.

Jarvis, L. and Lister, M. (2013a) 'Disconnected citizenship? The impacts of anti-terrorism policy on citizenship in the UK', *Political Studies*, 61:3, 656–675.

Jarvis, L. and Lister, M. (2013b) 'Vernacular securities and their study: a qualitative analysis and research agenda', *International Relations*, 27:2, 158–179.

Jarvis, L. and Lister, M. (2015a) *Anti-Terrorism, Citizenship and Security.* Manchester: Manchester University Press.

Jarvis, L. and Lister, M. (2015b) '"I read it in the FT": "everyday" knowledge of counter-terrorism and its articulation', in Jarvis, L. and Lister, M. (eds.) *Critical Perspectives on Counter-Terrorism.* Abingdon: Routledge, 109–129.

Jarvis, L. and Lister, M. (2016) 'What would you do? Everyday conceptions and constructions of counter-terrorism', *Politics*, 36:3, 277–291.

Jarvis, L. and Lister, M. (2017) '"As a woman …"; "As a Muslim …": subjects, positions and counter-terrorism powers in the United Kingdom', *Critical Social Policy*, 37:2, 245–267.

Jarvis, L., Marsden, L. and Atakav, E. (2020) 'Public conceptions and constructions of "British values": a qualitative analysis', *The British Journal of Politics and International Relations*, 22:1, 85–101.

Jerome, L., Elwick, A. and Kazim, R. (2019) 'The impact of the Prevent Duty on schools: a review of the evidence', *British Educational Research Journal*, 45:4, 821–837.

Johnson, A., Lawson, C. and Ames, K. (2018) '"Use your common sense, don't be an idiot": social media security attitudes amongst partners of Australian Defence Force personnel', *Security Challenges*, 14:1, 53–64.

Kaleem, A. (2021) 'The hegemony of Prevent: turning counter-terrorism policing into common sense', *Critical Studies on Terrorism*, 15:2, 267–289.

Kitzinger, J. and Barbour, R. S. (1999) 'Introduction: the challenges and promise of focus groups', in Kitzinger, J. and Barbour, R. S. (eds.) *Developing Focus Group Research.* London: Sage, 1–20.

Krause, K. and Williams, M. C. (1996) 'Broadening the agenda of security studies: politics and methods', *Mershon International Studies Review*, 40:2(Suppl 2), 229–254.

Kuhn, T. S. (2012) *The Structure of Scientific Revolutions: 50th Anniversary Edition.* Chicago, IL: Chicago University Press.

Kundnani, A. (2009) *Spooked: How Not to Prevent Violent Extremism.* London: Institute of Race Relations.

Kundnani, A. (2012) 'Radicalisation: the journey of a concept', *Race & Class*, 54:2, 3–25.

Kundnani, A. (2014) *The Muslims are Coming! Islamophobia, Extremism, and the Domestic War on Terror.* London: Verso.

Kuzel, A. J. (1992) 'Sampling in qualitative inquiry', in Crabtree, B. F. and Miller, W. I. (eds.) *Doing Qualitative Research.* Newbury Park, CA: Sage, pp. 31–44.

Laclau, E. (1990) *New Reflections on the Revolution of Our Time.* London: Verso.

Langford, J. and McDonagh, D. (2003) 'Introduction', in Langford, J. and McDonagh, D. (eds.) *Focus Groups: Supporting Effective Product Development.* London: Taylor & Francis, pp. 1–17.

Lathen, L. and Laestadius, L. (2021) 'Reflections on online focus group research with low socio-economic status African American adults during COVID-19', *International Journal of Qualitative Methods.* https://journals.sagepub.com/doi/full/10.1177/16094069211021713

Lester, E. G., Popok, P. J., Grunberg, V. A., Baez, A., Herrawi, F. and Vranceanu, A. (2021) 'Stopping to listen: using qualitative methods to inform a web-based platform for adults with Neurofibromatosis', *Journal of Patient Experience*, 8, 1–8.

Liamputtong, P. (2011) *Focus Group Methodology: Principles and Practice*. London: Sage.

Lister, M. and Jarvis, L. (2013) 'Disconnection and resistance: anti-terrorism and Citizenship in the UK', *Citizenship Studies*, 17:6–7, 756–769.

Lobe, B. (2017) 'Best practices for synchronous online focus groups', in Barbour, R. and Morgan, D. L. (eds.) *A New Era in Focus Group Research*. Abingdon: Palgrave, 227–250.

Löfflmann, G. and Vaughan-Williams, N. (2018) 'Vernacular imaginaries of European border security among citizens: from walls to information management', *European Journal of International Security*, 3:3, 382–400.

Luckham, R. (2017) 'Whose violence, whose security? Can violence reduction and security work for poor, excluded and vulnerable people?', *Peacebuilding*, 5:2, 99–117.

Mac Ginty, R. (2019) 'Circuits, the everyday and international relations: connecting the home to the international and transnational', *Cooperation and Conflict*, 54:2, 234–253.

Mac Ginty, R. and Firchow, P. (2016) 'Top-down and bottom-up narratives of peace and conflict', *Politics*, 36:3, 308–323.

Macdonald, S. (2006) 'A suicidal woman, roaming pigs and a noisy trampolinist: refining the ASBO's definition of "anti-social behaviour"', *The Modern Law Review*, 69:2, 183–213.

Macdonald, S. (2008) 'Why we should abandon the balance metaphor: a new approach to counterterrorism policy', *ILSA Journal of International and Comparative Law*, 15:1, 95–146.

Maguire, M. and Westbrook, D. A. (2020) 'Security by design: counterterrorism at the airport', *Anthropology Now*, 12:3, 122–135.

Makki, M. and Tahir, M. (2021) 'Mapping normalcy through vernacular security-development in post-conflict North Waziristan', *Conflict, Security & Development*, 21:5, 565–592.

Marsden, L., Jarvis, L. and Atakav, E. (2022) '"That still goes on, doesn't it, in their religion?" British values, Islam and vernacular discourse', *Nations and Nationalism*. https://doi.org/10.1111/nana.12849

Martin, T. (2014) 'Governing an unknowable future: the politics of Britain's Prevent Policy', *Critical Studies on Terrorism*, 7:1, 62–78.

Martin, T. (2018) 'Identifying potential terrorists: visuality, security and the Channel project', *Security Dialogue*, 49:4, 254–271.

Mays, N. and Pope, C. (1995) 'Rigour and qualitative research', *The British Medical Journal*; 311:6997, 109–112.

McDonald, M. (2008) 'Securitization and the construction of security', *European Journal of International Relations*, 14:4, 563–587.

McGlynn, C. and McDaid, S. (2019) 'Radicalisation and Higher Education: students' understanding and experiences', *Terrorism and Political Violence*, 31:3, 559–576.

McGuiness, A. (2021) 'Prevent: why key part of government's counter-terrorism strategy is under scrutiny after murder of MP Sir David Amess', *Sky News*, 20 October. Available online at: https://news.sky.com/story/prevent-why-key-part-of-governments-counter-terrorism-strategy-is-under-scrutiny-after-murder-of-mp-sir-david-amess-12439347 Last accessed 29 November 2022.

Merton, R. K. and Kendall, P. L. (1946) 'The focussed interview', *American Journal of Sociology*, 52, 541–557.

Milliken, J. (1999) 'The study of discourse in international relations: A critique of research and methods', *European Journal of International Relations*, 5:2, 225–254.

Mitzen, J. (2006) 'Ontological security in world politics: state identity and the security dilemma', *European Journal of International Relations*, 12:3, 341–370.

Moffat, A. and Gerard, G. F. (2020) 'Securitising education: an exploration of teachers' attitudes and experiences regarding the implementation of the Prevent duty in sixth form colleges', *Critical Studies on Terrorism*, 13:2, 197–217.

Monaghan, J. and Molnar, A. (2016) 'Radicalisation theories, policing practices, and "the future of terrorism?"', *Critical Studies on Terrorism*, 9:3, 393–413.

Morgan, D. L. (1996) Focus Groups as Qualitative Research. London: Sage.

Morgan, D. L. (1998) *The Focus Group Guidebook*. London: Sage.

Morgan, D. L. (2019) *Basic and Advanced Focus Groups*. London: Sage.

Mortimer, C. (2016) 'Eight-year-old boy questioned after teachers mistake t-shirt slogan for Isis propaganda', *Independent*, 1 August. Available online at: www.independent.co.uk/news/uk/home-news/isis-propaganda-t-shirt-boy-east-london-teachers-mistake-terrorism-terror-a7164941.html Last accessed 29 November 2022.

Mueller, J. E. and Stewart, M. G. (2016) *Chasing Ghosts: The Policing of Terrorism*. Oxford: Oxford University Press.

Mueller, J. E. and Stewart, M. G. (2021) 'Terrorism and bathtubs: comparing and assessing the risks', *Terrorism and Political Violence*, 33:1, 138–163.

Mughal, S. (2019) 'As a survivor of 7/7 I support anti-radicalisation, but the Prevent strategy has become toxic', *Metro*, 28 January. Available online at: https://metro.co.uk/2019/01/28/as-a-survivor-of-7–7-i-am-supportive-of-the-idea-of-prevent-but-it-has-become-toxic-8384687/ Last accessed 29 November 2022.

Muncey, T. (2005) 'Doing autoethnography', *International Journal of Qualitative Methods*, 4:1, 69–86.

Muro, D. (2016) 'What does radicalisation look like? Four visualisations of socialisation into violent extremism', *Notes Internacionals,* 163, 1–5.

Muslim Council of Britain (2016) *The Impact of Prevent on Muslim Communities*. Available online at: http://archive.mcb.org.uk/wp-content/uploads/2016/12/MCB-CT-Briefing2.pdf Last accessed 29 November 2022.

Mythen, G. and Walklate, S. (2006) 'Criminology and terrorism: which thesis? Risk society or governmentality', *British Journal of Criminology*, 46:3, 379–398.

National Offender Management Service (2011) *Extremism Risk Guidance: ERG22+ Structured Professional Guidelines for Assessing Risk of Extremist Offending*. London: Ministry of Justice.

Neumann, P. R. (2003) 'The trouble with radicalization', *International Affairs*, 89:4, 873–893.

Neumann, P. R. (2008) *Perspectives on Radicalisation and Political Violence*. London: International Centre for the Study of Radicalisation and Political Violence. Available online at: www.nonviolent-conflict.org/wp-content/uploads/2016/11/Perspectives-on-Radicalisation-Political-Violence.pdf Last accessed 29 November 2022.

New Zealand Government (2022) *New Zealand's Countering Terrorism and Violent Extremism Strategy*. Available online at: https://dpmc.govt.nz/sites/default/files/2021-10/New%20Zealands%20Countering%20Terrorism%20and%20Violent%20Extremism%20Strategy.pdf Last accessed 29 November 2022.

Newman, E. (2001) 'Human security and constructivism', *International Studies Perspectives*, 2:3, 239–251.

Newman, E. (2010) 'Critical human security studies', *Review of International Studies*, 36:1, 77–94.

Nyman, J. (2016) 'What is the value of security? Contextualising the negative/positive debate', *Review of International Studies*, 42:5, 821–839.

Nyman, J. (2021) 'The everyday life of security: capturing space, practice, and affect', *International Political Sociology*, 15:3, 313–337.

O'Connor, C. and Joffe, H. (2020) 'Intercoder reliability in qualitative research: debates and practical guidelines', *International Journal of Qualitative Methods*, 19. https://doi.org/10.1177/1609406919899220

O'Loughlin, B. and Gillespie, M. (2012) 'Dissenting citizenship? Young people and political participation in the media-security nexus' *Parliamentary Affairs*, 65:1, 115–137.

O'Toole, DeHannas, D. N. N. and Modood, T. (2012) 'Balancing tolerance, security and Muslim engagement in the United Kingdom: the impact of the "Prevent" agenda', *Critical Studies on Terrorism*, 5:3, 373–389.

O'Toole, T., Meer, N., DeHannas, D. N. N., Jones, S. H. and Modood, T. (2016) 'Governing through Prevent? Regulation and contested practice in state-Muslim engagement', *Sociology*, 50:1, 160–177.

Open Society Foundations (2016) *Eroding Trust: The UK's PREVENT Counter-Extremism Strategy in Health and Education.* New York, NY: Open Society Foundations.

Opiyo, L. M. (2015) 'Music as education, voice, memory and healing: community views on the roles of music in conflict transformation in Northern Uganda', *African Conflict and Peacebuilding Review*, 5:1, 41–65.

Oren, I. and Solomon, T. (2015) 'WMD, WMD, WMD: securitisation through ritualised incantation of ambiguous phrases', *Review of International Studies*, 41:2, 313–336.

Orock Rogers, T. E. (2014) 'Crime, in/security and mob justice: the micropolitics of sovereignty in Cameroon', *Social Dynamics*, 4:2, 408–28.

Oyawale, A. (2022) 'The impact of (counter-)terrorism on public (in) security in Nigeria: a vernacular analysis', *Security Dialogue*, 53(5), 420–437.

Pantazis, C. and Pemberton, S. (2009) 'From the "old" to the "new" suspect community: examining the impacts of recent UK counter-terrorist legislation', *The British Journal of Criminology*, 49:5, 646–666.

Pantazis, C. and Pemberton, S. (2011) 'Restating the case for the "suspect community": a Reply to Greer', *The British Journal of Criminology*, 51:6, 1054–1062.

Paris, R. (2001) 'Human security: paradigm shift or hot air?', *International Security*, 26:2, 87–102.

Pech, L. (2021) 'The concept of chilling effect: its untapped potential to better protect democracy, the rule of law, and fundamental rights in the EU', *Open Society Foundation*. Available online at: www.opensocietyfoundations.org/uploads/c8c58ad3-fd6e-4b2d-99fa-d8864355b638/the-concept-of-chilling-effect-20210322.pdf Last accessed 29 November 2022.

Pennick, E. (2022) 'How Sir David Amess' killer went from model student to violent extremist', *Independent*, 11 April. Available online at: www.independent.co.uk/news/uk/crime/david-amess-ali-harbi-ali-london-kentish-town-old-bailey-b2055477.html Last accessed 29 November 2022.

Pettinger, T. (2020) 'British terrorism preemption: subjectivity and disjuncture in Channel "deradicalization" interventions', *The British Journal of Sociology*, 71:5, 970–984.

Prevent Watch (n.d.) *About Prevent Watch*. Available online at: www.preventwatch. org/about/ Last accessed 29 November 2022.

Puchta, C. and Potter, J. (2004) *Focus Group Practice*. London: Berg.

Puwar, N. (2004) *Space Invaders: Race, Gender and Bodies Out of Place*. King's Lynn: Berg.

Qurashi, F. (2017) 'Just get on with it: implementing the Prevent duty in higher education and the role of academic expertise', *Education, Citizenship and Social Justice*, 12:3: 197–212

Ragazzi, F. (2015) 'Policed multiculturalism? The impact of counter-terrorism and counter-radicalization and the "end" of multiculturalism', in Heath-Kelly, C., Baker-Beall, C. and Jarvis, L. (eds.) *Counter-Radicalisation: Critical Perspectives*. Abingdon: Routledge, 156–174.

Ragazzi, F. (2016) 'Suspect community or suspect category? The impact of counter-terrorism as "policed multiculturalism"', *Journal of Ethnic and Migration Studies*, 42:5, 724–741.

Ramsay, P. (2017) 'Is Prevent a safe space?', *Education, Citizenship and Social Justice*, 12:3, 143–158.

Reed, A., Ingram, H. J. and Whittaker, J. (2017) *Countering Terrorist Narratives*. Brussels: European Parliament. Available online at: www.europarl.europa.eu/RegData/etudes/STUD/2017/596829/IPOL_STU(2017)596829_EN.pdf. Last accessed 29 November 2022.

Rengger, N. and Thirkell-White, B. (2007) 'Still critical after all these years? The past, present and future of Critical Theory in International Relations', *Review of International Studies*, 33:Suppl 1, 3–24.

Revell, L. and Bryan, H. (2018) *Fundamental British Values in Education: Radicalisation, National Identity and Britishness*. Cheltenham: Emerald Publishing.

Richards, A. (2015) 'From terrorism to "radicalization" to "extremism": counter-terrorism imperative or loss of focus?', *International Affairs*, 91:2, 371–380.

Richardson, L. (2006) *What Terrorists Want: Understanding the Terrorist Threat*. London: John Murray.

Rights Watch and Liberty (2017) *Briefing on the Higher Education and Research Bill: An Independent Review of Prevent*. Available online at: www.libertyhuman rights.org.uk/wp-content/uploads/2020/02/Rights-Watch-UK-and-Liberty-briefing-an-independent-review-of-Prevent.pdf Last accessed 29 November 2022.

Risør, H. (2010) 'Twenty hanging dolls and a lynching: defacing dangerousness and enacting citizenship in El Alto, Bolivia', *Public Culture*, 22:3, 465–485.

Robinson, L., Cotten, S. R., Ono, H., Quan-Haase, A., Mesch, G., Chen, W., Schulz, J., Hale, T. M. and Stern, M. J. (2015) 'Digital inequalities and why they matter', *Information, Communication & Society*, 18:5, 569–582.

Robinson, N. (2015) 'Have you won the war on terror? Military videogames and the state of American exceptionalism', *Millennium*, 43:2, 450–470.

Robinson, N. (2016) 'Militarism and opposition in the living room: the case of military videogames', Critical Studies on Security, 4:3, 255–275.

Roe, P. (2012) 'Is securitization a "negative concept? Revisiting the normative debate over normal versus extraordinary politics', *Security Dialogue*, 43:3, 249–266.

Rogers, C. (2020) 'V for Vendetta as vernacular critique: the exceptional state of liberal political economy', *New Political Economy*, 25:1, 107–121.

Rogers, P. (2008) 'Contesting and preventing terrorism: on the development of UK strategic policy on radicalisation and community resilience', *Journal of Policing, Intelligence and Counter Terrorism*, 3:2, 38–61.

Rowley, C. and Weldes, J. (2012) 'The evolution of international security studies and the everyday: suggestions from the Buffyverse', *Security Dialogue*, 43:6, 513–530.

Sabaratnam, M. (2011) 'IR in dialogue … but can we change the subjects? A typology of decolonising strategies for the study of world politics', *Millennium*, 39:3, 781–803.

Sageman, M. (2016) *Misunderstanding Terrorism*. Philadelphia, PA: University of Pennsylvania Press.

Salter, M. (2011) 'When securitization fails: the hard case of counter-terrorism programs', in Balzacq, T. (ed.) *Securitization Theory: How Security Problems Emerge and Dissolve*. Abingdon: Routledge, 116–132.

Saul, B. (2006) *Defining Terrorism in International Law*. Oxford: Oxford University Press.

Schmid, A. P. (2013) *Radicalisation, De-Radicalisation, Counter-Radicalisation: A Conceptual Discussion and Literature Review*. Available online at: www.icct.nl/app/uploads/download/file/ICCT-Schmid-Radicalisation-De-Radicalisation-Counter-Radicalisation-March-2013.pdf Last accessed 29 November 2022.

Schuurman, B. and Taylor, M. (2018) 'Reconsidering radicalization: fanaticism and the link between ideas and violence', *Perspectives on Terrorism*, 12:1, 3–22.

Sedgwick, M. (2010) 'The concept of radicalization as a source of confusion', *Terrorism and Political Violence*, 22:4, 479–494.

Seymour, J., Gott, M., Bellamy, G., Ahmedzai, S. H. and Clark, D. (2004) 'Planning for the end of life: the views of older people about advanced care statements', *Social Science and Medicine*, 59, 57–68.

Shaykhutdinov, R. (2018) 'The terrorist attacks in the Volga region, 2012–13: hegemonic narratives and everyday understandings of (in) security', *Central Asian Survey*, 37:1, 50–67.

Silva, D. M. (2018) 'Radicalisation: the journey of a concept, revisited', *Race & Class*, 59:4, 34–53.

Singer, J. D. (1961) 'The level-of-analysis problem in international relations', *World Politics*, 14:1, 77–92.

Sjoberg, L. (2019) 'Failure and critique in critical security studies', *Security Dialogue*, 50:1, 77–94.

Sjoberg, L., Cooke, G. D. and Neal, S. R. (2011) 'Introduction: women, gender and terrorism', in Sjoberg, L. and Gentry, C. (eds.) *Women, Gender and Terrorism*. Athens, GA: University of Georgia Press, 1–27.

Smith, S. (1999) 'The increasing insecurity of security studies: conceptualizing security in the last twenty years', *Contemporary Security Policy*, 20:3, 72–101.

Smith, S. (2005) 'The contested concept of security', in Booth, K. (ed.) *Critical Security Studies and World Politics*. London: Lynne Rienner, 27–62.

Spiller K., Awan I. and Whiting A. (2018) 'What does terrorism look like? University lecturers' interpretations of their Prevent duties and tackling extremism in UK universities', *Critical Studies on Terrorism*, 11:1, 130–150.

Stanley, L. and Jackson, R. (2016) 'Introduction: everyday narratives in world politics', *Politics*, 36:3, 223–235.

Steele, B. J. (2008) *Ontological Security in International Relations: Self-Identity and the IR State*. Abingdon: Routledge.

Steerpike (2021) 'Fact check: what did Michael Gove actually say about "experts"?', *The Spectator*, 2 September. Available online at: www.spectator.co.uk/article/fact-check-what-did-michael-gove-actually-say-about-experts- Last accessed 29 November 2022.

Stein, J. and Townsend, M. (2021) 'Muslim boy, 4, was referred to Prevent over game of Fortnite', *The Guardian*, 31 January. Available online at: www.theguardian.com/uk-news/2021/jan/31/muslim-boy-4-was-referred-to-prevent-over-game-of-fortnite Last accessed 29 November 2022.

Stevens, D. (2009) 'In extremis: a self-defeating element in the "preventing violent extremism" strategy', *The Political Quarterly*, 80:4, 517–525.

Stevens, D. (2011) 'Reasons to be fearful, one, two, three: the "preventing violent extremism! agenda', *The British Journal of Politics and International Relations*, 13:2, 165–188.

Stewart, D. W., Shamdasani, P. N and Rook, D. W. (2007) *Focus Groups: Theory and Practice*. Sage: London.

Stewart, K. and Williams, M. (2005) 'Researching online populations: the use of online focus groups for social research', *Qualitative Research*, 5:4, 395–416.

Struthers, A. (2017) 'Teaching British Values in our schools: but why not human rights?', *Social & Legal Studies*, 26:1, 89–110.

Sylvester, C. (2013) 'Experiencing the end and afterlives of International Relations/theory', *European Journal of International Relations*, 19:3, 609–626.

Taylor, D. (2021) 'Boy, 11, referred to Prevent for wanting to give "alms to the oppressed"', The *Guardian*, 27 June. Available online at: www.theguardian.com/uk-news/2021/jun/27/boy-11-referred-to-prevent-for-wanting-to-give-alms-to-the-oppressed Last accessed 29 November 2022.

Taylor, J. D. (2020) '"Suspect categories", alienation and counterterrorism: critically assessing PREVENT in the UK', *Terrorism and Political Violence*, 32:4, 851–873.

Thomas, P. (2009) 'Between two stools? The government's "preventing violent extremism" agenda', *The Political Quarterly*, 80:2, 282–29.

Thomas, P. (2010) 'Failed and friendless: the UK's "preventing violent extremism" programme', *The British Journal of Politics and International Relations*, 12:3, 442–458.

Thomas, P. (2012) *Responding to the Threat of Violent Extremism: Failing to Prevent*. London: Bloomsbury.

Thomas, P. (2014) 'Divorced but still co-habiting? Britain's Prevent/community cohesion policy tension', *British Politics*, 9:4, 472–493.

Thomas, P. (2016) 'Youth, terrorism and education: Britain's Prevent programme', *International Journal of Lifelong Education*, 35:2, 171–187.

Thornton, A. and Bouhana, N. (2019) 'Preventing radicalization in the UK: expanding the knowledge-base on the Channel programme', *Policing: A Journal of Policy and Practice*, 13:3, 331–344

Tingle, R. (2022) 'Why did Prevent fail to stop David Amess killer? Islamist "lone wolf" Ali Harbi Ali was able to secretly plot his murderous act for years despite being referred to "politically-correct" anti-terror programme', *Mail Online*, 11 April. Available online at: www.dailymail.co.uk/news/article-10707959/Yet-Prevent-failure.html Last accessed 29 November 2022.

Tonkiss, K. (2016) 'Experiencing transnationalism at home: open borders and the everyday narratives of non-migrants', *Politics*, 36:3, 324–337.

Toros, H. (2016) 'Dialogue, praxis and the state: a response to Richard Jackson', *Critical Studies on Terrorism*, 9:1, 126–130.

UK Home Office (2019) 'Government announces independent review of Prevent', 22 January. Available online at: https://homeofficemedia.blog.gov.uk/2019/01/22/government-announces-independent-review-of-prevent/ Last accessed 29 November 2022.

UK Home Office (2021a) *Official Statistics: Individuals Referred to and Supported Through the Prevent Programme, England and Wales, April 2020 to March 2021*, 18 November. Available online at: www.gov.uk/government/statistics/individuals-referred-to-and-supported-through-the-prevent-programme-april-2020-to-march-2021/individuals-referred-to-and-supported-through-the-prevent-programme-england-and-wales-april-2020-to-march-2021 Last accessed 29 November 2022.

UK Home Office (2021b) *Independent Review of Prevent: Terms of reference.* Available online via: www.gov.uk/government/publications/independent-review-of-prevent-terms-of-reference/independent-review-of-prevent-terms-of-reference Last accessed 29 November 2022.

UK Home Office (2023) *Official Statistics: Individuals Referred to and Supported Through the Prevent Programme, England and Wales, April 2021 to March 2022*, 26 January. Available online at: www.gov.uk/government/statistics/individuals-referred-to-and-supported-through-the-prevent-programme-april-2021-to-march-2022/individuals-referred-to-and-supported-through-the-prevent-programme-april-2021-to-march-2022 Last accessed 24 May 2023.

UNDP (1994) *Human Development Report.* Oxford: Oxford University Press.

Vaughan-Williams, N. (2008) 'Borderwork beyond inside/outside? Frontex, the citizen-detective and the war on terror', *Space and Polity*, 12:1, 63–79.

Vaughan-Williams, N. (2021) *Vernacular Border Security: Citizens' Narratives of Europe's' Migration Crisis.* Oxford: Oxford University Press.

Vaughan-Williams, N. and Stevens, D. (2016) 'Vernacular theories of everyday (in)security: the disruptive potential of non-elite knowledge', *Security Dialogue*, 47:1, 40–58.

Venhaus, J. M. (2010) *Why Youth Join al-Qaeda.* Washington, DC: United States Institute of Peace. Available online at: www.usip.org/sites/default/files/resources/SR236Venhaus.pdf Last accessed 29 November 2022.

Vidino, L. and Brandon, J. (2012) 'Europe's experience in countering radicalisation: approaches and challenges', *Journal of Policing, Intelligence and Counter Terrorism*, 7:2, 163–179.

Wæver, O. (1995) 'Securitization and desecuritization', in Lipschutz, R. D. (ed.) *On Security.* New York: Columbia University Press, 46–86.

Waldron, J. (2003) 'Security and liberty: the image of balance', *Journal of Political Philosophy*, 11:2: 191–210.

Waldron, J. (2010) *Torture, Terror and Trade-Offs: Philosophy for the White House.* Oxford: Oxford University Press.

Walker, R. B. J. (1997) 'The subject of security', in Krause, K. and Williams, M. C. (eds.) *Critical Security Studies: Concepts and Cases.* London: UCL Press, 61–82.

Walt, S. M. (1991) 'The renaissance of security studies', *International Studies Quarterly*, 35:2, 211–239.

Weldes, J. (1999) 'Going cultural: Star Trek, state action, and popular culture', *Millennium*, 28:1, 117–134.

Whiting, A. (2020) *Constructing Cybersecurity: Power, Expertise and the Internet Security Industry*. Manchester: Manchester University Press.

Whiting., A., Spiller, K. and Awan, I. (2021a) *A Disproportionate Response: Five Years of the Prevent Duty in Higher Education*. Available online at: https://bcuassets.blob.core.windows.net/docs/a-disproportionate-response-final-report-132640783134972833.pdf Last accessed 29 November 2022.

Whiting, A., Campbell, B., Spiller, K. and Awan, I. (2021b) 'The Prevent Duty in UK higher education: insights from freedom of information requests', *British Journal of Politics and International Relations*, 23:3, 513–532.

Whittaker, K., Looney, S., Reed, A. and Votta, F. (2021) 'Recommender systems and the amplification of extremist content', *Internet Policy Review*, 10:2. https://doi.org/10.14763/2021.2.1565

Wibben, A. T. (2008) 'Human security: toward an opening', *Security Dialogue*, 39:4, 455–462.

Wibben, A. T. (2011) *Feminist Security Studies: A Narrative Approach*. Abingdon: Routledge.

Wibben, A. T. (2016) 'Opening security: recovering critical scholarship as political', *Critical Studies on Security*, 4:2, 137–153.

Wibben, A. T. (2020) 'Everyday security, feminism, and the continuum of violence', *Journal of Global Security Studies*, 5:1, 115–121.

Wichum, R. (2013) 'Security as a dispositif: Michel Foucault in the field of security', *Foucault Studies*, 15, 164–171.

Wight, C. (2009) 'Theorising terrorism: the state, structure and history', *International Relations*, 23:1, 99–106.

Wilkinson, S. (1998) 'Focus groups in feminist research: power, interaction, and the co-construction of meaning', *Women's Studies International Forum*, 21:1, 111–125.

Williams, M. C. (2003). 'Words, images, enemies: securitization and international politics', *International Studies Quarterly*, 47:4, 511–531.

Winch, B. (2021) 'Vernacular human security and Moris Diak in Timor-Leste: a social contract between the living and spirit actants', *Asian Journal of Peacebuilding*, 9:1: 183–207.

Winter, C., Heath-Kelly, C., Kaleem, A. and Mills, C. (2022) 'A moral education? British Values, colour-blindness, and preventing terrorism', *Critical Social Policy*, 42:1: 85–106.

Wolfendale, J. (2016) 'The narrative of terrorism as an existential threat', in R. Jackson (ed.) *Routledge Handbook of Critical Terrorism Studies*. Abingdon: Routledge, 130–139.

Wolfers, A. (1952) '"National security" as an ambiguous symbol', *Political Science Quarterly*, 67:4, 481–502.

Younis, T. and Jadhav, S. (2019a) 'Keeping our mouths shut: the fear and racialized self–censorship of British healthcare professionals in PREVENT training', *Culture, Medicine, and Psychiatry*, 43:3: 404–424.

Younis, T. and Jadhav, S. (2019b) 'Islamophobia in the National Health Service: an ethnography of institutional racism in PREVENT's counter-radicalisation policy', *Sociology of Health and Illness*, 42:3: 610–626.

Zalewski, M. (1996) '"All these theories yet the bodies keep piling up": theory, theorists, theorising', in Smith, S., Booth, K. and Zalewksi, M. (eds.) *International Theory: Positivism and Beyond*. Cambridge: Cambridge University Press, 340–353.

Zedner, L. (2005). 'Securing liberty in the face of terror: reflections from criminal justice', *Journal of Law and Society*, 32:4, 507–533

Zedner, L. (2018) 'Counterterrorism on campus', *University of Toronto Law Journal*, 68:4, 545–587.

Zempi, I. and Tripli, A. (2022) 'Listening to Muslim students' voices on the Prevent Duty in British universities: a qualitative study', *Education, Citizenship and Social Justice*. https://doi.org/10.1177/17461979221077990

Index

7/7 16, 92
9/11 16, 24, 92, 98, 130

Action Counters Terrorism 92
aims of the book 3
Al Qaeda 8, 10, 99
Ali Harbi Ali 8, 9
Amnesty International 16

Bangladesh 123
Bashar al-Assad 9
Bethnal Green Trio 104
Boko Haram 17, 120
Brexit 133

Cage Advocacy 16
Channel 9, 10, 13, 22
    criticisms of 22–23
    effectiveness 22
    guidance 10–11
    lack of transparency 22
    risk assessment 22
    and young people 23
chilling effect 27, 28, 122, 123, 139, 146
Christchurch Attack 17
Coalition government 14
Cold War 33, 148
Community Cohesion Agenda 13, 21, 128
CONTEST 10, 12, 92, 122
contributions of the book 3–4
Copenhagen School 35, 147
Counter Terrorism and Border Security Act 16
counter-extremism 17, 154
    disengagement 17

Muslim experience of 15
    with prisoners 18
counter-radicalisation 11, 12, 17, 23, 24, 26, 31, 46, 101, 110
    consequences of 23
    as defined in Prevent 11
    effectiveness 21
    expansion of 24, 29
    international strategies 17–18
    and safeguarding 27
    vernacular approach towards 32, 43
    as 'whole-of-society' approach 17
counter-terrorism 1, 12, 20, 21, 24, 98, 101
    and dissent 24
    expansion of 25
Counter-Terrorism and Security Act 2015 12, 14, 26, 31
Counter-Terrorism and Security Bill 14
COVID-19 vii, 12, 35, 54, 154, 158
critical security studies 39, 40

Dal Babu 14
David Amess 8, 9
de-radicalisation 19, 80, 83
duty of care 14, 26

European Court of Human Rights 121, 122
Extreme Risk Guidance (ERG 22+) 22, 119

extremism 2, 11, 14, 16, 17, 26,
27, 32, 72, 98, 138
as defined in Prevent 11
far-left 120
far-right 107, 120, 146
and ideology 10, 118
Incel 13
Islamic 1, 13, 14, 124
mixed, unstable and unclear 13
non-violent 14, 15
right-wing 1, 13
school massacre ideology 13
violent extremism 17, 118

Facebook 97, 126
feminist scholarship 37
focus groups 50–56
benefits to our study 52–53
distinguishing features 51
flexibility of 52
interaction between participants 51
limitations and consideraations for
our study 54–56
virtual setting 53
fundamental British values 11, 17,
26, 42, 98, 127, 138
criticisms of 26

governmentality 24, 25

Handyside v United Kingdom 121
higher education 17, 26, 27,
53, 122, 138
higher education institutions 31,
46, 54, 94, 110
Higher Education and Research Bill 16
Home Office 94, 97, 104, 129, 143

ideology 68, 78
as root cause for terrorism 118, 119
violent 69
Independent Review of Prevent 1,
14, 16, 140, 152, 154
boycott of 16, 153
Independent Reviewer of Terrorism
Legislation 16
Instagram 107
International Centre for the
Study of Radicalisation 18
international relations 36, 38, 40, 59

Iraq 82
ISIS 8, 9, 10, 15, 85, 104, 127
Islamophobia 14, 16, 23, 29

jihadism 95, 107, 120
Jo Cox 8

Liberty UK 16
London Bridge Attack 99,
100, 101, 105
Lord Carlile 14, 16
Lord Shawcross 1, 16, 140, 152
Lord Sheikh 14

Manchester Arena
Bombing 99, 100, 115
Martin Luther King Jr 79
Microsoft Teams 53, 55, 59
Muslim Council of Britain 15
Muslims 16, 21, 22, 95
alienation and stigmatisation
of 23, 86
co-opted into counter-extremism 24
and experience of
counter-radicalisation 27
'paranoia narrative' 20
as securitised 21
as suspect community 16,
23–24, 124–76, 139
as target of Prevent 94, 117

NHS 103, 110
Nigeria 120

People's Review of Prevent 16
Prevent Duty 12, 14, 23, 25, 29,
31, 96, 101, 106, 110,
119, 120, 122
criticisms of 26–27
deputisation 12, 14, 23, 25
and education sector 27
expectations 12
and free expression 122
and health sector 25
and higher education 28
impact across public sector 121, 125
legality of 27
as 'pragmatic compromise' 28
and secondary education 12
and securitisation 25

Prevent Strategy 1, 9, 11, 12,
    13, 16, 17, 19, 21, 22,
    23, 25, 26, 28, 31, 47,
    49, 50, 64, 86, 88, 97, 110
  awareness raising 107–126, 141
  as 'best practice' 17, 18
  as beyond repair 129–130
  brief history of 13–14
  challenging misconceptions 107
  as community cohesion 22
  as conflated with welfare
      support 128
  as counter-productive 117, 124, 145
  as counter-terrorism 14
  criticisms of 1–2, 10, 14–16,
      21–22, 23–24, 25
  delivery model 11
  and difficulties evaluating success
      115–117
  and education sector 96, 108–126
  effectiveness 9, 21, 118
  empirical and theoretical
      underpinnings 118–119
  employment and training as source
      of knowledge 102–104
  family and friends as source of
      knowledge 97–98, 144
  and free expression 122
  and gender 129
  'hearts and minds' 21
  higher education as source of
      knowledge 101–102, 142
  ideology and early intervention 93
  media as source of knowledge
      104–106, 142
  media coverage 15, 95, 104–106,
      107, 116
  misunderstandings of 95–96
  as multi-agency approach 96
  objectives 10
  operation of 96–97
  as proactive 114, 115
  proposed reforms 126–130
  as public duty 95
  rationale 64
  referrals, 11, 30, 31, 30–32, 213,
      236, 292
  resilience of 2
  as safeguarding 14, 64
  secondary education as source of
      knowledge 98–101, 142
  and social media 96–97, 107
  as 'softer' approach 114
  support for 2, 114–115
  as targeting Muslims 21, 124
  as toxic brand 14, 29
  training 96, 97, 101, 102–104,
      119–121, 138
  what is Prevent? 92–93
  where is Prevent targeted? 93–96
  as 'whole-of-society' approach 11
Prevent Watch 2

radicalisation 2, 8, 9, 11, 13, 17, 18,
    28, 31, 32, 37, 64, 92, 94, 98,
    110, 115, 119, 125, 138, 140
  as absolute and relative concept 19
  and agency 68–69
  as agency denying 83–84, 137
  ambiguity and conceptual
      complexity 19, 75–76,
      80–81, 138
  behavioural and cognitive 19, 20
  as 'brainwashing' 69, 86, 137
  causes 72–75
  and community 72
  conceptual moorings of 18
  conceptual resilience 82, 136
  debate on meaning 18–21
  as defined in Prevent 11
  as depoliticising 83, 137
  drivers and dynamics 68
  and 'echo chambers' 73
  epidemiological logic of 20
  and freedom of speech 83
  as gendered discourse 137
  gendered logic 72
  geometric conception 68
  and grievance 74
  as 'grooming' 72, 86, 137
  as ideational 21, 137
  inconsistent application 19, 84–86
  as inextricable 69
  as interchangable with Islamic
      terrorism 76
  and the internet 73, 96, 115
  and mental illness 69, 84
  models 65
  and neoliberal governmentality
      20, 145
  as non-linear 68, 70
  pejorative connotations 77–78

as politically instrumental 18,
    20, 82–83
power and subjectivity 78–81
as process 65–70
as productive 20
racialised opitcs of 27
and 'radical' 70, 77, 78, 139
role of wider social contexts 20
'self-radicalisation' 9
subjectivity and power 76
as violent attitude 70–71
Religious Rehabilitation and
    Disengagement Programme 17
Rights Watch 16
risk 24
    assessment and mitigation 24, 25
    dispositif of precautionary
        risk management 24
    risk knowledge 25

safeguarding 1, 12, 17, 20, 26, 86
    as politically instrumental 26, 27
school shootings 101
securitisation 34–36, 144
security
    'bottom up' 31, 32, 48
    broadening and deepening 39
    as constitutive 31, 34, 37, 134, 143
    constructivist approaches 34
    discourse 31, 36, 37
    elite constructions 31, 36
    as 'essentially contestable' 32, 33
    'everyday' constructions 36–37
    'everyday security' 40
    as everyone's concern 25
    feminist approaches 32, 34, 39, 49
    human security 40
    national security 34, 42
    post-colonial approaches 32, 34, 40
    sectors of 33
    'security speak' 45
    as 'thick signifier' 34
security studies 33
    critical 3, 35
sedimentation 141
Shamima Begum 85–86, 104,
    119, 123, 137, 139
Snapchat 108
Somalia 120
surveillance 2, 24, 27

Sylvia Pankhurst 83
Syria 8, 72, 85, 86, 104, 139
    civil war 9

Taliban 99
terrorism 10, 11, 14, 16, 32,
    34, 37, 93, 98
    far-right 14, 95
    as ideational 10–11
    Islamic 95
    state terrorism 24
    victims of 14
The Open Society 16
The Today Programme 14
Theresa May 10
Thomas Mair 8
TikTok 107, 108
Tony Blair Institute for Global
    Change 110, 114
Trojan Horse Scandal 26
Twitter 4, 41, 49

Uighurs 82
UNDP Report 39

vernacular security 32, 40–41
    assumptions of 42–46
    strengths and applications 42
    value for investigating counter-
        radicalisation 47–50, 155–157
Vladimir Putin 35
vulnerability 9, 13, 20, 26,
    28, 68, 119, 120
    and 'brainwashing' 94
    as politically instrumental 26
    understandings of 93–94
    vulnerable people 1, 10, 12,
        23, 86, 93, 119
    young people 17, 28, 69,
        94, 107, 114

Wales 99, 108
War on Terror 16, 23, 26, 86

Xinjiang 82

YouTube 4, 41, 48, 94, 97, 129, 143

Zoom 55

Milton Keynes UK
Ingram Content Group UK Ltd.
UKHW021418280524
443389UK00008B/196